Battleground
From the Channel to the Ypres Salient

King Albert of the Belgians and his Queen, Elisabeth of Bavaria, played a vital part in the portrayal of Belgium to the world and in maintaining the morale of a nation that had been reduced by the end of 1914 to a faint shadow of its pre-August 1914 self. They represented Belgium's courage and endurance in adversity. He had a physical advantage in that he was a very tall man, which made him easily recognisable in group photographs of allied commanders or political personalities. Albert, beside his constitutional role (which was substantial), was also a military commander: in September 1918 he led the attack from the sea to Ypres, commanding Army Group Flanders, against Germany's northern flank. It was Belgian troops, for example, that finally liberated Passchendaele.

Battleground series:

Stamford Bridge & Hastings *by* Peter Marren
Wars of the Roses - **Wakefield / Towton** *by* Philip A. Haigh
Wars of the Roses - **Barnet** *by* David Clark
Wars of the Roses - **Tewkesbury** *by* Steven Goodchild
Wars of the Roses - **The Battles of St Albans** *by*
Peter Burley, Michael Elliott & Harvey Wilson
English Civil War - **Naseby** *by* Martin Marix Evans, Peter Burton
and Michael Westaway
English Civil War - **Marston Moor** *by* David Clark
War of the Spanish Succession - **Blenheim 1704** *by* James Falkner
War of the Spanish Succession - **Ramillies 1706** *by* James Falkner
Napoleonic - **Hougoumont** *by* Julian Paget and Derek Saunders
Napoleonic - **Waterloo** *by* Andrew Uffindell and Michael Corum
Zulu War - **Isandlwana** *by* Ian Knight and Ian Castle
Zulu War - **Rorkes Drift** *by* Ian Knight and Ian Castle
Boer War - **The Relief of Ladysmith** *by* Lewis Childs
Boer War - **The Siege of Ladysmith** *by* Lewis Childs
Boer War - **Kimberley** *by* Lewis Childs

Mons *by* Jack Horsfall and Nigel Cave
Néry *by* Patrick Tackle
Retreat of I Corps 1914 *by* Jerry Murland
Aisne 1914 *by* Jerry Murland
Aisne 1918 *by* David Blanchard
Le Cateau *by* Nigel Cave and Jack Shelden
Walking the Salient *by* Paul Reed
Ypres - **1914 Messines** *by* Nigel Cave and Jack Sheldon
Ypres - **1914 Menin Road** *by* Nigel Cave and Jack Sheldon
Ypres - **1914 Langemarck** *by* Jack Sheldonand Nigel Cave
Ypres - **Sanctuary Wood and Hooge** *by* Nigel Cave
Ypres - **Hill 60** *by* Nigel Cave
Ypres - **Messines Ridge** *by* Peter Oldham
Ypres - **Polygon Wood** *by* Nigel Cave
Ypres - **Passchendaele** *by* Nigel Cave
Ypres - **Airfields and Airmen** *by* Mike O'Connor
Ypres - **St Julien** *by* Graham Keech
Ypres - **Boesinghe** *by* Stephen McGreal
Walking the Somme *by* Paul Reed
Somme - **Gommecourt** *by* Nigel Cave
Somme - **Serre** *by* Jack Horsfall & Nigel Cave
Somme - **Beaumont Hamel** *by* Nigel Cave
Somme - **Thiepval** *by* Michael Stedman
Somme - **La Boisselle** *by* Michael Stedman
Somme - **Fricourt** *by* Michael Stedman
Somme - **Carnoy-Montauban** *by* Graham Maddocks
Somme - **Pozières** *by* Graham Keech
Somme - **Courcelette** *by* Paul Reed
Somme - **Boom Ravine** *by* Trevor Pidgeon
Somme - **Mametz Wood** *by* Michael Renshaw
Somme - **Delville Wood** *by* Nigel Cave
Somme - **Advance to Victory (North) 1918** *by* Michael Stedman
Somme - **Flers** *by* Trevor Pidgeon
Somme - **Bazentin Ridge** *by* Edward Hancock
Somme - **Combles** *by* Paul Reed
Somme - **Beaucourt** *by* Michael Renshaw
Somme - **Redan Ridge** *by* Michael Renshaw
Somme - **Hamel** *by* Peter Pedersen
Somme - **Villers-Bretonneux** *by* Peter Pedersen
Somme - **Airfields and Airmen** *by* Mike O'Connor
Airfields and Airmen of the Channel Coast *by* Mike O'Connor
In the Footsteps of the Red Baron *by* Mike O'Connor
Arras - **Airfields and Airmen** *by* Mike O'Connor
Arras - **The Battle for Vimy Ridge** *by* Jack Sheldon & Nigel Cave
Arras - **Vimy Ridge** *by* Nigel Cave
Arras - **Gavrelle** *by* Trevor Tasker and Kyle Tallett
Arras - **Oppy Wood** *by* David Bilton
Arras - **Bullecourt** *by* Graham Keech
Arras - **Monchy le Preux** *by* Colin Fox
Walking Arras *by* Paul Reed
Hindenburg Line *by* Peter Oldham
Hindenburg Line - **Epehy** *by* Bill Mitchinson
Hindenburg Line - **Riqueval** *by* Bill Mitchinson
Hindenburg Line - **Villers-Plouich** *by* Bill Mitchinson
Hindenburg Line - **Cambrai Right Hook** *by* Jack Horsfall & Nigel Cave
Hindenburg Line - **Cambrai Flesquières** *by* Jack Horsfall & Nigel Cave
Hindenburg Line - **Saint Quentin** *by* Helen McPhail and Philip Guest
Hindenburg Line - **Bourlon Wood** *by* Jack Horsfall & Nigel Cave

Cambrai - **Airfields and Airmen** *by* Mike O'Connor
Aubers Ridge *by* Edward Hancock
La Bassée - **Neuve Chapelle** *by* Geoffrey Bridger
Loos - **Hohenzollern Redoubt** *by* Andrew Rawson
Loos - **Hill 70** *by* Andrew Rawson
Fromelles *by* Peter Pedersen
The Battle of the Lys 1918 *by* Phil Tomaselli
Accrington Pals Trail *by* William Turner
Poets at War: Wilfred Owen *by* Helen McPhail and Philip Guest
Poets at War: Edmund Blunden *by* Helen McPhail and Philip Guest
Poets at War: Graves & Sassoon *by* Helen McPhail and Philip Guest
Gallipoli *by* Nigel Steel
Gallipoli - **Gully Ravine** *by* Stephen Chambers
Gallipoli - **Anzac Landing** *by* Stephen Chambers
Gallipoli - **Suvla August Offensive** *by* Stephen Chambers
Gallipoli - **Landings at Helles** *by* Huw & Jill Rodge
Walking the Gallipoli *by* Stephen Chambers
Walking the Italian Front *by* Francis Mackay
Italy - **Asiago** *by* Francis Mackay
Verdun: **Fort Douamont** *by* Christina Holstein
Verdun: **Fort Vaux** *by* Christina Holstein
Walking Verdun *by* Christina Holstein
Verdun: **The Left Bank** *by* Christina Holstein
Zeebrugge & Ostend Raids 1918 *by* Stephen McGreal

Germans at Beaumont Hamel *by* Jack Sheldon
Germans at Thiepval *by* Jack Sheldon

SECOND WORLD WAR

Dunkirk *by* Patrick Wilson
Calais *by* Jon Cooksey
Boulogne *by* Jon Cooksey
Saint-Nazaire *by* James Dorrian
Walking D-Day *by* Paul Reed
Atlantic Wall - Pas de Calais *by* Paul Williams
Atlantic Wall - Normandy *by* Paul Williams
Normandy - **Pegasus Bridge** *by* Carl Shilleto
Normandy - **Merville Battery** *by* Carl Shilleto
Normandy - **Utah Beach** *by* Carl Shilleto
Normandy - **Omaha Beach** *by* Tim Kilvert-Jones
Normandy - **Gold Beach** *by* Christopher Dunphie & Garry Johnson
Normandy - **Gold Beach Jig** *by* Tim Saunders
Normandy - **Juno Beach** *by* Tim Saunders
Normandy - **Sword Beach** *by* Tim Kilvert-Jones
Normandy - **Operation Bluecoat** *by* Ian Daglish
Normandy - **Operation Goodwood** *by* Ian Daglish
Normandy - **Epsom** *by* Tim Saunders
Normandy - **Hill 112** *by* Tim Saunders
Normandy - **Mont Pincon** *by* Eric Hunt
Normandy - **Cherbourg** *by* Andrew Rawson
Normandy - **Commandos & Rangers on D-Day** *by* Tim Saunders
Das Reich – **Drive to Normandy** *by* Philip Vickers
Oradour *by* Philip Beck
Market Garden - **Nijmegen** *by* Tim Saunders
Market Garden - **Hell's Highway** *by* Tim Saunders
Market Garden - **Arnhem, Oosterbeek** *by* Frank Steer
Market Garden - **Arnhem, The Bridge** *by* Frank Steer
Market Garden - **The Island** *by* Tim Saunders
Rhine Crossing – **US 9th Army & 17th US Airborne** *by* Andrew Rawson
British Rhine Crossing – Operation Varsity *by* Tim Saunders
British Rhine Crossing – Operation Plunder *by* Tim Saunders
Battle of the Bulge – St Vith *by* Michael Tolhurst
Battle of the Bulge – Bastogne *by* Michael Tolhurst
Channel Islands *by* George Forty
Walcheren *by* Andrew Rawson
Remagen Bridge *by* Andrew Rawson
Cassino *by* Ian Blackwell
Anzio *by* Ian Blackwell
Dieppe *by* Tim Saunders
Fort Eben Emael *by* Tim Saunders
Crete – The Airborne Invasion *by* Tim Saunders
Malta *by* Paul Williams
Bruneval Raid *by* Paul Oldfield
Cockleshell Raid *by* Paul Oldfield

Battleground

From the Channel to the Ypres Salient

The Belgian Sector 1914–1918

Chris Baker

Series Editor
Nigel Cave

Pen & Sword
MILITARY

First published in Great Britain in 2021 by
Pen & Sword Military
An imprint of
Pen & Sword Books Ltd
Yorkshire – Philadelphia

Copyright © Chris Baker 2021

ISBN 978 1 52674 931 4

The right of Chris Baker to be identified as Author of this work has been asserted by him in accordance with the Copyright, Designs and Patents Act 1988.

A CIP catalogue record for this book is available from the British Library.

All rights reserved. No part of this book may be reproduced or transmitted in any form or by any means, electronic or mechanical including photocopying, recording or by any information storage and retrieval system, without permission from the Publisher in writing.

Typeset by Mac Style
Printed and bound in the UK by CPI Group (UK) Ltd, Croydon, CR0 4YY

Pen & Sword Books Limited incorporates the imprints of Atlas, Archaeology, Aviation, Discovery, Family History, Fiction, History, Maritime, Military, Military Classics, Politics, Select, Transport, True Crime, Air World, Frontline Publishing, Leo Cooper, Remember When, Seaforth Publishing, The Praetorian Press, Wharncliffe Local History, Wharncliffe Transport, Wharncliffe True Crime and White Owl.

For a complete list of Pen & Sword titles please contact

PEN & SWORD BOOKS LIMITED
47 Church Street, Barnsley, South Yorkshire, S70 2AS, England
E-mail: enquiries@pen-and-sword.co.uk
Website: www.pen-and-sword.co.uk

Or

PEN AND SWORD BOOKS
1950 Lawrence Rd, Havertown, PA 19083, USA
E-mail: Uspen-and-sword@casematepublishers.com
Website: www.penandswordbooks.com

Contents

Introduction vii
Series Editor's Introduction x

Chapter 1   The Strategic Context 1
Chapter 2   The Last Stand on the Yser 6
Chapter 3   Inundation 52
Chapter 4   The Northernmost Part of the Western Front 77
Chapter 5   Politics and the Shaping of Memory 125
Chapter 6   The Tours 137
Tour A   Nieuwpoort, Lombardsijd and Ramskapelle 143
Tour B   Diksmuide 161
Tour C   The Belgian Rear of the Yser Front 179
Tour D   Drie-Grachten, Merkem and Steenstraat 201
Tour E   The Towns of the Belgian Rear 219

Other Notable Sites in the Area 240
Appendix: The Belgian Army 244
Selective Bibliography 247
Index 249

List of Maps

1. Movement across Flanders, 1914 7
2. Attack on the Yser, 1914 25
3. French and Belgian defences, 26 October 1914 49
4. Nieuwpoort waterways and inundated areas 56
5. The recapture of Ramskapelle, 30 October 1914 62
6. The Second Battle of Ypres, April–May 1915 92
7. Drie-Grachten, Luigem and Merkem 101
8. Defences north of Diksmuide 110
9. German defences of Diksmuide and the Minoterie 114
10. The defences of the Grote Wacht 122
11. Tour A Route Map 144
12. Tour B Route Map 162
13. Tour C Route Map 180
14. Tour D Route Map 202
15. Tour E Route Map 220

Introduction

This is a book that has been long in gestation. The work of researching and writing it has taken time enough, but my journey of discovering the fascinating history, geography, art, architecture, food, language and people of West Flanders began when I first visited in the early 1980s. The period of the Great War is but one in this place of continual turmoil, conflict and change but it left a physical legacy and memory that is deeply ingrained in the region.

Touring the area described is a relatively easy business. It is easily reached, is geographically compact, has an excellent road network and an abundance of accommodation and places of refreshment to suit any budget. Many of the sites can be visited by using the extensive public transport network of buses and the coastal tram operated by 'De Lijn'. The towns of Diksmuide, Veurne and Nieuwpoort have particularly rich history and are worth visiting regardless of their Great War connections. De Panne, Koksijde and the coastal strip, a run of apartment blocks which is now effectively continuous as far as the Yser estuary, are very busy with seaside tourists and perhaps not as attractive, but they too have a wealth of history hidden away and should not be missed. My own preference, though, is to leave the towns and spent time on the land. Flat, criss-crossed by canals and ditches lined by reeds and pollarded trees, and dotted with the towers and spires of village churches, the West Flanders landscape has an undeniable beauty and charm.

The Westhoek area of West Flanders has the historically noteworthy claim to being the one piece of Belgium that was not captured and occupied by the German forces during the Great War. Hostilities arrived in the area as the Belgian army carried out a desperate withdrawal from its 'national redoubt' of Antwerp in early October 1914 and soon came under a heavy and sustained attack in the Battle of the Yser. Once the front line between opposing forces had stabilised in late October and early November 1914, it remained the Belgian army's desolate home until late September 1918 and has assumed symbolic significance as its place of martyrdom and sacrifice.

The French army played a key role, holding for a long period the northernmost four kilometres or so, a vital flank edging onto the dunes and beach of the North Sea, until it was replaced in the summer of 1917 by an element of the British Expeditionary Force ready to take part in an audacious operation that, in the event, never took place. To some extent the operation was shelved due to a surprise attack by a first class, all arms element of the German forces known as the *MarineKorps Flandern* that was established in the coastal strip of this sector.

This book is principally about the years of war fought between the two sides in what was essentially static, positional, entrenched warfare but in a landscape like no other on the Western Front. It is aimed squarely at a British readership and I hope that Belgian, French and German readers will forgive me for this, for I am conscious that I have sometimes sacrificed operational detail for explanation at a higher level.

The geographic scope of the book extends from the North Sea coast down to the very edge of that most ghastly battlefield known as the Ypres Salient. Its timeline covers the period from the beginning of the war up to, but excluding, the final offensive operations from late September 1918 that finally drove the invader out of the province. It has always seemed to me to be rather odd that many British histories of the Ypres fighting have effectively ignored what was happening on its northern flank, especially given the unique, curious nature of much of the fighting there. The book is also slanted towards the role of the Belgian army, for it also appears to receive only passing attention in English-language histories. I can only hope that I have done it justice and that the book engenders increased interest.

Present day modernised Flemish place name spellings are used throughout the book, with certain exceptions, notably the River Yser and the cities of Ypres, Bruges and Ghent. These are just too familiar to an English language readership to be replaced with the modern Ijzer, Ieper, Brugge and Ghent unless really necessary. Most of the modern names are obvious and minor variants of the spellings used during the Great War but it may help readers to be aware of the following changes: Coxyde is now Koksijde; Dixmude (Diksmuide); Nieuport (Nieuwpoort); La Panne (De Panne); Saint-Georges (Sint-Joris); and Furnes (Veurne). One type of infantry unit in the Belgian army was known as *Jagers te voet* (Flemish) or *Chasseurs à Pied* (French). The French army also used the latter term. To avoid confusion, the term Foot Jager has been used when it is applied to a Belgian unit.

Battleground Europe series editor Nigel Cave has always proved to be a source of encouragement and expertise. For their courtesy and assistance with my research I would also like to thank the staffs of the British Library and National Archives, the Belgian War Heritage Institute, Centre de la mémoire urbaine d'agglomération (Dunkirk),

Centrum Agrarische Geschiedenis (Leuven), Erfgoed Alveringem, Kusterfgoed, KU Leuven Libraries Special Collections, North Carolina Museum of History, Westhoek Verbeelt and Jeremy Banning, Bart Debeer, Simon Jones and Simon Verdegem.

All efforts have been made to trace the copyright holder of photographic and map works incorporated within the book and to obtain their permission. In some cases this has not proved possible. I invite those with claims on copyright to make themselves known to the publisher.

The landscape

The geographic area described in this book stretches north-south from the sea to Steenstraat and Lizerne near Ypres, and west-east from the French border to a kilometre or two east of the River Yser. As a rectangle this amounts to around thirty kilometres by twenty-six kilometres. This ground lies within the Belgian province of West Flanders, and for the most in an area known as the Westhoek (west corner). The land is generally very flat, cut by a dense and complex network of streams, drainage channels, canals and the River Yser. It was, and remains to this day, a farmland of rich soil. The only towns of any great size at the time of the Great War were Nieuwpoort and De Panne on the coast, Diksmuide on the Yser and Veurne in the hinterland and near the border with France. Except where the Yser meets the sea – the only river estuary on this coast – there is an almost unbroken ribbon of coastal dunes.

The area over which the battles described would be fought lies within a region of West Flanders known as *Veurne-Ambacht*, an ancient area of forty-two parishes stretching from the sea almost to Ypres. North of the Yser it is often known as *Bachten de Kupe*. To the north, the coastal strip of dune land is known as de Bare; to the west lies *de Moeren*, a former swampy peatland area now a polder. Elsewhere it was a flat, rich agricultural land of many isolated farms, ditches and small waterways and a few villages clustered around churches, each with a characteristic spire or tower. Good roads were few and troop movements off the road not easy.

The geography is little changed today, although the road system is more extensive, the main towns are larger and some of the villages were not rebuilt exactly on their previous position.

Series Editor's Introduction

Over the years it has been possible to find excellent authors who have been able to extend the coverage of the First World War volumes of the *Battleground Europe* series on the Western Front beyond the activities of the British Expeditionary Force: one thinks, amongst others, of Christina Holstein's work on the French army and Verdun; of Maarten Otte on the American Expeditionary Forces; and of Jack Sheldon on the German army. The only significant army on this Front that still lacked some coverage was that of Belgium and I have spent the last ten years or so trying to find someone who felt up to the challenge of writing about it. So at last and with great pleasure I welcome this addition to the series on the Belgian army; the author, Chris Baker, will need no introduction to anyone interested in the Great War. To him we owe the first rate online community of those interested in it, *The Great War Forum*; this originated as part of *The Long, Long Trail*, now the go-to website for anyone seeking information on Britain's army and campaigns and associated matters. He had already contributed much to those of us with this great interest through his work on the committee of the Western Front Association, culminating in a period as its chairman. Finally, he has already published on the war, in this context with two volumes in the series on the Battle of the Lys 1918. Chris has brought to the task of writing about the Belgian army that invaluable (and possibly essential?) attribute, the ability to read Dutch/Flemish; whilst his passionate area of interest in the war lies in Flanders.

Although the book's main thrust relates to the operations of the Belgian army along the Yser, that is from October 1914 to September 1918, Chris provides a very useful background to Belgium's pre-1914 political and military situation; and then takes the reader through the opening weeks of the war before bringing them to the action along what was really the last defensible line in Belgium, based on the Yser and the North Sea. The fraught days of mid October to mid November 1914 are described in some detail, along with the vital part played by the French forces that were despatched to the area (not with quite the speed that the Belgians might have wanted). Although the intensity of fighting died down very substantially once the inundations had taken effect and the last German attacks beaten off (what might have happened if only the German command had managed to coordinate themselves better and launch the attacks of 10 November to the north of Ypres and that of 11 November to the east and south of that 'martyred' town simultaneously?), there was some intensive fighting but it was very local and involved limited resources of manpower and *materiel* and was never on the sort of scale that characterised what took place in the Salient in the following years. The only part of Belgium's military contribution not covered in the book relates to the two months of the offensive of Army Group Flanders under the overall command of King Albert.

Chris also provides an insight into the international medical efforts to assist 'plucky little Belgium' and how the battered remnants of the Belgian state operated in the very straitened circumstances in which it found itself for four years. Then he turns his attention to the complex (to most British readers) matter of how the war was commemorated by a nation that has always been noted for its cultural division between its Flemish and Walloon populations.

It is strange to relate, but I think true nevertheless, that there is a sort of *terra incognita* (and certainly amongst the great majority of British battlefield visitors) about the front, more or less north of Boesinghe, that was held for most of the war by the Belgians – albeit with a strong presence of the French army for nearly all the war and a chunk of time when the British held the line immediately adjacent to the North Sea, mainly in 1917. It is almost as if there is a border, across which the British visitor rarely crosses, unless there is a particular interest in, say, the Zeebrugge and Ostend Raids or Operations Hush and *Strandfest*.

I am certainly no exception to this attitude. Until about ten years ago I would say that the only places I had ventured to in this area was the Trench of Death, just north of Diksmuide, and a pilgrimage to the German cemetery at Vladslo. Whilst working with Jack Sheldon on our trilogy of Battleground books on Ypres 1914 a few years back we spent some time in the area whilst preparing the volume on Langemarck [sic]. Because these books were meant to give as much detail as practicable to the German side of the story, we explored quite a bit into those almost unknown, to us, areas around Houthulst and then west to Diksmuide. I remain struck by our visit to Esen, a medium sized village east of the Yser Canal; this was a scene of what would nowadays certainly be considered an atrocity, when some forty-five civilians were killed by the Germans during the fraught days of mid October 1914; many of the remaining men were deported to Germany. Perhaps unusually, the events are well commemorated by an exhibition in the south transept of the large church, along with some commemorative stained glass windows.

The 'Trench of Death' provided my enduring memory of the Belgian sector, however. I first visited here with my father, probably in 1970, on a fairly miserable day in August, as I recall. It was then 'managed' by the equivalent of the Belgian Royal Automobile Club and had seen far, far better days. I seem to recall a ticket office (entry fee very little) and an observation room, with helpful map, though the windows were so grubby and the skies so dark that I am not sure that I appreciated what I was seeing; and then there was the great length of trench and associated works in concrete. I am not sure that I was all that much the wiser by the time that we left. And that was my sum knowledge of the Belgian front on the ground for many years. I am pleased to say that the Trench of Death has had a wonderful restoration (associated with the Centenary), a completely rebuilt visitors centre, an excellent exhibition space and the preserved section now has photographs from the war positioned in appropriate places. After being fully manned during the commemoration years, it has now a somewhat Byzantine means of entry – but it is a place that should not be missed as it gives by far the best explanation on the ground of something of what the Belgian soldiers went through during the war.

The explorations mentioned above revealed quite clearly that driving in this part of Belgium along the Front presents its challenges, a consequence in large measure of the complex system of water management and the relatively small size of the local communities: there are numerous narrow roads – altogether too narrow for a bus and challenging, quite frankly, in anything much bigger than a saloon car or a small minibus. As is quite clear from Chris' text, there is much to see and much to appreciate; his tours are exhaustive and comprehensive. It is clear that three or four days can usefully be spent in this northernmost part of the Western Front; time spent on the ground makes all too evident (even lacking the inundations) the unique challenges that the topography provided, in particular to the Germans. When I was last there, in March 2020 and immediately preceding the first 'lockdown' in Belgium as a result of the Covid pandemic, it rained unceasingly – so it appeared – for several days, so I actually had an inkling of what the ground conditions might have looked like in, say, the Spring of 1915.

I can warmly recommend this book, from which I have learnt much: it quite lives up to my highest hopes and expectations when I approached Chris to write it. He has served the memory of the Belgian army of 1914 – 1918 well and has provided the means to enable tourers, particularly Anglophone readers, to find their way around this very different landscape, to follow the events of '14-18' on the ground and – perhaps not least – to understand the complexities of post war commemoration.

Nigel Cave
Ratcliffe College, Summer 2021

Chapter One

The Strategic Context

The Belgian state and neutrality
The Kingdom of Belgium came into existence in 1830, separating it from the Kingdom of the Netherlands. Final settlement of its position came with the signing of the Treaty of London, also known as the Quintuple Treaty, on 19 April 1839. Amongst the many provisions and definitions of this treaty, the most important as far as its position in 1914 was concerned was that Belgium would 'form an independent and perpetually neutral State', which 'shall be bound to observe such neutrality towards all other States'. The external signatories were France, Great Britain, the Netherlands, Russia and Prussia (for the German Confederation, Germany not being unified until 1871). They undertook to recognise and guarantee the position.

Belgium itself signed with some reluctance, accepting neutrality as a price of independence but only after months of negotiation in which it had resisted the idea. There were voices within the country in the years of increasing tension before 1914 that demanded international discussion, with a view to the legal abandonment of the enforced neutrality and that Belgium step up its military preparedness. In practice, Belgium had already comprised its neutrality when it entered into quiet discussions on military co-operation with Great Britain and when, in 1907, the latter consented to Belgium's annexation of the Congo Free State, previously a territory personal to the King. By 1913, after recent crises when war looked increasingly likely, it was openly discussed in Belgium that the treaty would not possess the least weight when compared to the strategic interests of the Great Powers of France, Germany and Great Britain. Chancellor Bethmann-Hollweg's characterisation of the treaty as a 'scrap of paper' when Germany invaded and breached her neutrality in August 1914 came as no genuine surprise to anyone in a position to know; but it handed Britain a justification for entry into the war and a propaganda asset of global value.

Newspapers in Britain printed the proclamation by Albert, King of the Belgians, on 6 August 1914: 'Soldiers! Without the slightest provocation from us, a neighbour, haughty in its strength, has torn up the treaty bearing its signature. It has violated the territory of our fathers. Because we have been worthy of ourselves, because we have refused to forfeit our honour, it has attacked us. But the whole world marvels at our loyal attitude, which its respect and esteem strengthen at these supreme moments.'

Belgian preparedness for war
It was understood by Belgian's political leadership from the outset that the commitment of its guarantors was far from certain and it was recognised that the country must be in a position to defend itself. By 1851 the primary threat to its existence stemmed from a resurgent France. With a field army of no great size in comparison with France, it was broadly agreed that Belgium could not hold the enemy at the border and would base its defence on the fortification of its 'national redoubt' of Antwerp. During the Franco-Prussian war of 1870 the Belgian army, at that point fairly modern and capable if small, was mobilised but was not called upon to come into action. Over the decades that followed, political and military disagreement about the nature of the threat and how to counter it, together with financial stringency and opposition to military expenditure, gnawed away at its capability.

With evidence of the growing might of the unified and militaristic Germany in Europe, the potential threat to Belgian sovereignty became more clearly focused on the county's south, for should either of the two great powers attack the other they would inevitably do so in the area of the valley of the River Meuse. France and Germany were developing field armies of enormous size; investment in border fortifications by both powers would force any potential action northwards towards the Meuse. However, it was not until 1887 that military engineer and architect Henri Alexis Brialmont was authorised to fortify the Belgian citadels of Liège and Namur, which together dominated the majority of the existing crossings over the river; but no steps were taken to increase the military manpower that one day might need to be called upon.

In the later decades of the reign of King Leopold II (1835–1909), Belgium enjoyed an economic boom. Capitalising on its position as an international trading place, ruthless exploitation of its possession of the Congo and with large sources of natural wealth in coal and iron at home, its population grew and its financial well-being blossomed. To a significant extent, this growth came mainly in the southern, French-speaking, Walloon half of the country, which became one of the most industrialised and urban areas of Europe. By 1914, for example, it included the most modern and productive steel making industry - but all based in the very area in which a major conflict might well take place.

Belgium passed a new military law in 1902, which ignored recommendations to enlarge the army significantly. It should be recognised that this was a relatively tranquil period, before a succession of crises brought Europe to the brink of war. The peace time strength (or establishment) was set at just 42,800 men, which would swell to a field force of 100,000 and fortress garrisons of 80,000 should the army be mobilised. An annual total of 13,300 men would be conscripted for national service. Individuals would be selected by lot from the available class (that is, by age) but the process was subject to 'remplacement', whereby those who could afford it might pay someone to take their place. This seems a strange and unequal practice but was often welcomed by the less well-off, particularly in Flanders, as a source of employment and income. It was assumed that the total force would be achieved by an appeal for volunteers: in other words the enlarged army would be part volunteer, part conscript. In spite of strong Christian-Democrat support for this military expansion, the ruling Catholic party vacillated in the face of opposition from the socialist *Parti Ouvrier Belge* and produced little by way of internal propaganda to entice volunteers to enlist.

By 1909 only one Belgian male in 400 was being recruited annually. In contrast, France was enlisting one in 170 and Germany one for every 241. In proportion to the respective populations, Belgium's forces were a pinprick and the country's overall military expenditure lagged well behind even that of Switzerland, let alone the great powers. The Swiss, whose population was only half of that of Belgium, had, for example, three times as many infantry battalions and twice the artillery. Belgium was ripe for the picking.

The crises, from Morocco in 1905 onwards, forced Belgium to reconsider its military approach. Talks quietly began with Great Britain and decisions began to be made; but in retrospect they were all too late and too small. A new fortress ring was to be constructed around Antwerp: it was still incomplete when it was besieged in 1914. One of Leopold II's final acts was to approve another military law, this time abolishing 'remplacement' and the lottery system and introducing universal (male) service but limiting it to one son per family. By this means, and various other enticements, which included shortening the period of service, the army now had a theoretical capacity of some 33,000 men becoming available per year. The proposed length of service differed by the arm of the service, but in all cases was cut remarkably short: infantrymen would serve only for fifteen, artillery twenty-one and cavalry for twenty-four months. All these men were then kept in the active reserve, up to a total service of fifteen years.

The Agadir Crisis of 1911 led to an emergency decision to increase expenditure on machine guns and ammunition and to call up three year classes of the reserve, but the latter was soon halted when Germany let it be known that it was pulling back from the brink. It was quite clear that Belgium's military preparedness was at a low ebb, but it still took time to react to what was becoming the clearest of challenges: the guarantee of neutrality was looking very threadbare. In 1913, the 'single-son' clause was lifted as part of further expansion plans but which, however, projected that it would take until at least 1918 to have available an army of 340,000 trained men. This was considered by some in the staff to be the minimum number required to defend the country from a serious attack. Orders were belatedly placed for modern artillery – but with the German firm Krupp and the national armament factory at Herstal, the major ownership of which was German. The orders remained unfulfilled when war came.

Germany monitored Belgian military developments; it considered Belgium incapable of offensive operations, would if attacked seek to avoid a decision in the field and would very quickly fall back to occupy the 'national redoubt', where its army could easily be contained. This appreciation of Belgian capabilities played a key part in the planning for attack.

In July 1914 the Belgian army was approximately 190,000 strong. It was organised as a field army of six divisions, along with the garrisons of the fortresses centred on Antwerp, Liège and Namur. Of the total, the field army numbered some 118,000 men of all arms, of which 14,000 were regular professional soldiers; the rest had or were serving obligatory national service, including being available in reserve. Some 40,000 did not become available in August 1914 for various reasons – not least that their home areas were soon overrun - so Belgium went to war with 104,000 men of the called-up classes and the 14,000 regulars. The fortresses at Liège, Namur and Antwerp were garrisoned by 5,000 regulars plus 60,000 older men of the 1899–1905 classes. In addition to the army, Belgium had a system of armed local militias as well as a *gendarmerie*.

The armament and equipment of the army reflected the decades of neglect and tight budgets. In all there were available only 93,000 rifles and 6,000 swords, which was bad enough, but the real problem in terms of the coming fight was the paucity of modern mobile artillery. There were only 324 obsolescent field guns and a paltry 102 machine guns. There was virtually no mechanised transport, the army relying on motive power provided by horses and dogs. There were also serious shortages of engineer stores, minor equipment and even uniforms, as the administration had struggled to gear up for the expansion of the classes of 1913 and 1914.

Disagreements at the highest levels about the strategy to be adopted continued until the very moment of crisis. General Antoine de Selliers de Moranville, in place as Chief of the General Staff only since 25 May 1914, was of a defensive mindset and proposed centring the whole army on Antwerp, leaving the fortress garrisons on the Meuse only as a delaying screen. General Louis de Ryckel, the Adjutant-General, favoured a more aggressive forward policy of strongly manning the Meuse border, snuffing out the intruders as they appeared and only falling back on Antwerp if necessary.

On 27 July 1914, in light of the deteriorating international situation, a precautionary measure was taken by the government to recall the 33,000 men of the 1913 class, who had gone on leave on 10 July. On the 31st, general mobilisation was ordered, following the German announcement of *Kriegsgefahrzustand* at 1.30pm that afternoon. The final decisions regarding deployment were taken on 2 August as the Germans were already rolling into Luxembourg.

Belgium had a reasonable expectation and hope of support from Great Britain and France, but a divergence of political and military thinking between the two ensured that it was unlikely to come, or at least to come any time soon. To a great extent, she would face the onslaught alone.

Chapter Two

The Last Stand on the Yser

The opening moves

The military plans and intentions of Germany and France that resulted in the initial manoeuvres of the war in Europe have been well described elsewhere. However, for the purposes of this book it is necessary to pick out the key points and in particular how they affected the Belgian army and brought the war to the Westhoek.

That Belgium received little immediate military support from Great Britain and France in the opening phase had its roots in the fundamental strategic concerns of the two powers. Britain fully recognised the imperative of friendly possession of the North Sea coast, yet had committed itself to send its small Expeditionary Force to support France and the latter's plan for an immediate offensive strike into the Ardennes, Luxembourg and Lorraine. It was only once Antwerp became seriously threatened that Britain sent military resources to support the Belgians there. With enormous reluctance, France was persuaded to allow the British Expeditionary Force to disengage on the Aisne and move to Flanders later in October 1914, but by then the die had been cast.

With tension at its height and France and Germany mobilising, the Belgian government issued orders for a general mobilisation of its army on 31 July 1914 and action began next day. Notices were posted in public places, newspapers ran headlines, bells were rung and the police and fire brigade went around the streets to call men out. The reservists began to report to their normal depots and war volunteers queued to enlist. Official announcements were at pains to say that Belgium was 'perpetually neutral' and that no hostile act that was likely to provoke hostilities in return would be tolerated and would even be severely repressed. They also stated that France had made a commitment to respect her neutrality. Dire warnings were given that reservists who had not reported by noon next day were liable to arrest. In Brussels, public transport was offered free of charge to enable the reservists to report. Privately owned horses and motor vehicles were being requisitioned for military use within a very short time. The Minister of the Interior, Paul Berryer, sent a circular to the provincial governors prohibiting any gathering of people whose purpose was to express 'sympathies or

Movement across Flanders, 1914. The small dots to the middle and top right of the map are forts.

antipathies' to any foreign country and all 'cinematographic or other' shows representing military scenes that were likely to inflame passions were banned. In Antwerp, military governor General Dufour stressed the need to monitor all foreigners, for there might be spies amongst them: an early manifestation of suspicion and spy mania that would lead to the loss of many an innocent life.

On 2 August 1914 German troops advanced into Luxembourg without opposition. The border posts along all Belgium's frontiers received an order to open fire on any hostile forces attempting to cross into Belgium. In the evening of the same day, the German Ambassador in Brussels presented the Belgian Foreign Office with a letter, an ultimatum demanding free passage for German forces through Belgian territory on the pretext that they had intelligence that France was about to attack Belgium. It was discussed by the Belgian Cabinet and was unanimously and courageously rejected. The Minister for Foreign Affairs, Henri Davignon, delivered the official rejection next morning: '… if, contrary to our expectation, Belgian neutrality should be violated by France, Belgium intends to fulfil her international obligations and the Belgian army would offer the most vigorous resistance to the invader. … The attack upon her independence with which the German Government threaten her constitutes a flagrant violation of international law. No strategic interest justifies such a violation of law. The Belgian Government, if they were to accept the proposals submitted to them, would sacrifice the honour of the nation and betray their duty towards Europe. … If this hope is disappointed the Belgian Government are firmly resolved to repel, by all the means in their power, every attack upon their rights.'

France commenced hostilities against Germany on 3 August, and Belgian General Headquarters issued orders to deploy the army. The 3rd Division, under General Gérard Leman, was ordered to reinforce and hold Liège, and the 4th, under Lieutenant-General Augustin Michel, went to Namur for the same purpose. The four other divisions were ordered to the area east of Brussels: the 1st Division left Ghent for Tienen; the 2nd went from Antwerp to Leuven; the 5th from Mons to Perwez; and the 6th moved on Wavre. The fortress cities were placed under martial law.

At dawn on 4 August orders were received by advanced German units that they should execute the next step of the plan: the capture of Liège. Units crossed into Belgium at six different places. A telegram was sent from the small border garrison of the Belgian 34 Brigade at Gemmenich to Leman, by now at Liège: *Le terroire Belge avait été envahi par les troupes Allemandes!* ('Belgian territory has been invaded by German troops!').

The immense forces of the German right wing, the First and Second Armies under Generals Alexander von Kluck and Karl Wilhelm Paul von Bülow respectively, advanced westwards into Belgium. They met with unexpectedly determined resistance but with such a weight of numbers and firepower it was inevitable that what Britain was soon calling 'Brave little Belgium' fell increasingly into German hands. It faced not only conventional forces but a new form of terror: during the night of 5–6 August Liège was bombed from the air by the Zeppelin LZ VI Köln and nine civilians lost their lives. Köln was damaged by anti-aircraft fire and crashed near Bonn on its return journey.

The fortress of Liège fell to the Second Army on 7 August, the ring of forts being overcome one by one by the unprecedented firepower of heavy 30.5cm Skoda and 42cm Krupp mortars, but only after initial attempts to attack using infantry and field artillery had met with a severe repulse. The Germans had planned to knock out the forts and capture Liège inside three days. As things turned out it was only on the eleventh day that final armed resistance from the last of the forts was overcome, several days after the city itself had been occupied. The remnants of the 3rd Division, less its commanding officer (Leman) who had been rendered unconscious by an explosion at his headquarters at Fort Loncin and taken as a prisoner of war to Magdeburg, withdrew to the next planned line of defence, the River Grote Gete. By 10 August, the 1st, 3rd and 5th Divisions lined the river south of Tienen; the 2nd Division and General Headquarters remained at Leuven; the 6th Division was behind the main force, positioned at Wavre; and the Belgian cavalry, under General Léon de Witte, was on the forward left flank around Loksbergen.

The news of the fall of Liège was very soon known by the public across Belgium, despite optimistic official communiqués. Namur, held by the 4th Division and its fortress garrison of some 37000 troops, lived in hope of significant support from the French Fifth Army: it never came. The French had given assurances that necessary military support would be given to Belgium whenever it was requested. During the morning of 7 August the Belgian military deputy in France reported to General Headquarters in Leuven with a message from Joffre. It said that the full French deployment would be complete by 11 August. At this time Joffre was still under the impression that Liège was securely in Belgian hands: he wanted it held until he could send four corps to the Meuse valley from the direction of Namur and insisted that if a retreat became necessary then it must be in a south-westerly direction (that is, towards France). But too late, for as this message was being received the Germans were already on both banks of the Meuse at Liège and the Belgian 3rd Division was beginning to withdraw to the Gete.

The German Second Army had learned quickly from its initial shock at Liège and deployed the heavy mortars as the first stage of the attack on Namur on 20 August. The Belgian garrison knew of the fate of Liège and there could be no surprise about what they were about to face. Within days the forts had suffered in the same crushing way as those at Liège and Belgian losses in killed, wounded and captured amounted to some 15000. A large proportion of the Belgian 4th Division managed to withdraw to the south and into France: it had the unusual experience of being moved immediately by rail to Le Havre, was put on shipping and transported by sea to Ostend on 27 August. It then proceeded to the 'national redoubt', where the rest of Belgian's field army was now concentrating. The last of Namur's forts fell on 25 August.

What was left of the 3rd Division, along with the others (except for the 4th Division at Namur) fought a number of localised but sharp defensive actions, with perhaps the most notable being that at Tongeren, where a company of cyclists, with help from the local *burgerwacht* (militia), drove off a brigade of *Liebeshuzaren* (Life Guards) on 9 August. Three days later, at Halen, units of the Belgian cavalry (the 4th and 5th *Lansiers* with a company of cyclists and another of pioneer engineers) under General Léon de Witte ambushed advanced squadrons of German cavalry under von Marwitz. It was almost certainly the last fight between mounted cavalrymen wearing the breastplates and plumed helmets of an earlier era: it became known as the 'battle of the silver helmets'. The battle lasted for most of the day and drew in reinforcements from both sides as the Germans mounted several waves of attacks. They met with a serious defeat in the village and in the surrounding farms, losing some 150 dead, 600 wounded and 200–300 prisoners. The number of dead horses was put at over 400. Belgian losses totalled around 500. The Germans withdrew, advancing days later with rather greater caution.

A refreshed German attack on 18–20 August forced the five Belgian divisions and their cavalry to withdraw through the Leuven area and turn north-westwards, avoiding battle and moving towards the safety of the 'national redoubt'. Again there were spots of intensive fighting: at Sint-Margriete-Houtem near Tienen on 18 August and at Aarschot the next day; but otherwise a relatively calm withdrawal was carried out as German focus began to move south-westwards. The Belgian force concentrated inside the 'national redoubt', where it was soon rejoined by the 4th Division. The main body of the German forces swept on westwards, leaving only General Hans von Beseler's III Reserve Corps as a screening force.

The Germans capitalised quickly on the Belgian withdrawal. On 19 August they marched into Leuven and flew the Kaiser's flag on the town hall, which until just a few hours previously had housed King Albert and the General Staff of the Belgian army. Next day came a triumphant, unopposed entry, impressive and threatening, into Brussels. American journalist Richard Harding Davies witnessed the scene.

> 'At eleven o'clock ... down the Boulevard Waterloo came the advance guard of the German army. It consisted of three men, a captain and two privates on bicycles. Their rifles were slung across their shoulders, they rode unwarily, with as little concern as the members of a touring-club out for a holiday. Behind them, so close upon each other that to cross from one sidewalk to the other was not possible, came the Uhlans, infantry, and the guns. For two hours I watched them, and then, bored with the monotony of it, returned to the hotel. After an hour, from beneath my window, I still could hear them; another hour and another went by. They still were passing. Boredom gave way to wonder. The thing fascinated you, against your will, dragged you back to the sidewalk and held you there open-eyed. No longer was it regiments of men marching, but something uncanny, inhuman, a force of nature like a landslide, a tidal wave, or lava sweeping down a mountain. It was not of this earth, but mysterious, ghostlike. It carried all the mystery and menace of a fog rolling toward you across the sea. ... For three days and three nights the column of grey, with hundreds of thousands of bayonets and hundreds of thousands of lances, with grey transport wagons, grey ammunition carts, grey ambulances, grey cannon, like a river of steel, cut Brussels in two.'

Mayor Adolphe Max, who had taken steps to ensure that no member of the public carried out any act that could be used as an excuse for German violence and destruction, refused to continue his duties under a German-appointed governor. He resisted the taxes and requisitions that were immediately imposed by the Germans and formed a national committee to manage supplies to the civilian population. Max was arrested in September and initially imprisoned at Namur before being sent to Germany for the duration of the war.

While Brussels escaped the worst of *schrecklichkeit* (terror), the period after the action at Aarschot was notable for a policy of German violence. A small force of Belgian infantry and field artillery held up the German advance for several hours, but after suffering heavy losses and being attacked from three sides, the survivors withdrew. Inevitably the Germans took prisoners, mostly wounded men. A significant number were marched to the banks of the River Demer, where they were shot.

Those that escaped were thrown in the river to drown. The Germans then turned on the citizens of Aarschot: some 400 houses were plundered and set on fire and 150 civilians were executed. During the next few days the fury continued and the towns of Diest, Schaffen and Tremelo were razed. It would not be long before the world would be outraged at similar atrocities at Dinant, Tamines and Andenne and at the burning of Leuven and the destruction of its priceless library.

The sorties from Antwerp
By 21–23 August 1914 the main body of the German right wing was engaged in a major battle against the French Fifth Army, with the newly arrived British Expeditionary Force on its north west flank at Mons. With the intention of ensuring that the German screening force could not be sent to reinforce it and to sever communications with Brussels, the Belgian force at Antwerp carried out an attack that is usually known as the 'first sortie'. After a reconnaissance, on 24 August the Belgian force advanced across the Rivers Dijle and Senne towards Mechelen and Vilvoorde. Only the 3rd Division, still recovering from its experiences at Liège, was held back in reserve. The 4th Division was still extricating itself from Namur. The remaining Belgian divisions advanced several kilometres, pushing back the thin German screen until they came against stouter resistance from artillery. At that time, a message was received from Joffre that a general withdrawal into central France had been ordered. King Albert ordered the divisions to disengage and to withdraw behind the outer fortress ring on 26 August. The Belgians had played their part: not only were they now fighting for Belgium, they were supporting the very armies whose support they needed so desperately.

A Belgian armoured car early in the war.

For a while the situation in Antwerp remained quiet and consequently gave the Belgians some time to reorganise. The divisions were deployed to hold the southern sector of the outer ring of forts, south of the Rivers Rupel and Nete and facing Mechelen, which was now in German hands. Antwerp was as yet not under fire but had been bombed by Zeppelin LZ25 on the night of 25–26 August.

By 1 September Belgian intelligence indicated that the Germans were preparing to advance past their western flank to reach the crossing of the River Scheldt at Dendermonde (Termonde). Any enemy movement across the Scheldt in that area would threaten the Antwerp Garrison with encirclement and so it was a threat that had to be taken with the utmost seriousness. The town was situated at a key strategic location, at the confluence with the River Dender, had been fortified in past centuries and artillery batteries had been added on the southern and eastern sides (clearly in anticipation of an attack from the direction of Germany); but these facilities were of little value in 1914. In the first days of the war Dendermonde had been an important mobilisation point for the army's reservists. Although many people had already fled, it had received many refugees from the east and was still thickly populated with civilians.

General Max von Boehn's IX Reserve Corps arrived in the area after a recent orgy of destruction of Leuven: it would soon repeat the exercise, with even greater rapacity. The intelligence that the Belgians had gathered was quite right. Von Beseler ordered IX Reserve Corps to attack Dendermonde on 4 September, after an initial demand for its surrender had been rejected.

Early on that day German artillery opened fire on the outlying villages of St. Gillies-bij-Dendermonde and Oudegem, which lay on the approach roads from the south and south west.

From 31 August they assembled forces for an attack on Dendermonde as a prelude to an assault on Antwerp. It began on 4 September, as IX Reserve Corps advanced to the mouth of the River Leie. Four battalions of Belgian infantry resisted, but could not hold for long against overwhelming numbers. They made a fighting withdrawal in the direction of Lokeren. By mid-day, the Germans had entered the old centre of Dendermonde, setting it ablaze. At the same time, the 12th Landwehr Brigade, together with the 6th Jagers, moved on Kapelle-op-den-Bos. They were soundly rebuffed, cut down by fire coming from the direction of Fort Breendonk.

IX Reserve Corps laid waste to Dendermonde, carrying out a systematic programme of destruction and plunder. More than 1200 buildings were burned, hostages were taken and many innocent civilians were executed. The orgy continued in the surrounding villages: the local war memorial in St. Gillies lists thirty-one of its soldiers who died in the Great War along with another thirty-two civilians. Most of the local population was herded up and moved out, many to prison camps at Soltau and Sennelager in Germany.

Four days later, by which date the main fighting had moved many days' march to the south and the French were beginning to strike back in the decisive Battle of the Marne, south east of Paris, it was noted that some German units appeared to be leaving Flanders: a 'second sortie from Antwerp' was launched to discourage any further movement. The cavalry, 2nd, 3rd and 6th Divisions advanced to cross the Demer and Dijle with the intention of outflanking the screening force on its eastern side. By 10 September lead elements of de Witte's cavalry had penetrated as far as Leuven; but it became increasingly clear that the Germans were reinforcing – for example, the 30th Division was identified and it was known that it had recently been in Alsace – and once again the operation was called off and the force withdrew to the fortress ring. The operation had cost some 8000 casualties.

While the German high command was now of the opinion that the Belgian army was incapable of serious, sustained offensive action, it had become clear that it still posed a threat to the northern German flank and the lateral communication lines and railways running across Belgium, the artery supplying the main fighting front with materials and men from Germany. These lines were all too vulnerable to a sudden attack from Antwerp.

The 'national redoubt' of Antwerp
Through its important position at the head of the long estuary of the Scheldt, Antwerp plays a major role in any strategic military considerations involving the Low Countries. It forms a natural supply base and military centre. The city had been fortified since 1851, originally by an entrenched encircling line. During the heightened tensions of the 1860s the line was greatly strengthened. Following the designs of the military engineer Brialmont, Forts 1 to 8 and Fort Merksem on the right bank of the Scheldt facing the Netherlands and Germany were constructed. On the left bank, protecting the city from a coastal attack from the direction of France or Great Britain, Forts Kruibeke, Zwijndrecht and St Marie were also built. They were extensive brick constructions, providing sufficient protection from the artillery of the day. The forts girdled the city, each three to four kilometres from the next. The experience of the Franco-Prussian war of 1870–71 made it plain that the ring needed to be widened and pushed further out from the city if the mass armies and increasingly heavy artillery then being

developed were to be withstood. At the same time, the Belgian economy was growing, and the harbour complex to the west of the city was pushing the limits of the populated areas outwards. It was, however, only in 1906 that the Belgian government agreed to a new scheme for the fortress.

The development plan featured a new defensive ring of concrete fortresses, which would be equipped with a selection of old artillery pieces to reduce the costs. The ring would be situated just forward of the natural borders formed by the Rivers Rupel and Nete, between Lier and the lower loop of the Scheldt. The plan also called for the strengthening of the old brick forts with concrete and for the establishment of new battery positions near Doel, able to fire from the lower Scheldt to the Dutch border. Endless planning debates and budget constraints ensured so that by August 1914 the construction work was far from complete. Much of the 1906 plan still existed only on paper. Many of the fortresses as yet comprised no more than the gun cupolas, whilst some of the rotating turrets were not fully set in concrete. There were gaps in the telephone and electricity supplies, and the 1859 forts of the inner ring were still only brick. Trenches, designed to run continuously between the forts, had not been started. The old gunpowder cannons gave off so much smoke on firing that they could be seen from miles away - and there was only one of them per kilometre of front. To add to all of these weaknesses, the forts were garrisoned by 65,000 of the oldest classes of troops, under-trained, poorly armed and poorly supplied. Recent experience made it evident that the forts were obsolete death traps. Observations of the effects of shelling in the Russo-Japanese war of 1905 revealed that the concrete would not withstand even 6-inch shell bursts, let alone the size of the mortars now possessed by the Germans.

On 8 September 1914 fortress engineer General Victor Deguise took over as military governor of the Antwerp district. He ordered immediate works on the entrenchments, including providing head cover using tree trunks and logs (which of course provided little chance of cover against all but small arms fire) and continuous barbed wire. Unfortunately, the work of clearing away buildings and trees to improve the field of fire for the garrisons of the forts also allowed improved observation from the German side,

Belgian General Deguise commanded the garrison of Antwerp.

improving the accuracy of their artillery. Belgian military engineers also arranged for riverside areas to be flooded, but this capability was not used in the forthcoming battle.

The Battle for Antwerp and the escape of the Belgian field army
The Germans had already shown at Liège and Namur that the old fortresses were no match for the heaviest artillery; but they had begun to have a healthy respect for the Belgian field army. They strengthened their forces in East Flanders and placed them under the orders of von Beseler, commander of III Reserve Corps. He had at his disposal more than the strength of five infantry divisions, along with 160 heavy and thirteen super-heavy artillery pieces.

Von Beseler chose the area between Mechelen and Lier, south-east of the city, for the frontal assault. The general plan was to break through the fortress line in one place and then extend northwards. Systematic shelling of the outer forts at Lier, Koningshoekt, St Katherine Wavre and Walem, together with the smaller shelters and posts between them, would open the way for a major infantry advance.

Meanwhile the Belgians were planning a third 'sortie', scheduled to take place on 25 September, between the Dender and the Willebroek Canal. Unfortunately, by this time the fighting on the Aisne had subsided and the Germans were able to release more troops for Antwerp. Belgian intelligence detected this movement and the sortie was postponed.

On Sunday 27 September 1914, the German attack on Antwerp began, with the 5th and 6th Reserve Divisions advancing on the city in the area between the Rivers Dijle and Nete. They were opposed by the Belgian 1st and 2nd Divisions but nevertheless made good progress, in large part as a result of superior artillery fire. Mechelen, a town of no military value but unlucky in that it was situated relatively near the outer fortress ring, suffered grievously from shelling, during which its 13th Century cathedral of St Rombold was almost completely destroyed. East of the town, Putte and Heist-op-den-Berg fell to the Germans, and 27th Landwehr Brigade pushed beyond them to capture the railway at Lier.

The next day the large mortars came into action in this area for the first time. Shortly after midday the first 420mm shells fell on Fort St Katherine Wavre, while 305mm shells hit Fort Walem. Within minutes the gun cupolas were knocked out, the two metres' thick concrete walls were ripped apart and the interiors of the forts devastated. At Fort Walem, the magazine exploded: of a hundred men inside the building, only ten escaped.

The morning of 29 September found the German 4th Ersatz Division and 38th Landwehr in full advance between the Dender and the Dijle.

Blaasveld, north west of Mechelen, was flattened by gun fire, and there was in general no let up from the previous day. The powder magazine at Fort St Katherine Wavre was hit and burned, resulting in a black column of smoke visible for miles around. The Belgian defences were powerless against such a crushing weight of artillery. The 420mm and 305mm mortars were well outside the range of counter-battery fire from the Belgian field guns and in any case were not spotted by the few aircraft and observation balloons. The attack carried on into the 30th, with the same results. Fort Walem was finally destroyed. Just behind it, shelling burst the banks of a large reservoir, drowning men in the fire trenches. The most advanced German units moved inexorably forward and broke through the fortress ring, pushing the increasingly fragmented 1st and 2nd Belgian Divisions closer in to the city proper. Behind them countless thousands of refugees were in flight from the city across the Scheldt, heading along the coast or crossing into the Netherlands. The further defence of Antwerp and the safety of the whole of the army still inside the perimeter looked increasingly perilous. It was reluctantly understood that it was essential to move the army out and along the coastal corridor before the Germans encircled them. But this would all take time and it was obvious that if any substantial part of the army was to escape then the fighting line must be held for another three days at least. During the night of 30 September–1 October orders were given to move GHQ west along the coast to Ostend. Antwerp itself would only finally be evacuated when the Germans were at the gates.

The British arrive
A token British force had already been briefly in Belgium when on 30 September, with the Germans breaking the outer ring of forts at Antwerp, King Albert requested urgent assistance from the French and British governments. Both had made reassuring promises about supporting the Belgians ever since the Germans began the attack on Liège, but precious little had yet arrived in terms of practical help. On 25 August an improvised brigade of Royal Marine Light Infantry and Royal Marine Artillery had been sent to Ostend, without specific orders and with precious little equipment. After establishing an outpost line around the town it was hurriedly withdrawn home after six days. It returned to Dunkirk in mid-September, now supplemented by the Oxfordshire Hussars and some Royal Engineers, but went to Lille to operate with the French. By the end of the month they were at Cassel.

Kitchener and Churchill, respectively the British Secretary of State for War and First Lord of the Admiralty, were all too aware of the strategic importance of the control of the Scheldt and the Belgian coast and were determined to encourage the Belgians to hold Antwerp as long as possible. Kitchener had already sent Colonel Alister Grant Dallas to act as liaison officer with the Belgians and was arranging to provide some heavy artillery support – not that he had much available to send. Disquieting news of continued German pressure and progress over the next days increased pressure to do something – indeed almost anything. Churchill cabled the Belgians via the British ambassador in the early hours of 3 October:

> 'The importance of Antwerp justifies a further effort till the course of the main battle in France is determined. We are trying to send you help from the main army and, if this were possible, would add reinforcements from here. Meanwhile a brigade of marines will reach you tomorrow to sustain the defence. We urge you to make one further struggle to hold out. Even a few days will make a difference. We hope that government may find it possible to remain, and field army to continue operations.'

The Belgian reply was to the effect that, if no serious help were forthcoming within three days, it would be necessary to evacuate the city and to move the army to Ostend.

Not untypically, but with Kitchener's support, Churchill temporarily abandoned his primary role at the Admiralty and went to Antwerp himself, arriving by special train later that day. The French were now arranging to send the 87th Territorial Division and a brigade of *Fusiliers-Marins* (marines). By coincidence, Britain would also send its sea soldiers: the brigade at Cassel was ordered onto trains that would take them via Dunkirk and Bruges into the inferno at Antwerp. Detraining at Vieux-Dieu (Oude-God), a few kilometres east of the city, at 11 pm on 3 October, the brigade marched out next morning to relieve the tired Belgian 21st Line Regiment in trenches near Lier and was ordered, along with the 7th Line Regiment, to hold the position. Churchill's offer to resign his post and take command of the British force was rejected. The Belgian government evacuated to Ostend on this day: it would eventually settle in exile at Sainte-Adresse, at Le Havre, on the French coast.

Two further British brigades were also now on the way, but what Churchill had taken care not to reveal to the Belgians was that this consisted of Royal Naval service reservists together with about 700 men who had only been serving for a few days, with precious little training and in some cases no weapons. The British *Official History* refers to one platoon as consisting entirely of 'pensioner sergeants and colour-sergeants'. The brigades reached Antwerp during the night of

5–6 October and the British force was formalised as the Royal Naval Division, under the command of Brigadier General Archibald Paris.

The British also prepared the newly formed 7th Division and the 3rd Cavalry Division to form a IV Corps of the British Expeditionary Force and sail it to Belgium. They arrived at Zeebrugge on 6–7 October, too late to save Antwerp, and were moved to Ghent. This city was certain to be the next to be attacked by the Germans after the fall of Antwerp and there was little time or manpower to put it into any form of defensive state.

Early in the morning of 7 October the Antwerp newspapers printed an official message from Deguise, saying that an attack on the city was imminent and those who could still leave the city should do so without delay. Little wonder that over the next few days some 500,000 civilians would leave the city in the directions of Ghent, Ostend and the Netherlands. Every road out of Antwerp and the surrounding towns was solid with refugees. A war correspondent reported seeing a crowd of at least 150,000 queuing to cross to the left bank of the Scheldt by a few pontoon bridges and ferries. It was said that some unscrupulous ferry owners were charging twenty francs a head to cross.

The Belgian 1st and 3rd Divisions clung bravely on to the River Nete positions until the last possible moment, but withdrawal became urgent and inevitable. Their losses were heavy. The German 1st Ersatz Brigade captured the banks of the River Scheldt to the west of the city and, two days later, completed the capture of Schoonaarde. This latter position was potentially of immense importance, as it threatened the coastal corridor and the route of the Belgian withdrawal.

Belgian headquarters, in conference with Churchill, proposed to evacuate the entire army to the west bank of the Scheldt on the night of 7–8 October. A small force would be left behind to cover the retreat, consisting of the garrison of the remaining forts, units of the 2nd Division and the three British brigades of the Royal Naval Division. They would hold positions at the older fortress line, within the outer suburbs of the city, for as long as possible. The proposed general move westwards was fraught with the danger of a German attack towards the coast, potentially cutting the army in two. There was by now only a thin corridor, about a hundred kilometres long, stretching towards Ostend and beyond into the Westhoek, along which the Belgians could retreat. King Albert and Queen Elisabeth reluctantly left Antwerp and, moving via Eekloo and Bruges, briefly took up residence in the royal chalet at Ostend.

During the evening of the 7th, von Beseler sent a communication to Deguise, an ultimatum to capitulate or be destroyed. The ultimatum was rejected. At midnight a deliberate bombardment of the old city began. The first shell fell in the southern suburb of Berchem, killing a boy and wounding his mother and sister. The next blew the head off a street-sweeper as he ran for shelter. Shells fell at five or six a minute. Fires began in many places and, with the city's water supply cut since 2 October, a strong wind blowing and with people more concerned with flight, the city was abandoned to its fate. It has since been calculated that 556 houses were partially and another 221 completely destroyed, along with public buildings and damage to many of its architectural jewels. The city centre area around Groenplaats, Schoenmarkt, Beddenstraat and Eiermarkt was particularly badly hit, including the gutting of the Au Quatre Saisons department store, the Hotel de l'Europe and the Taverne Royale. Vanbreestraat, known for its large patrician houses, was also destroyed. Old Antwerp would never be the same again. On the left bank, Belgian troops set huge petrol and oil storage tanks ablaze in order to deny their contents to the Germans.

Early on 8 October German infantry began a fresh assault, this time on the force holding the older fortress line. The 305mm and 420mm mortars had been moved up and fired on the old brick forts. Even before dawn, Forts 1, 2 and 4 were reported to have fallen. Approximately at the same hour, the French 87th Territorial Division detrained at Poperinge and moved forward to take up positions near Ypres.

During the evening the brigades of the Royal Naval Division were ordered to withdraw. Not all of the units received the order and there was some confusion. With incredible congestion on the few roads heading north-west, it proved practically impossible even for signal runners to move back and forth between headquarters and front line units. The 1st Naval Brigade suffered especially badly. Eventually, the men of the brigade made their way to St Gillies Waes, where a train had been sent to evacuate them, just as the Germans were attacking at Moerbeke, cutting the line to the west. The men were ordered to march to cross the Dutch frontier, three miles to the north, where some 1,500 of them were disarmed and interned. One unit of marines, the Portsmouth Battalion, went by another route to Kemzeke, the next station down the line to the east. While there they fought with advance units of the 37th Landwehr Brigade. About half eventually got away, and finally did get a train at Zelzate. The remainder, along with some 400 Belgians, surrendered. Deguise ordered the remainder of the 2nd Division to concentrate around Fort St Marie and make a last stand. The few remaining forts on the right bank were ordered to hold out to the last man.

On 9 October Antwerp city council decided to deal with the enemy. Mayor Jan De Vos signed the city's surrender later that day. The last forts were overcome the next day and the remnants of Deguise's headquarters and the 2nd Division surrendered at Fort St Marie. 25,000 Belgian troops, finding themselves isolated on the left bank and surrounded by the Germans, crossed the border into Zeeuwse Vlaanderen, the part of the Netherlands south of the Scheldt, where they were interned until the end of the war. In a final effort to round up the Belgian troops still in the city, the Germans advanced. Von Beseler ruefully remarked, as 60,000 German troops marched into the city, that for all their effort and not inconsiderable losses in front of Antwerp, all he had won was *ein solche Festung und kein General* (essentially 'a sorry fortress and no general').

In all, some 2,600 British troops were lost at Antwerp. Only seven officers and fifty men were killed, but 138 were wounded, 936 became prisoners of war and 1,479 were interned in the Netherlands.

The covering force
The hastily-constituted British IV Corps was landed on 6 and 7 October under orders to proceed to Antwerp for offensive operations against the German heavy artillery in the area of Mechelen, but on no account was it to allow itself to be bottled up in Antwerp. Its units proceeded to concentrate around Bruges; but it immediately became evident that the original plan could not be carried out. The Belgians and British marines were stuck in Antwerp and there was no sign of the promised French 87th Territorial Division.

Intelligence about the actual situation at Antwerp was most unclear and, with only part of his force yet available, instead of advancing towards the objective, the corps commander, Lieutenant General Sir Henry Rawlinson, withdrew his troops westwards in order to cover further landings taking place at Ostend. Hearing that a promised force of French marines had reached Ghent, on 8 October he ordered his force to move to the same area but to avoid becoming seriously involved in action.

The Belgians had already received assistance from one scratch force of naval men, and a second was now to enter the fray. On 4 October a 6000-strong brigade of French Fusiliers-Marins gathering in Paris received orders to proceed to Dunkirk. This brigade was largely made up of surplus naval troops from Cherbourg, Lorient and Brest, the ports of Brittany, who had received little training for land warfare and had no heavy artillery. Its commanding officer *Contre-Amiral* (Rear-Admiral) Pierre-Alexis Ronarc'h (pronounced Ronar), a 49 year-old Breton and a veteran of the Boxer Rebellion in China, had only had about a week to organise his brigade into two regiments, each of three battalions, and a machine gun company. The brigade entrained on 7 October; but by the time it arrived at Dunkirk later that day it found that the situation was changing fast. Rather than being given time to organise and train it was to be sent straight away to reinforce the garrison at Antwerp. The French General Paul Pau had been sent by Joffre on a co-ordinating mission. When Ronarc'h met the 65 years-old, one-armed Pau next day at Ghent, he found from him that the Belgians were already evacuating Antwerp and that his brigade was to co-operate with the British IV Corps, now landing at Ostend and Zeebrugge, in covering the Belgian withdrawal.

Contre-Amiral Pierre-Alexis Ronarc'h commanded the Franco-Belgian force in the defence of Diksmuide.

Over the next twenty-four hours, Ronarc'h deployed near Melle, where his force had its first, short but sharp clash with German forces. He received orders to disengage and withdraw to Thielt, covered by the British 7th Division while this was carried out. Next day, 10 October, his orders were to withdraw again, this time to Diksmuide, an ancient market town of about 4,000 inhabitants on the eastern bank of the River Yser. These were days of hard marching for men unaccustomed to such work, in rain and with the roads congested by the flight of thousands of refugees, the air alive with rumours of the nearby enemy. As the brigade approached the town, Ronarc'h deployed the 2nd Battalion of his 1st Regiment near the village of Esen to hold the roads leading from Klerken, Vladslo and Roeselare; the 3rd Battalion of 2nd Regiment went to Woumen to cover the approach to Ypres; and the rest of the force retired to and through

The 'red pompoms', the French Fusiliers-Marins, proved to be formidable fighters.

Diksmuide. The artillery was eventually found a suitable location south of the chapel of Notre-Dame de Bon Secours, half way to Esen, and Ronarc'h moved his headquarters into the chapel there. Detachments of Belgian engineers and infantry joined the brigade to create improvised defences, just as an enemy cyclist patrol (and, it is said, an armoured car) clashed with the outposts on the Esen road.

By 9 October the bulk of what was left of the Belgian field army, with the remnants of the Royal Naval Division, had reached the west bank of the Ghent-Terneuzen canal. They desperately needed rest and their position in terms of supplies – of food, forage and ammunition – was precarious. The main supply depots and railways had fallen into German hands. Intelligence showed that the Bavarian cavalry was on the move westwards and that a column of at least 20,000 infantry was moving on Kortrijk and Menen. Joffre asked that the Belgians move south-westwards, in the direction of Deinze and Thielt. The Belgians thought differently, agreeing to fall back on to the River Yser, the last possible defence line in Belgium. The British IV Corps covered their move and took up positions at Roeselare, before eventually moving south westwards to form a defensive line in front of Ypres.

By the time it was approaching the Yser the entire Belgian force was down to around 70000 men, of whom 48000 were rifles. The mixed brigades were reduced to three battalions each and the men of the disbanded units were redeployed to bring units back up to something approaching their establishment. Artillery, transport and medical support was similarly depleted; while on paper the army consisted of six infantry divisions, it more resembled perhaps three in fighting strength. No part of the allied line that now stretched down as far as Switzerland looked as vulnerable and gave such concern as the twenty miles or so from Ypres to the Yser estuary.

Last stand

With only a narrowing strip of West Flanders still free, on 13 October King Albert issued an inspirational order. He had no choice. If any part of Belgium was to be saved, the time had come to make the last stand.

> 'Soldiers, for two months and more you have been fighting for the most just of causes, for your homes, for national independence. You have contained the enemy armies, suffered three sieges, carried out several withdrawals, operated without losses a long retreat through a narrow corridor. Until now you have been isolated in this immense struggle. You are now standing alongside the valiant French and English (sic) armies. It is up to you, through

the tenacity and bravery of which you have given so much proof, to uphold the reputation of our arms. Our national honour is committed to it. Soldiers, look to the future with confidence, fight with courage. That, in the positions in which I will place you, your gaze will be directed only forward and consider as a traitor to the fatherland the one who will speak the word retreat without the formal order being given. The time has come, with the help of our powerful allies, to drive from our dear homeland the enemy who invaded it in defiance of its commitments and the sacred rights of a free people.'

There was only one potential natural line of defence for the last stand and that was the River Yser. At the time the order was given, Albert's army was east of the river, on the line Eernegem to Wynendale Forest, prolonged on the right by the Fusiliers-Marins to Kortemark, and screened by cavalry on the Lys and the Terneuzen Canal. Standing alongside the river estuary was the fishing port town of Nieuwpoort, which was, according to the *Dover Express* in 1889, '... an old decayed haven very much on a par with Sandwich ... this old port is hardly worthy of being taken into account at all as it could not be used for any offensive or defensive military purpose.' How wrong this was to prove to be.

On the same day a large body of recently-raised, fresh and enthusiastic but wholly inexperienced, troops began to arrive from Germany and concentrate west and southwest of Brussels. Comprising the XXII, XXIII, XXVI and XXVII Reserve Corps (each of two divisions), it was placed under orders of Albrecht, Duke of Württemberg, commanding the reorganised Fourth Army. Taken together with the III Reserve Corps, 4th Ersatz Division and 37 Landwehr Brigade at Antwerp, it brought the available force in Flanders to 140 battalions of infantry and approximately 500 guns. Fourth Army was tasked with by-passing Lille to its north, clearing the Belgians out of Flanders and to advance with its right flank west of Saint-Omer. General von Falkenhayn, now the German chief of the general staff, instructed Albrecht that this was to be achieved without consideration of casualties.

The British IV Corps at this stage was withdrawing towards Ypres and the remainder of the British Expeditionary Force was in the process of moving to Flanders, having disengaged from the stabilised front on the River Aisne, east of Paris. French cavalry was in Houthulst Forest, with the 87th and 89th Territorial Infantry Divisions at Poperinge and Ypres respectively.

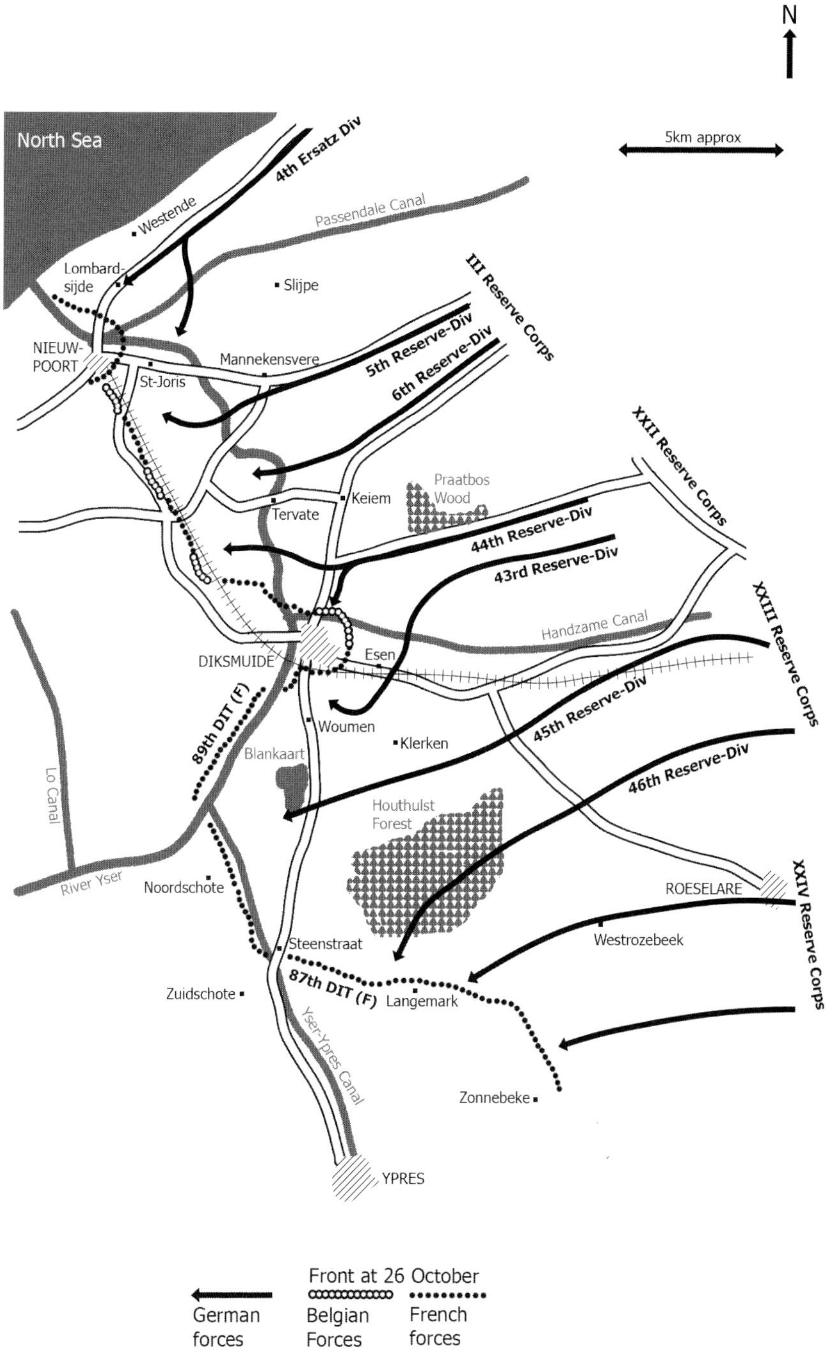

Attack on the Yser, 1914.

The Belgian deployment

As the army streamed into the Yser area from the east, the units were reorganised and the divisions deployed. The 2nd Division, under General Émile Dossin, held a line from the sea to the Yser bridge east of Sint-Joris, with advanced posts at Lombardsijde, Rattevalle and Mannekensvere: the latter pair protected key bridges over the Plassendale Canal and the Yser respectively. The 1st Division continued the line down along the river to Schoorbakke Bridge with an outpost about a kilometre away at Schore. From there, the 4th Division held the river bend past Tervate to Den Toren Farm, east of Oud-Stuivekenskerke, with posts at Keiem and Beerst. The brigade of Fusiliers-Marins held the salient that snaked around to the east of Diksmuide, with two brigades of the 3rd Division in reserve at Lampernisse. From St-Jans-Kapelle, south of Diksmuide, the 5th Division held the line down to Drie-Grachten, with a forward post at Luigem; and the 6th Division carried it on past Merkem to Boesinge, where it met the French territorials. The cavalry of the Belgian 1st Cavalry Division cavalry operated around Houthulst Forest and the 2nd Cavalry Division was held in reserve at Nieuwpoort.

From right (north) to left, the German forces were deployed as follows: III Reserve Corps marched from Antwerp and was positioned on the extreme right (north) of the German force, with its right on the coast; to its left came, in turn, XXII, XXIII and XXVI Reserve Corps. This would be the force that would engage the Belgians and French. South of them, XXVII Reserve Corps would march on Ypres and in due course engage with the British Expeditionary Force. All came under the command of Fourth Army.

Tervate Bridge. Note the damage to houses nearby.

Support from the North Sea
On 15 October III Reserve Corps seized Ostend. The historical architectural gem that is Bruges also fell into its hands, along with the sea canal to another vital harbour and dock area at Zeebrugge. This was a most serious loss as far as British interests were concerned. At a stroke, the lines of communication across the English Channel could be threatened. By good fortune this eventuality had been foreseen and while British land forces could do little about it its greater naval power could: the British Official History of Naval Operations explains the steps that had already been taken.

'On 12 October a new command was instituted out of that of the Admiral of Patrols. The [Dover] Straits were removed from his jurisdiction and made a separate command under Rear-Admiral the Hon. HLA Hood, with the designation of 'Rear-Admiral Commanding the Dover Patrol and Senior Naval Officer, Dover'. The force under his orders was to consist of the 6th or Dover Destroyer Flotilla (twenty-four 'Tribal' class), with its attached light cruisers *Attentive* (Captain Charles D Johnson in command), *Adventure*, *Foresight* and *Sapphire*; the 3rd and 4th Submarine Flotillas (thirteen 'B' and 'C' class), together with the Downs Boarding Flotilla and all trawlers and auxiliary patrol vessels within his area. At the same time, the command of the Admiral of Patrols – who was left all to the northward and now shifted his headquarters to the Humber – was reorganised in order to deal with its immense extension that was on foot to cope with submarine attack. The submarine, indeed, was at the root of the reorganisation.

For the new Dover Patrol no coastal operations were in immediate anticipation, and of the few vessels on the Navy List adapted for that purpose none had been attached to Admiral Hood's Command; but the three monitors were still at Dover and, within an hour of the Belgian request coming to hand, he asked for them. They were given to him immediately, but although this went beyond what the Belgians had asked, the Admiralty did not stop there. During the night news came in of vast bodies of Germans swarming westward against the Belgian line, and next day, 16 October, a fuller request came from General Joffre himself. Apparently he did not count on the Belgians being able to stem the flood; for what he saw was operations extending to the North Sea between Ostend and the outer defences of Dunkirk. He asked that the Allied fleets should take part in them by supporting the

The monitor HMS *Humber* provided fire support from the sea.

extreme left and acting with long-range guns against the German right if that flank was extended to the dunes; and he expressed a wish that the naval officer in command would concert operations through Dunkirk with General Foch, who was now in command of the French *Détachement d'Armée en Belgique*. Within two hours Admiral Hood had his orders. The three monitors, with a division of destroyers to protect them, were to proceed at once to Dunkirk under Commander Eric Fullerton of the *Severn*. The French also offered a division to protect 'the cruisers', but it had been explained that cruisers were not to be risked on so hazardous a service. It was a resolution the Admiralty soon saw cause to change.'

The 'three monitors' were new ships: the HMS *Humber*, *Mersey* and *Severn*. They were odd looking, eighty-one metres long, very shallow draught vessels, each with a crew of 140. They had been recently built for the Brazilian Navy but at the outbreak of the war were hurriedly purchased from Vickers for use by the Royal Navy. Fitted with a pair of 6-inch and two 4.7-inch guns, they possessed considerable firepower but were unstable and difficult to manoeuvre, certainly in any difficult sea conditions. On the other hand, HMS *Severn* went on to survive a torpedo attack because the weapon passed below her shallow keel.

16 October: skirmishes as advanced screens of both sides meet
During the morning mounted troops of the 1st Belgian Division clashed with enemy patrols at Sint-Pieters-Kapelle, some eleven kilometres

east of Nieuwpoort. They found that they were facing elements of the 5th Reserve Division of III Reserve Corps, which had marched from Bruges through Jabbeke and Gistel.

Later in the day, east of Diksmuide, after a bombardment of the rudimentary trenches, German infantry advanced against the Fusiliers-Marins, who were supported by six Belgian batteries. It proved to be but the beginning of an intensive, concerted and bloody fight for possession of the town and its all-important river crossing. The advance failed to penetrate the French line in the face of effective support by the fire of field artillery, although certain spots changed hands on occasion during the day without changing the overall situation.

The Diksmuide sector was now held on the left (that is, north of the Kaaskerke – Diksmuide – Esen road) by the 1st Regiment under *Capitaine de Vaisseau* (Captain) Joseph Delage and on the right by the 2nd Regiment under *Capitaine de Vaisseau* Georges Varney. They were supported by Belgian artillery, which had set up an observation post on the high concrete tower of the Minoterie (flour mill) on the river bank on the west side of the town. Another battery arrived on the second day of the battle, 17 October, bringing the total artillery force up to seventy-two guns. Ronarc'h established his headquarters at the railway station at Kaaskerke.

During the day Lieutenant General Michel, of the Belgian 4th Division, issued a special order to his men:

The Minoterie was an imposing agro-industrial complex dominating the banks of the Yser at Diksmuide. (*University of Ghent*)

'The fate of the whole campaign probably depends on our resistance. I implore officers and men, notwithstanding what efforts they may be called upon to make, to do even more than their mere duty. The salvation of the country and therefore of each individual among us depends on it. Let us then resist to our utmost.'

Although his brigade had deployed in front of Diksmuide after withdrawing from Melle, it had quickly become clear to Ronarc'h that he was holding too long a line for the number of men available. After consultation with Michel, under whose command he had now been placed, he took steps to withdraw to a shorter, tighter line. Knowing that his force of some 6000 men, reinforced by about 5000 Belgians but with no prospect of reinforcement, faced three German army corps, he implored his men to hold out for four days to buy time for significant allied forces to come in behind them. As things turned out, the brigade fought in the defence of Diksmuide from 16 October until the town finally fell on 10 November. It is rightly regarded as an epic of the Great War, in which the French marines, wearing caps that gave the brigade its nickname of the 'red pompoms', earned lasting acclaim.

The 16th October proved to be a disappointing and enlightening day for the German; in some ways similar to the recent experience of German cavalry cut down by Belgian guns at Halen, the unexpectedly stiff resistance they encountered in the skirmishes introduced a new note of caution. It may have played a part in a tactical switch the next day, for the weight of attack was shifted northwards against Belgian-held positions along the line between Leke, Keiem and Beerst.

During the day Ferdinand Foch met with King Albert in Veurne. The French general outlined his intention to attack and turn the German right wing and requested Belgian assistance in this operation. He left disappointed, although he appreciated that the King simply could not squander any appreciable portion of his army in offensive operations and thus risk the fall of his country. This question of the continued existence of a part of free Belgium defended by a Belgian army was a point to which Albert would return on numerous occasions during the Great War.

17 October 1914
On this misty day King Albert visited the front line at Diksmuide at the very time that Fourth Amy commenced its operations to outflank the main allied body as it had been ordered. III Reserve Corps was already west of Ostend, while the rest of Fourth Army began from the line Oostkamp – Tielt – Waregem. Four strong German columns advanced

from Bruges and Ostend, others from Zarren and Staden, towards the Yser. Contact was still mainly confined to cyclist and cavalry reconnaissances.

French cavalry engaged enemy patrols north of Houthulst Forest. The 1st Division of Belgian cavalry supported them on the right and south of the forest, moving through Langemark to Vijfwegen and Ondank. At about 10am a clash developed with a column advancing from Staden. German artillery came into action and the Belgians wisely withdrew to the edge of the forest, leaving behind two medical men: 50 year old *Médecin de Régiment* Léon Debongnie of 2 Guides Regiment, killed by a shell which burst under his horse, and *Médecin-Adjoint (*assistant physician) Richard Camille Baudoux of the division's horse artillery. The presence of the cavalry allowed some adjustment of the Belgian disposition and the beginnings of the creation of a secondary defensive line: 5th Division was relieved and moved to Lampernisse. The 3rd Division, which it replaced there, moved to the rear area of Avekapelle, east of Veurne, and a brigade of the 6th Division moved forward to Luigem.

Rear Admiral Horace Hood reached Nieuwpoort in HMS *Attentive* at about midnight and established communication with the shore. On his way he had received from Belgian headquarters the latest information regarding the military situation. What was required of his force was, first, to prevent any landing of German troops behind the Belgians (that is, between Nieuwpoort, De Panne and Dunkirk) and, secondly, to check with gun fire the forces of the enemy that were advancing on Nieuwpoort. Hood's despatch of 11 November 1914 later explained the role played by his force.

> 'Operations commenced during the night of 17 October when the *Attentive*, flying my flag, accompanied by the monitors *Severn*, *Humber* and *Mersey*, the light cruiser *Foresight* and several torpedo boat destroyers, arrived and anchored off Nieuwpoort pier. Early on the morning of the 18 October information was received that German infantry were advancing on Westende village, and that a battery was in action at Westende-Bad. The flotilla at once proceeded up past Westende and Middelkerke to draw their fire and endeavour to silence the guns. A brisk shrapnel fire was opened from the shore which was immediately replied to and this commenced the naval operations on the coast that continued for more than three weeks without intermission".

Sunday, 18 October 1914
By 3am Hood was able to report that the three monitors would be in position at daylight, and that he was sending back the scouts and all but four of the destroyers but was remaining himself on the *Attentive*.

As the Royal Navy was heading in the direction of the Belgian coast, many thousands of people were heading the opposite way by whichever means possible. The first refugees to reach Ireland did so on this date; most others settled in England. During the day, in an act of military logic but showing undeniable signs of impending defeat, Belgian engineers destroyed the ancient tower of the old Vierboete lighthouse at Nieuwpoort; a building that traced its history back to 1284 but which had been replaced by a new, nearby construction.

At an early hour the German attack began in earnest against the Belgian advanced posts at Lombardsijde, Rattevalle, Mannekensvere, Schore, Keiem and Beerst. All came under sustained artillery fire, as did the area of Schoorbakke Bridge, and soon German infantry began to probe forward.

At 10am, in response to urgent Belgian messages for assistance, Hood's attention was focused on the area of Rattevalle and the hamlet of Lovie and Blockhuis Farm, a few hundred metres to its north east. This was held by the right-hand elements of 6 Mixed Brigade of the 2nd Division and was the most easterly of the advanced posts. Rattevalle was a bridging point on the Plassendale Canal, north east of Nieuwpoort, and is less than three kilometres from the sea. Advancing towards it was the German 4th Ersatz Division, marching along the coast road through Middelkerke, after which it diverged to form columns advancing on Westende, Lombardsijde and Rattevalle.

The *Attentive*, as well as the monitors and the *Foresight* with her destroyers, bombarded the enemy column attacking Rattevalle and were hotly engaged all day once German artillery began to return fire. Despite being unable to directly observe the effect of its shelling (mainly due to the height of the dunes, which blocked the line of sight), the ships played a key part in the failure of the 4th Ersatz Division to advance on Lombardsijde. In the afternoon King Albert sent Hood a special message of thanks. Hood now moved to HMS *Amazon* as his flag ship and *Attentive* returned to Dover.

The outpost at Mannekensvere was held by the 7th Line Regiment of 7 Mixed Brigade, 2nd Division. It had recently been brought up to strength by merging with the 27th Line Regiment of the same brigade. Only some 800 metres behind it, the Union Bridge (Uniebrug) crossed the Yser, after which there was a straight three kilometres' march through the village of Sint-Joris to Nieuwpoort: a wheel leftwards would then roll up the Belgian front from behind. It was a position that simply had to be held. Under its commanding officer, Colonel Hector Delobbe, the regiment performed its duty so well in defending Mannekensvere that it was decorated with the Order of Leopold by King Albert. A few days before, on 15 October, a detachment of Belgian engineers had blown up the tower of the village church to deny it to the enemy as a potential aiming and observation point. The explosion was of such force that fifteen nearby houses became uninhabitable and those villagers thus made homeless joined the throngs of refugees making their way westwards. They may, in retrospect, perhaps be considered lucky.

German troops, approaching from the direction of Slijpe, going along the Vladslovaart through the area of a large farm, 't Geuzengat, engaged the detachments that had been posted by Delobbe to hold the small ditch bridges at Molenbrug and Busbrug in front of Mannekensvere at about 10.30am. A sustained firefight of small arms and artillery commenced, in which soldiers of both sides were killed. The village fell briefly into German hands but was recaptured by a counter attack by 7th Line Regiment during the evening. *De Duinengalm*, a weekly magazine about the Belgian coastal land published from 1920, later reported that four local people who had decided not to flee but to take shelter also lost their lives on this day: Henri Maes, a local councillor, and his wife Nathalie, who had earlier left but took the chance of returning, both died when a shell exploded near a cart beneath which they had taken cover; farmer Camiel Spegelaere was killed near the Busbrug when taking his cows out – the Germans later buried him near his house; and a labourer, Désiré De Vlaemynck, was killed instantly by a shell. Others found by the Germans were prohibited from leaving their homes. They woke next day to find that doors, window frames, blankets, mattresses and clothing had all been removed for German soldiers to use. Over the next days the buildings in and around Mannekensvere were wrecked and burned by shellfire; some were turned over as machine-gun posts or used for other front line purposes. Some thirty-five people were rounded up by the Germans and held in a vaulted room of a large farm, left to live for eight days on potatoes stored there. When they emerged they found that their land was securely in German hands. On 24 November they were forcibly evacuated to Sint-Pieters-Kapelle.

The Schore outpost fell to the Germans but no progress could be made beyond it. A Belgian 1st Division counter-attack in the evening was beaten off. Keiem was held by 10th Line Regiment and captured by the 6th Reserve Division. The Belgian unit retreated south-westwards towards Kasteelhoek, from which it counter-attacked during the night and regained the edge of the village. Its commanding officer, Colonel

Antoine Michel Jules Funck, was wounded during the action: mortally so, for he died in the hospital that was operating at Sophie-Berthelot College in Calais on 22 October.

During the day the 87th and 89th Territorial Infantry Divisions relieved the Belgian 6th Division south of the old Fort Knokke, where the Ieperlee meets the Yser.

19 October

The German attack recommenced with greater force and now included deeper shelling from longer-range heavy artillery. The Belgian chain of advanced posts once again came under renewed pressure but continued to hold for some hours. Weight of numbers and firepower gradually had their inevitable effect: the capture of Keiem was completed, during which the commanding officer of the 13th Line Regiment, 48 year old Major Henri Delcourt, was killed. Possession of Keiem was key to being able to attack the river loop between Schoorbakke and Tervate.

At about 10am the Uniebrug, behind the Mannekensvere outpost, was destroyed by a large calibre shell: the detachment of the 7th Line Regiment eventually managed to withdraw and cross to the left bank of the Yser. The regiment suffered the loss of Capitaine-Commandant Henri Joseph Dungelhoef, killed near the bridge. Further south, Belgian engineers destroyed the river bridge at Tervate.

The Belgian 5th Division received orders to carry out an attack on the flank of the Diksmuide salient towards Esen and Vladslo, aimed at relieving the pressure on the defenders of Beerst and the area west of Keiem. It was to be co-ordinated with actions of Ronarc'h's force of Fusiliers-Marins and French and Belgian cavalry and was to attack the southern flank of the 6th Reserve Division. A brigade of Moroccan Goumiers, exotically attired mounted troops, was sent to patrol towards Bovekerke.

Indications had come from the British I Corps (under Lieutenant General Sir Douglas Haig and just arriving in the Ypres area from the River Aisne sector in France) that it was about to commence an advance. It was also understood that a screen of French cavalry was in the area of Klerken. A battalion of the 1st Regiment of Fusiliers-Marins, supported by two armoured cars, consequently ventured out from the Diksmuide line, passing dead lying on the road, and were surprised to reach Esen without trouble. They found much evidence that the Germans had been there but had withdrawn.

The heavy German attack falling a few kilometres to the north, in the area of the Belgian outposts between Leke and Beerst, immediately threatened to break through the thinly held defence and cut the

Diksmuide-Middelkerke-Ostend road and even the Diksmuide-Pervijze-Nieuwpoort road. Such an advance would cross the Yser and outflank Diksmuide, exposing the force there to the threat of encirclement. Conceivably it could mean that the German would make a breakthrough that could see them push on to the coast and the Channel ports. Such dire consequences were clear to the Belgian and French commands: Ronarc'h had little choice but to make the courageous move of sending the main body of the 1st and 2nd Battalions of the 1st Regiment forward to the attack, moving along on either side of the road to Beerst; the third battalion also advanced, aiming at the area between Vladslo and Beerst in the hope of outflanking the German attack. The precise situation was largely unknown to Ronarc'h and the troops advanced until they came into contact.

On approaching within a few hundred metres of Beerst, the lead companies came under a hail of machine gun and small arms fire. Completely exposed on the flat, open land, the survivors took to the ground and found whatever cover they could in drainage ditches. Urged on by the importance of the situation, attempts were made to rise and charge the guns with bayonets: they were inevitably most costly in lives, particularly to the junior officers leading the companies and platoons. Even so, in places the marines' counter-attack forced its way into Beerst, house to house fighting took place and it even seized control of the village. Steps were taken as night fell to put the place into a coherent state of defence, but events elsewhere were overtaking the possibility of holding the position and orders came to disengage and withdraw, abandoning Beerst to the enemy.

Alongside the French, the Belgian 3rd Foot Jager (17 Mixed Brigade) and 1st Line Regiment (1 Mixed Brigade), both of the 5th Division, had somewhat greater initial success, advancing along the north of the Handzame Canal through Vladslo and in the direction of Bovekerke. News of the arrival of the German XXIII Corps, detraining at Roeselare, quickly quashed any hopes of exploiting this small success. The Belgian 1st Cavalry Division and French 4th Cavalry Division, operating with elements of the Belgian 6th Division towards Staden, came into contact with this force as it began to deploy: the Belgian 2nd Regiment of Grenadiers (18 Mixed Brigade, 6th Division) lost two officers, Major René Elisée Dubreucq and Lieutenant Joseph Césaire de Rossart.

By the day's end the Belgians no longer held any ground east of the Yser north of Diksmuide except at the small bridgeheads and the salient around the town. In the rear, the intensifying fighting and instructions from the military high command led to a greater flow of people from the area. The mayor of Pervijze was organising the

GUERRE 1914-1915. — En Belgique. — L'Église de Pervyse après le 2ᵉ bombardement.
Visé Paris n° 437   In Belgium. — The church of Pervyse after the second bombardment. — LL

Pervijze Church was a target for German artillery and was soon reduced to rubble.

departure of refugees when shells began to fall on the village at about 10am. It had been receiving refugees from Liège, Lier, Mechelen and Hofstade from as early as 20 August and their numbers were about 150 when the attack began. Many had taken shelter in the convent of the *Zusters van Liefde* (Sisters of Charity), which was later also used by military staff and troops for the same purpose. The nuns were eventually and reluctantly evacuated on 24 October, by which time the village was an inferno and the front line very near. According to Sister Ermelinda Pauwelyn, one of a number of nuns to have reached Pervijze from Schore the previous day, the shell fire was aimed at blocking the village crossroads with rubble from the monastery and Sint-Niklaaskerk Church. The nuns continued their work as nurses at Alveringem and Avekapelle.

20 October
The day saw continued German efforts to eliminate the Belgian bridgeheads and complete the deployment of XXII and XXIII Reserve Corps along the river. Leaving the central river loop alone, the weight of attack fell against the Lombardsijde and Diksmuide sectors. To the south, the British Expeditionary Force commenced an attempted advance from the Ypres area towards Menen, meeting greatly superior forces coming towards it and was obliged to retire and attempt to hold a defensive line: this is regarded as the start of the First Battle of Ypres.

Two battalions of the Belgian 6th Line Regiment held the Lombardsijde front: on the left, in the coastal dunes, on the right at Grote Bamburgh Farm. Possession of the latter was key to this sector of the front, for it lay in the path of assault towards the estuary and the town of Nieuwpoort on the far bank. The regiment's 3rd Battalion continued the line and connected with the 7th Line Regiment, which was holding the north of Sint-Joris.

III Reserve Corps, which one German account called 'the battering ram of the Fourth Army', took centre stage in this attack, spearheaded by the 5th Reserve Division, which was supported by almost the whole of the corps artillery, against the river line between the Union and Schoorbakke bridges. To its north was the 4th Ersatz Division; to the south the 6th Reserve Division.

At dawn, elements of the 4th Ersatz Division began to advance from the Westende area, quickly capturing Grote Bamburgh Farm but then lost it to a counter attack by 9th Line Regiment, sent as a reserve from the 3rd Division. During this fighting, a small British naval party arrived in support.

The Royal Naval monitors had continued to fire in aid of the Belgian defence and had taken the unusual step of sending a landing party under Lieutenant Edward Selby Wise RN of *HMS* Severn. Reports vary as to exactly how many men landed but it appears to have been around ten from each vessel. Disembarking at the pier at Nieuwpoort, they proceeded towards Grote Bamburgh Farm, having been informed that Germans were threatening the place by working around it after advancing from the direction of Slijpe (that is, through Rattevalle and along the Plassendale canal). On 26 October 1914 *The Times* carried an article by a special correspondent:

> 'I was told the story of his [ie Lieutenant Wise] forlorn hope by some Belgian officers who saw him killed. "We were in the trenches behind the Grote Bamburgh," they said, "when we saw him coming along with his twenty men carrying the mitrailleuses [machine guns]. He was walking straight across the fields with his map in his hand, shouting to his men where to go as calm as if nothing were happening. We called out to him not to go on, as we knew the Germans had got their own mitrailleuses into the farm and that it was too late. But he didn't seem to understand. He went right on. It was fine to see how calm he was. Then when he was about fifty yards from the farm the Germans suddenly opened fire, and he fell, killed by the first bullets."'

The Times suggested that in addition to Wise, five men were wounded, six others were missing and that the detachment had quickly been destroyed. By 31 October the same newspaper was reporting that *Hood's* naval force had sustained in total the loss of one officer and eleven men killed, three officers and thirty-eight men wounded and one man missing: this would have included any casualties on board the vessels.

Another attack was beaten off at about 1pm but two hours later a repeated effort broke the Belgian defence in the area of the farm, forcing the Belgians to retire 600 metres to the old fortress site at Palingbrug once an attempted and costly counter-attack by the 9th Line Regiment failed. They now had their backs quite literally to the river, with the town of Nieuwpoort on the far side and the Goose Foot lock complex close by on the right. Lombardsijde village was gradually prised from Belgian hands after thirteen hours of incessant attack. Meanwhile, in the centre of the line, Belgian engineers of the 1st Division destroyed Schoorbakke Bridge.

Down at Diksmuide, Belgian troops under Colonel Jean-Baptiste Meiser had been grouped under Ronarc'h's overall command, in addition to his own force of marines. He now had some four kilometres of front to defend, from where the dyke road from Oostkerke met the river near what would soon become known as the *Dodengang* (Trench of Death), down past the town to Sint-Jacobs-Kapelle. Half of the 11th Line Regiment was in a reserve position at Kaaskerke; the other half was with 12th Line Regiment holding the west bank of the Yser in the vicinity of the main road bridge and under the command of Colonel Jules Marie Alphonse Jacques. Their machine guns had been placed forward, to cover the approaches from Beerst, Esen and Woumen. The Fusiliers-Marins held the salient. French cavalry, patrolling towards Zarren, were driven back early in the day as the German attack recommenced. Heavy artillery, located at Praatbos Wood, north of Vladslo, began bombarding the town centre of Diksmuide at around 6.30am (some accounts, including Ronarc'h's, say it was later in the morning). Soon enough, infantry of the 44th and 43rd Reserve Divisions of XXI Reserve

General Jules Marie Alphonse Jacques was created 1st Baron Jacques of Diksmuide in recognition of his role in the town's defence.

Corps began to advance, capturing and clearing Beerst and Vladslo and entering Esen in two columns, converging on the defences east of the town. This was by no means an easy operation, for the only way to achieve it was by advancing on foot across the rather swampy meadows and (in the northern pincer) crossing the Handzame Canal whilst under the fire of about eighty Belgian guns. Nonetheless progress was made such that the attack intensified during the afternoon, causing severe losses to the 11 and 12th Line Regiments (both of the 3rd Division), breaking into the front of the former, and also the line held by companies of the marines. Any reserves to hand, including cyclists, were added to the increasingly desperate defence. At around 8pm the attack died down but was resumed several times during the night, in particular a vigorous assault at 2am, straddling the Esen road.

21 October
Having by now completed its deployment, the German Fourth Army began its attempt to cross the Yser with a heavy and sustained bombardment and launched attacks on Diksmuide and Ypres. Shelling by some 400 guns began during the night and lasted all day, falling on the front line and deep into the Belgian rear. The air concussion was such that windows were reported broken from its effect as far away as forty-five kilometres. On some occasions during the day it was claimed that thirty shells a minute fell on Diksmuide.

From north to south, the attacking force now had in line: the 4th Ersatz Division facing Nieuwpoort; III Reserve Corps down as far as Keiem; XXII Reserve Corps from Keiem to the north of Diksmuide; XXVI Reserve Corps continued the line past Diksmuide; XXVI Reserve Corps took it down to Houthulst Forest; and XXVII Reserve Corps faced the British between Westroozebeek and Becelare. Facing the assault of seven mainly fresh divisions, the Belgians had the 2nd Division holding from the sea and around Nieuwpoort to Sint-Joris; the 1st Division held the river line down to Schoorbakke; the 4th Division held the river loop around Tervate. Part of the 3rd Division was in reserve behind the northern part of this line; the 6th Division was at Pervijze, behind the Diksmuide front; and the 5th Division was behind the French Fusiliers-Marins (with the Belgian 11 and 12nd Line Regiments of the 3rd Division and joined during the day by two battalions of 2 Foot Jager) holding Diksmuide. The Belgian artillery of 350 field guns included none larger than 150mm calibre. Help was on its way, however, in the form of the French 42nd Division, which began to move forward from its overnight billeting places around Dunkirk and De Panne.

Troops marching through De Panne.

Despite the shelling and under enormous pressure, the Belgians held on at the key points. The bridgeheads at Schoorbakke (defended by the 3rd Line Regiment) and Tervate (8th Line) held, and the 6th Line Regiment, supplemented by two battalions of Foot Jager, even managed to regain some ground in the direction of Lombardsijde. Two tentative German attempts to cross the river south of Mannekensvere were beaten off.

Diksmuide was attacked four times during the day and at one point German troops got into the marines' trenches south east of the town before being ejected at bayonet point. Their losses were very considerable, for the inexperienced reserve units advanced in a rigid mass of eight ranks and were exposed to machine-gun, rifle and shell fire as they moved across open ground. Ronarc'h would note:

> 'I had to put two more companies of sailors in the bridgehead. On the 21st, the shelling resumed, very violent, and became general on the trenches, the city, the bridges, Kaaskerke Station and the back roads. Our losses are great and I must ask the navy to fill them as quickly as possible. In the evening, I am informed that trenches occupied by sailors and Belgians have just been taken by the Germans, and that a movement of withdrawal is taking shape. I immediately order the recapture of the lost trenches, and

I send as reinforcement to the bridgehead three companies of sailors and two Belgian companies. [They] dislodged the enemy from the captured trenches and the situation was restored, but another attack from the south was immediately launched. Finally, the fighting stopped at 9pm and we had kept all our positions, but we had lost a lot of men and officers.'

The situation along the whole line was becoming increasingly critical, with losses mounting, ammunition dwindling and with no prospect of large scale help coming from the French or British. The latter were by now under similarly overwhelming attack before Ypres.

22 October
This proved to be one of the Belgian army's worst days in terms of casualties. Army chaplain Jozef Pauwels, who was working at Stuivekenskerke, noted in his diary that it was a bloodbath. It also saw a dramatic turn of events. The river loop north of the destroyed Tervate Bridge had been under the most intense artillery fire for two days, with batteries arced around it from Schore to Kasteelhoek, near Beerst. Under its cover, during the night 21–22 October, 800 metres south of Schoorbakke Bridge, the German 26th Reserve Infantry Regiment managed to seize a plank footbridge and slipped men across to the west bank. They soon got a dozen machine guns across the river and began to construct more foot bridges, enabling three battalions to advance. The dreadful truth was known at Belgian headquarters at about 8.30am: the consequences were too hideous to contemplate and, despite the weakened and tired condition of the army on the Yser, it was clear that every effort had to be made to halt any further progress from this incursion.

Several Belgian attempts to counter attack and drive the enemy back across the river met only with bloody defeat. The 8th Line Regiment, which had been holding the Tervate area, sustained heavy casualties, losing two of its battalion commanders: Majors Louis Joseph Blairon was killed and Adolphe Leopold Salpetier seriously wounded; the latter was evacuated to England, where he died in hospital in Bristol on 7 November. He was given a funeral with full military honours and which was attended by large crowds. The regiment held on to the Tervate bridgehead until about mid-day; but by afternoon the Belgian front now ran from Schoorbakke down to the long-abandoned village of Stuivekenskerke and the nearby Chateau Vicogne.

The 1st Grenadiers of the 6th Division was another unit flung into the counter attack. It reached the river bank near Tervate but was there cut off by German forces and surrounded. Amongst its losses was its aristocratic commanding officer, the 48 year-old Count Major Henri François-Marie d'Oultremont. In his 1958 memoir, *The Battle of the Yser*, veteran Marcel Senesael recalled,

Count Major Henri François-Marie d'Oultremont of the Belgian Grenadiers was killed in the attempt to hold Tervate Bridge.

'There are now 200 to 250 grenadiers, the diminished 1 Company of 2 Battalion of the 8th Line, as well as thirty men of the 4th Line and a handful of carabiniers. It is a soggy, numb, jaded and meagre group, holding a three kilometre line that it must defend against an enemy in front of them, on the flanks and in the rear. The threat comes mostly from the farms, which have now become real fortresses, making any reconnaissance impossible. They ask for support, for help, but the heavy barrage prevents it. Confusion arises, commands are not understood; grenadiers are retreating, other detachments remain or wander around until the new day arrives at this tragic place of misery and death. A last handful of men, from different regiments, fires from the Yser dyke, shrinks, shoots, crawls back and reduces until the remaining ones reach burning Stuivekenskerke or shelled Pervijze.'

These men had now been under bombardment for about 120 hours and engaged in heavy fighting for three days. The situation was reaching a critical climax.

23 October

At Diksmuide the town and the approaches to it had become a death trap and the last civilians were evacuated from it.

To the north, the line from Schoorbakke and up through Sint-Joris also came under the heaviest of bombardment and direct attack, but without a German breakthrough. Beyond it, the Belgians even regained ground when 9th Line Regiment and 1 Foot Jager counter attacked at Lombardsijde: they captured large numbers of enemy and two machine guns. Later in the day, the French 151 Infantry Regiment arrived, relieved the Belgians and pushed on somewhat towards Westende. This unit was under command of 84 Brigade of Grossetti's 42nd Division. French artillery came into action at about 4pm, the battery having arrived at Booitshoeke, south west of Ramskapelle. While it came as a most welcome reinforcement to the hard pressed Belgian 2nd Division, the French arrival was hardly what the Belgian command had hoped for or requested: they were desperate to shore up the fragmenting defence in the Tervate Loop.

During the day the growing German force on the west bank pushed forward to the south of Stuivenkenskerke and gained Vicogne and Kloosterhoek. Grossetti reported to the headquarters in Veurne at around 5.30 pm and announced that he had been instructed that he was not under Belgian authority and that he was to attack at Nieuwpoort. It was only during the night that he authorised his 83 Brigade to proceed towards the area where the enemy breakthrough had occurred. During the night more German bridges were placed across the Yser and southward advances were made from the bridgehead that captured Den Toren and a pair of petroleum tanks situated on the river bank near Diksmuide.

Major-General Paul François Grossetti commanded the French 42nd Division in the Battle of the Yser; he had arrived with a different plan of action to the Belgians.

The 7th Line Regiment was finally relieved after its unrelenting defence at Mannekensvere and Sint-Joris. In a week of fighting it had lost eighteen officers and 600 men.

24 October
At an address given in London in 1915, the Belgian Minister of Justice, Henry Victor Marie Ghislain, Count Carton de Wiart (a cousin of the notable British officer, Lieutenant General Adrian Carton de Wiart VC), recalled:

> 'On 23 October the first French reinforcements arrived on our left, and on the 24th the six Belgian divisions were supported by one French division and a few battalions of Territorials. On the night of the 23rd a furious attack upon Diksmuide was repelled by the Marin-Fusiliers (whose heroism will forever remain legendary, and with justice) and a couple of Belgian regiments. This was the sixth time that the German army had attacked Diksmuide within a week; and at each of these repeated assaults there were frightful

hand-to-hand combats and hecatombs of dead; and each time our valiant soldiers remained masters of the field.

The area conquered by the Germans on the 23rd, lying within the bend of the Yser between Schoorbakke and Tervate, was violently bombarded and recaptured. Here it was that a notebook was found on a German corpse in which an officer of XXII Reserve Corps recorded the dreadful moral and physical sufferings endured in that hell of bullets and fire and blood; companies reduced to half their strength, units mixed together, the officers nearly all killed, famine and thirst and a sense of the uselessness of all efforts against our redoubtable little army: such was the balance-sheet on the German side. Yet the Kaiser's troops seemed to rise out of the ground. Fresh reinforcements came to fill the frightful gaps made by our fire and our bayonet attacks. Foot by foot the Belgian army defended the soil lying between the left bank of the Yser and the railway from Nieuwpoort to Dixmude, behind which it organized a new line of defence.'

The straight railway line was the only geographic feature that provided any valuable natural defence once the enemy was across the Yser. Behind it, the army endeavoured to restore order, reorganising the units that had been dislocated, confused and mixed up during the repeated attacks of recent days. In many cases these units had to be sent back into the melée. It was vital to hold the line between Schoorbakke and Stuivenkenskerke to give the arrival of the French 83 Brigade time for its deployment and entry into action.

The Germans had by now erected three heavy bridges and more plankways across the Yser, enabling a greater flow of troops and material into the river loop. It proved to be a day of heavy losses for both sides and the gradual advance of the front westwards towards the railway. The Belgian front line was defended by the tired and depleted 2nd and 3rd Line Regiments holding the line of the small Klein Beverdijk stream; the 8th and 13th took it down to Stuivenkenskerke and Kloosterhoek Farm; whilst south of that the 10th Line clung onto the river bank.

Continued attacks during the day caused the Belgians to withdraw from Stuivenkenskerke, and the German front pushed inexorably if slowly forward. Two battalions each from 9th Line Regiment and 1 Foot Jager were moved to form a line of resistance east of Pervijze, with their backs to the railway line and French units begin to arrive alongside them; 10th Line Regiment and a mix of carabiners and grenadiers took up a line along the Reigersvliet Stream and the paved road alongside it down to Oud Stuivekenskerke. A local counter attack was attempted by 1st Line Regiment and Fusiliers-Marins towards Den Toren Farm, which lies beyond Oud Stuivenkenskerke and near another German plank bridge that had been placed overnight: it was swiftly destroyed by artillery fire.

In the north there was again heavy shell fire in the area of Sint-Joris and infantry attacks from the Schoorbakke direction that forced 14th Line Regiment to withdraw some way in the afternoon, with the hope of holding the line of the Noordvaart Stream. In so doing, it had to abandon Sint-Joris to the enemy. Grossetti's Frenchmen were similarly forced to concede ground in the face of multiple attacks by the 4th Ersatz Division, giving up Lombardsijde: it was only by intensive artillery fire that the enemy was kept at bay from the Yser estuary and Nieuwpoort. Orders were given for the force to shorten its line by pulling back to a small bridgehead around the Palingbrug, an old fort on the Yser from which men could look directly into the houses of Nieuwpoort and dominate the canal complex.

To the south, intense artillery fire continued to crush Diksmuide and its defenders; five times during the night infantry attacks were only held off by close-in fighting. At about 10am a German breakthrough came in the French-held trenches south of the town but the situation was restored by counter attack. Over nine days of almost constant firing and being everywhere out-gunned, the Belgian artillery was approaching collapse. More and more guns experienced mechanical breakdowns and wear, while the supply of shells was running increasingly short: the stock was now down to fewer than a hundred rounds per gun by the end of the following day.

Sunday, 25 October
A somewhat quieter day but there were still German attacks at Diksmuide and against Nieuwpoort, the latter by means of an attempt to advance over the Groote Noord Nieuwland Polder. This area was now partially flooded after the first Belgian efforts to inundate these flat lands: it was but a small precursor to a much larger and more effective flooding action which is explained in detail in the next chapter. Even so, it was another day of heavy losses for the Belgians: at least 439 officers and men are believed to have lost their lives on this date.

Grossetti's force was by now deployed along the front and had relieved Belgian units at the most sensitive points: Lieutenant Colonel Henri Claudon commanded a group consisting of 162 Infantry Regiment and a battalion of Tirailleurs, holding Nieuwpoort and facing Lombardsijde. South of Ramskapelle, which was still in Belgian hands, 151 Infantry Regiment had taken up the railway line down as far as

French artillery crosses the square at Veurne.

Booitshoeke Bridge, over the Venepevaart. Beyond another stretch held by the Belgians, the 8th Chasseurs à Pied (Sidi Brahim) and 94 Infantry Regiment of 83 Brigade defended Pervijze. Behind them, a brigade of French cavalry was held in reserve. Ronarc'h's command, now consisting of the Fusiliers-Marins, 19th Chasseurs à Pied and Tirailleurs Sénégalais, held from Lettenburg, round Diksmuide to as far as Sint-Jacobs-Kapelle. This had brought a significant contribution – not only of fighting strength but recent battle experience.

The two French regiments of 83 Brigade, together with the Belgian 1st Line and 2 Foot Jager, carried out a localised counter attack that reoccupied Stuivekenskerke and Den Toren Farm. To the south, the action at Diksmuide began later in the day. A German official account, written in the autumn of 1917 by Captain Otto Schwink, a General Staff Officer, recalled:

> 'A very heavy thunder of guns rumbled incessantly from the south: the German artillery, including 42-centimetre guns, had bombarded Dixmude throughout the 24th October and morning of the 25th, and now the 43rd Reserve Division had begun its assault on the town. It resulted in the most violent street fighting; fast and furious came the bullets from the machine guns posted in

the houses along the edge of the town, and from the shells from the batteries massed west of the Yser, but nothing could hold up our attack. The Belgians have given the following description of the power of the German assault: "What plunder must not they have been promised, to allow themselves to be killed in such a way? What drink must they not have taken to give themselves such animal courage? Like devils, thirsting for blood, they storm forward with the howls of wild beasts; lusting to massacre, they tread the wounded under foot and stumble over the dead: and, though shot down in hundreds, they keep coming on. Then follow isolated fights with bayonets and the butts of rifles: some are impaled, others strangled or have their skulls bashed in."

The fight swayed backwards and forwards till well into the night: guns brought up into the front line fired at point-blank range: both sides put in their last reserves. During the night, rifles were unloaded, bayonets fixed, and we attacked again. A small German detachment of about fifty men advanced across the Yser bridge but, in endeavouring to assault the enemy's batteries, it succumbed to greatly superior numbers. Thus the morning of 26th October found the attackers back in their assault-positions: their courage, spirit and indifference to death having added another leaf of fame to the chaplet of the Guards.'

This account tells only part of the story. It was at 7pm that the 43rd Reserve Division launched its attack against the 11th and 12th Line Regiments from the direction of Esen. Although the attack was in the main held in front of Diksmuide by Belgian machine gunners, a detachment, said to be up to 300 strong, broke through the town and perhaps fifty of them crossed the river to reach Kaaskerke. Too few in numbers to exploit their breakthrough, they appear to have done so largely unnoticed until 2.30am, when firing was heard. The situation was most unclear so

'[Ronarc'h] sent one of his officers, Lieutenant Durand-Gasselin, to reconnoitre. He got as far as the Yser without finding the enemy; the fusillade had ceased; the roads were clear. He set out on his way back to Kaaskerke. On the road he passed an ambulance belonging to the brigade going up towards Diksmuide, which, on being challenged, replied: "Rouge Croix". Rather surprised, he stopped the ambulance; it was full of Germans, who, however, surrendered without offering any resistance. But this capture suggested a new train of thought to the Staff: they were now certain that there had been an infantry raid upon the town; the Germans in the ambulance probably belonged to a troop of mysterious assailants who had made their way into Diksmuide in the night and had vanished no less mysteriously after this extraordinary deed of daring. One of our covering trenches must have given way, but which? Our [Belgian] allies held the railway line by which the enemy had penetrated into the defences, sounding the charge.... The riddle was very disturbing, but under the veil of a thick damp night, which favoured the enemy, it was useless to seek a solution. It was found next morning at dawn, when one of our detachments on guard by the Yser suddenly noticed in a meadow a curious medley of Belgians, French Marines, and Germans. Had our men been made prisoners? This uncertainty was of brief duration. There was a sharp volley; the [marines] fell; the Germans made off. ... Various versions have been given of this incident, one of the most dramatic of the defence, in the course of which the heroic Commander Jeanniot and Dr. Duguet, chief officer of the medical staff, fell mortally wounded, along with several others.'

Many reports suggest that 51 year-old *Capitaine de frégate* Roch Louis Jeanniot, who had commanded 1 Battalion of 2nd Regiment of the Fusiliers-Marins, and the other prisoners had been murdered in cold blood. Jeanniot now lies in the French national cemetery at Dunkirk.

Some of the Germans found their way to the large industrial flour mill, the Minoterie, which stood on the bank of the Yser at the road bridge to Kaaskerke. They were discovered by patrols and shot. The remainder of the German detachment made their way south, where they encountered Belgian artillery and were rounded up and taken into captivity. It is believed by some that, under Ronarc'h's orders, thirty of them were executed for their crimes.

Behind the front line the situation was growing increasingly desperate. The French were preparing for an assumed imminent Belgian collapse and a major German advance and were taking steps to flood a large area east and south of Dunkirk. There was no definite knowledge of the potential extent of such floods but its implementation would certainly have cut the only supply routes for the Belgians and might imperil those forces still fighting in the Nieuwpoort area.

Coming as both unexpected and shocking, it impelled further and more urgent Belgian efforts to consider flooding the Yser as a means of defence. Poor weather, the presence of the French brigades at Lombardsijde and increasing fire from German artillery rendered support from the Royal Navy impotent. Some thousand Belgian casualties of recent days could only find medical care in improvised

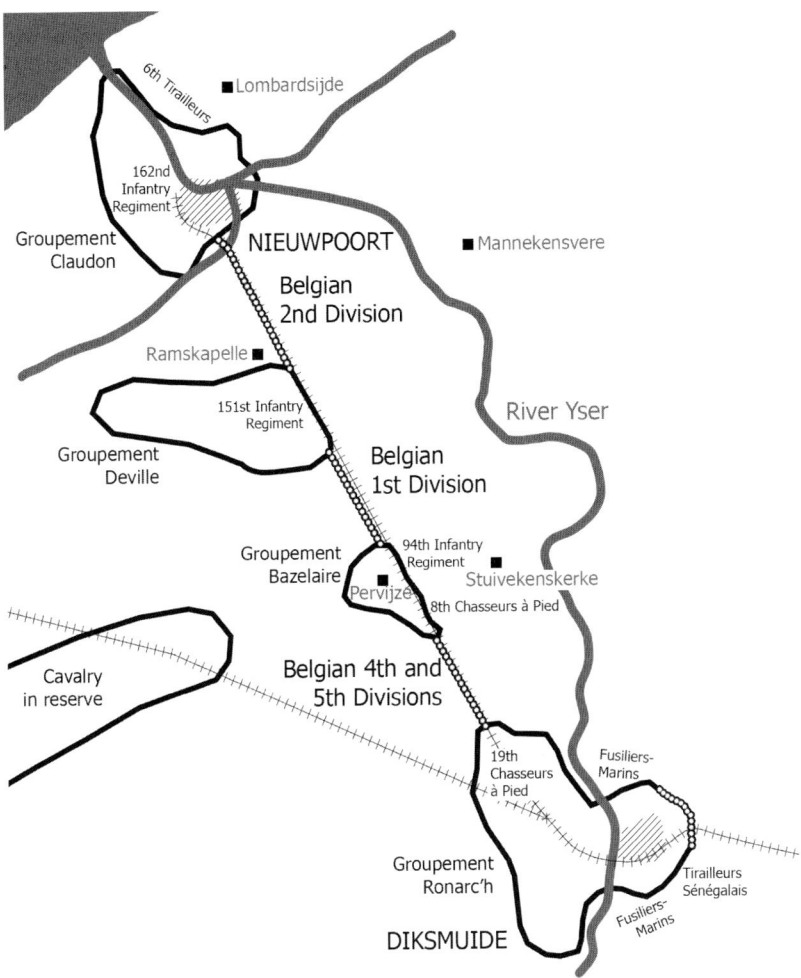

French and Belgian defences, 26 October 1914.

dressing stations which were full to overflowing. Those 9000 or so who had made it as far as the hospitals in Veurne began to be evacuated by railway to Adinkerke, for the town was now threatened. The proportion of men who lost their lives during these few days and who have no known grave today is testament to sheer inability to know of and then record their fates.

26 October

This was another day of intense and deep German artillery bombardment. The Belgians, now being enfiladed on their position of the Klein Beverdijk Line, were obliged to make a further withdrawal towards Nieuwpoort and beyond to the railway embankment. German guns began to cross the Yser and reached Stuivekenskerke. The village and its long-abandoned predecessor Oud-Stuivekenskerke were seized, as was Grote Beverdijk.

German attacks in the Nieuwpoort area, carried out by the 5th and 6th Reserve Divisions from 9am onwards, with the intention of cutting off the garrison in that area from the rest of the allied force and destroying it in detail, met with severe handling. Within range of Hood's naval squadron, every attempt was cut to pieces. Further south, the 44th Reserve Division met with the same fate. Unknown to the allies, German morale and will was stuttering as a consequence of the repeated effort, lack of success and the continued miserable weather.

Emile de Jonghe, parish priest at Sint-Joris, was killed in his village on 26 October 1914 during the Battle of the Yser.

Despite having held the attack, at 11pm Henri Claudon, who considered his numerical strength inadequate to maintain the Palingbrug Bridgehead, withdrew his three battalions of 162 Infantry Regiment across to the left bank of the estuary, leaving the Palingbrug and the canal lock complex to the enemy. Under his orders a Belgian officer, Lieutenant Lucien Alfred François, blew up the swing bridge at the Veurne Lock. The Germans failed to notice (or at least did not move to exploit it) this critical moment. During the night of 26–27 October the first serious efforts were made at putting a large scale inundation into effect. With the utmost bravery, the manipulations of the lock mechanisms were carried out by the opeators while they were effectively in No Man's Land and covered only by the guns of some forty carabinier-cyclists. Their efforts would totally change the nature and outcome of the battle.

It was also during the night that King Albert's headquarters issued the simple order 'Tomorrow the army, reinforced by French troops, will continue the defence of the positions it currently occupies – at all costs'. It was issued just as German attacks were being beaten off, if only just, by the 4th Line and 1st Grenadiers in the areas of Booitshoeke and Pervijze, and as intelligence indicated a large scale renewed German effort in the morning.

27 October
The Alveringem schoolmaster, Emiel Selschotter, wrote in his diary:

> 'A hurricane of explosions woke us. The wounded tell horrifying stories.... Pervijze, Ramskapelle, Nieuwpoort, Diksmuide, everything is burning. There are not twenty seconds between the explosions. And neither the Germans nor ours give away a thumb's breadth of ground.'

The German fire also swept the rear area. Three long range shells exploded at Veurne Station: it was an unnerving signal that there was now no significant element of Belgian soil not under enemy occupation or fire, certainly within the area behind the Yser. Selschotter had written the day before that men were talking about the sea sluices being opened and the whole Westhoek being flooded. He was right: it had already begun, and it would not be long before the Germans had no further chance of seizing even a thumb's breadth more ground, despite their advantage of firepower.

Chapter Three

Inundation

The hinterland of the coastal strip of the Westhoek is naturally vulnerable to flooding. The general elevation of the ground is below high tide level but above low tide. In other words, without its high dunes, man-made sea defences and dykes it would flood from the sea when the tide comes in. Any ingress of sea water would tend to flow over a wide area, for the ground is remarkably flat for several miles from the beach. Water also flows across the area towards the sea from higher ground inland, via the River Yser and several sizeable creeks and streams. In Flanders the water level has been managed since at least the 12th Century by a system of dykes, ditches, canals, locks and pumps. In that sense it is polder land not unlike that of parts of the Netherlands. For the most part, this arrangement held the water back and protected a very fertile agricultural plain. There had been several periods in history when a deadly combination of very high tide and bad weather had caused serious flooding. It was also well known that the land had on several occasions been deliberately flooded for military purposes, going as far back as the Hundred Years War of the 14–15th centuries. Such actions were the result of hard decisions, for the lasting effect of sea water on the soil is most undesirable. Desperate times in the autumn of 1914 caused for similarly desperate measures.

Six waterways come together near Nieuwpoort: although there has been much recent development, particularly of an inner harbour along the Yser, the pattern of six coming together at the *Ganzepoot* (Goose Foot) is today essentially as it was constructed in 1876–78 and when it played such a crucial role in October 1914. There have been some changes to the width, position and format of some of the sluices and locks and many of the buildings that stood in places around the Goose Foot were never rebuilt after the war-time destruction. From north to south, the waterways are:

- The *Nieuwbedelf*, a channel draining the area of land east of Lombardsijde, meeting the estuary at a sluice (a gate which can be opened to control the flow out to the sea);
- The 17th Century Plassendale Navigation Canal or *Brugsevaart*, with a sea lock known as *Écluse de Comte* or *Gravensluis* (the Count's lock);

- The *Nieuwendamme* Creek, a former, meandering course of the Yser, also known as the Old Yser, that flows along the north side of the Groote Noord Nieuwland Polder and which was equipped with a sluice known as *Springsas*;
- The *River Yser*, on a shortened and straightened course between high embankments, with a sluice and a sea lock: the *Écluse d'Ypres* or *Iepersluis*. The Yser is the only river with an estuary in Belgium;
- The *Noordvaart* drainage channel, which at its Goose Foot end is known as the Veurne-Ambacht Canal and meets the sea at a sluice;
- The 17th Century Nieuwpoort-Dunkirk Navigation Canal, also known as the *Veurnevaart*, with a sluice and a sea lock: the *Écluse de Furnes* or *Veurnesluis*.

Each of the six waterways was bridged by a single loop known as the Five Bridges Road. On 16 October 1914 the lifting bridges were opened and Belgian engineers installed explosive changes below the bridge over the Veurnevaart.

A smaller waterway, the *Old Veurnevaart* or *Arkevaart*, flowed into the Yser estuary some 900 metres downstream and nearer to Nieuwpoort. It had an old and rarely opened lock known as the Old Furnes Lock, *Kattensas* or *Spaansesas* (Spanish Lock).

The origin of the decisions to flood the area is disputed, with several individuals being given credit and various discussions were said to have taken place as early as 10 October. Nieuwpoort came under fire on 18 October and, with the continuing withdrawal of the French and Belgians to the west bank of the Yser, the Goose Foot was left in No Man's Land. Next day, with German troops now as near to the Goose Foot as 1600 metres away at Grote Bamburgh Farm, and Nieuwpoort itself coming under heavy artillery fire, chief lock keeper Geraard Dingens and his staff followed most of the local population and left. With them went crucial local expertise about water level control in the area and it later transpired that no one knew where they had gone. Dingens had already been consulted by Belgian and British staffs about the locks and how the area might be inundated and he appears to be central to the early discussions; but it would be others that would develop the idea and ultimately succeed in carrying it out. By 20 October the Belgian front line had been further withdrawn and was now only 600 metres or so from the Goose Foot.

Deliberately flooding the hinterland in a controlled manner was a complex business – a matter of managing a delicate balance between flows, tides and wind. That it was eventually accomplished, especially when the sluices and gates that needed to be manipulated at the right times were under fire, was a notable and decisive achievement. It was a matter of fortune that the need to do so coincided with a period of particularly high tides.

The first move took place on 21 October, when at 9.15am the Belgian 2nd Division ordered its engineers to flood the Groote Noord Nieuwland Polder by opening the Springsas Sluice of the Nieuwendamme Creek and if necessary to cut through the embankments or higher banks on either side of it. The instructions also said that the rising water must not spread east of the Old Yser (which suggests a purely tactical action and that widespread inundation as a matter of strategy was not yet foreseen). But there was a problem. The sluice was rather complex, for it had initially been designed as a military feature specifically to flood the polder but also had the peaceful function of land drainage. The necessary technical expertise had left and crucial tools and equipment for operating the various gates could not be found, putting the problem squarely in the hands of the military engineers. High tide was at 1.20pm that day and time was pressing.

The engineers in question would become part of the legend of the defence of Nieuwpoort and of the inundations. Initially a *Compagnie de Sapeurs-Pontonniers*, it later became established as the *Service des Inondations*. It soon became evident that the tide was going to be missed.

The job was given to Lieutenant Lucien François, whose small detachment worked with a local man, Hendrik Geeraert, a tugboat operator, waterman and – by all accounts – a wily character. Through Geeraert they soon found enough tools and equipment and during the night opened the sluice and locked it open: by morning much of the polder was flooded. Water had also flowed through a small culvert below the canalised Yser and flooded the ground between the Yser and the slightly higher ground of the Bruges road. It had the immediate effect of providing an effective defence on the south eastern flank of Nieuwpoort and the Goose Foot and ensured that

Hendrik Geeraert, hero of Nieuwpoort in 1914.

German infantry was unlikely to be able to approach it in force. The detachment was ordered to raise the doors at each high tide to increase the depth of flood water, which it continued to do until 26 October.

Despite this tactical success it only seems to have been on 24 October 1914 that the realisation that a need for large scale flooding was now certain and urgent. With the Yser Line already compromised, Foch advised King Albert of emergency French plans to flood the low lying area between Dunkirk, Bergues and Veurne, and so the subject took greater significance and centre stage.

On 25 October, Charles (Karel) Cogge discussed the situation with the aptly named Prudent Nuyten when they met at Veurne Town Hall. The two were well placed: Cogge was the highly experienced superintendent of the *Noordwetering*, the drainage area of the Veurne-Ambacht region, and Nuyten was a senior army staff officer attached to General Headquarters; a Fleming born in Ypres. They appreciated that the fundamental point to ensure the flooding of the area was the necessity to allow sea water into the system at high tide and to ensure it did not flow out again at low tide. Simply stopping the outflow would not achieve the necessary raising of the levels, certainly not in any short timescale.

Cogge's advice was to open the Noordvaart Sluice at high tide, but the risk to life would be great as the sluice was under fire and close to the enemy. The men considered a secondary but less effective option: to open the old Kattesas, further away from the enemy but controlling a much slower rate of flow over a longer route. Putting into action the inundation plan now began to gather pace: at 4pm engineering work began to close all places where water might flow below the railway and embankment.

During the night of 26–27 October Captain Robert Thys of the engineer battalion of the 2nd Division went with Cogge to open the Kattesas Sluice, having received authorisation from the Chief of the General Staff, Lieutenant General Félix Maximilien Eugène Wielemans. The effort failed, as the pressure of the rising tide of estuarial sea water pushed the gates closed again. They tried again the next night, this time roping the gates open, but water ingress proved to be slow. Cogge judged that it would take at least three days for any appreciable flooding of the hinterland to result from it: time the hard-pressed army was unlikely to have. There was a noticeable rising of the water in the ditches and drainage canals inland on 28 October but it was clear that more drastic measures had to be taken if a genuine inundation was to be effected. It was decided to go back to Cogge's original idea.

The Noordvaart is a meandering drainage channel; further inland it is known as the Grote Beverdijkvaart. It lies between the Yser and

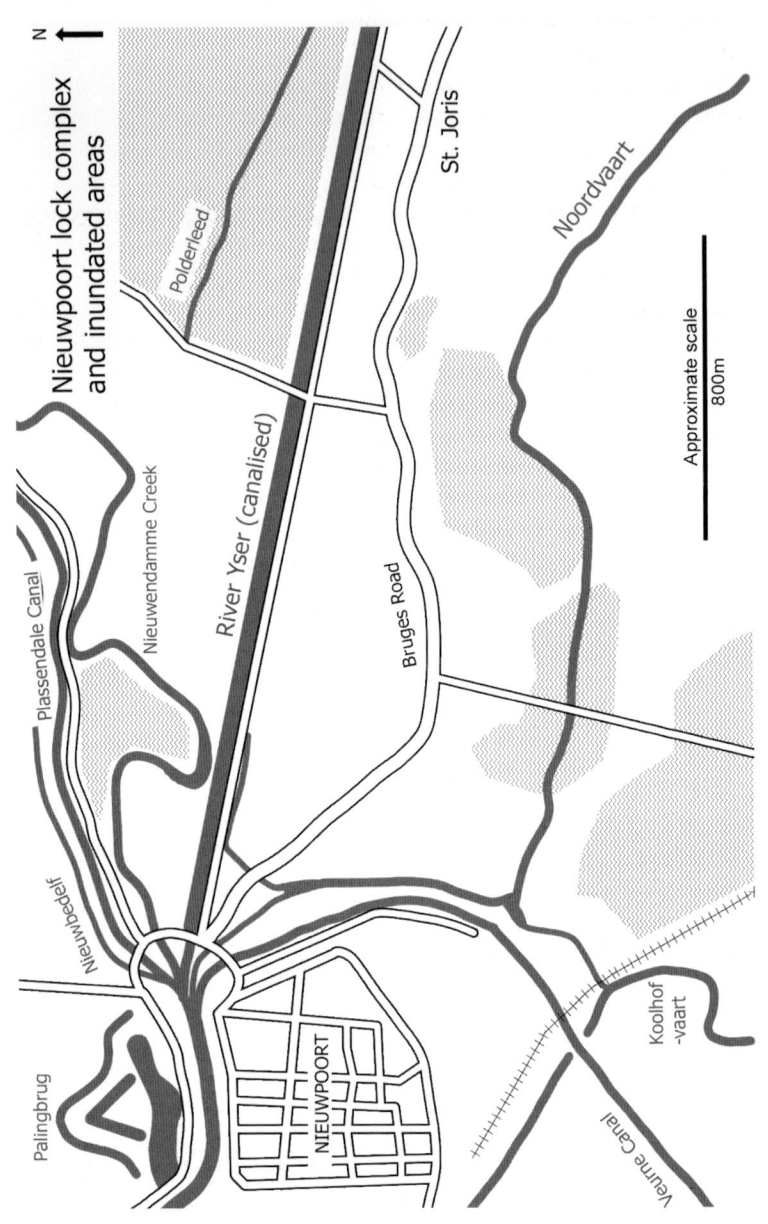

the straight Nieuwpoort-Diksmuide railway embankment. The former has raised embankments on both sides, with that on the western bank being the taller. If the many culverts and other passageways below the railway embankment could be blocked, the two would form boundaries that would constrain floodwater rising from the Noordvaart. Such inundation would mean giving up the line of the Yser to the Germans but would also render impractical any serious advance westwards across from the river to the railway; only much later on (practically four years, as it turned out) did it matter that it would also form a barrier to any potential Belgian advance.

On 29 October Geeraert and a detachment under Captain Fernand Umé of the engineers opened the exposed sluice of the Noordvaart. Sea water flowed in for several hours until the detachment closed the gates at low tide. This effort was repeated over three more nights, each allowing millions of tons of water into the area. The level rose slowly: the Germans at first believed it was the result of heavy rainfall but this impression soon dissolved as the Yserland became inundated to a depth of over a metre, eventually covering an area averaging three kilometres wide and up to thirty-two kilometres in length.

The whole area between the railway embankment and the west bank of the Yser was now under water. The depth varied with the slight undulations of ground below it, with some relatively small islands that were exposed or

A contemporary postcard celebrating the defeat of German ambitions by the inundation.

Officers of the Sapeurs-Pontonniers at Nieuwpoort. (*Europeana*)

were barely covered. The Bruges road was a watershed between the northern floods of the Nieuwendamme Creek and the greater southern waters of the Noordvaart. In chapter seven, the war across the water, it is explained that many farm buildings, churches and other features that stood proud of the inundation became the focus of positional warfare.

During November 1914 French troops dammed the Yser south of Diksmuide, raising the water level and flooding more of the area of the Blankaart. There was further local dam construction that increased the flooded area north east of Nieuwpoort and around Fort Knokke during 1915. Work by the *Service des Inondations* to manage the levels and to repair shell and other damage to sluices, locks and embankments, continued throughout the war.

A diver of the Sapeurs-Pontonniers, Francois van der Vreecken, lost his life at the Goose Foot on 5 November 1916. He is buried in the Belgian military cemetery at Adinkerke.

A long nightmare begins

War came to the village of Esen, east of Diksmuide, on 12 September 1914, when a detachment of German cavalry of Ulanen-Regiment 11 entered the area. They manoeuvred through and around thousands of civilian refugees moving west, fleeing from the fighting elsewhere with many terrifying stories circulating of German atrocities at Dinant, Aarschot and Leuven. This was at the time when the main body of the Belgian Army was besieged at Antwerp but was in the process of carrying out the second sortie: outside the city there were detachments and garrisons in other places yet to be over-run by the invaders.

Between Esen and nearby Zarren were men of the Belgian 13th Line Regiment and some thirty volunteers (*oorlogsvrijwilligers*) of 2 Company of 2 Battalion, the 6th Regiment of Volunteers, under the command of Lieutenant F Dresse. There was an exchange of firing, in which six Belgian and two German troops lost their lives: the first to do so in the Diksmuide sector. Of the Belgians, two were initially buried in Esen and the rest in Zarren: in September 1918 the latter were relocated to Esen.

On 6 October the decision was taken to withdraw the Belgian force from Antwerp: a second wave of refugees came towards Diksmuide and by 16 October German forces were arriving in strength and Esen came under fire as part of the German advance on Diksmuide. A bitter struggle of attack and counter-attack effected the village for four days, while the many hundreds of civilians took shelter as best they could in the Costenoble Brewery (now the Dolle Brouwers), the distillery, church and any cellar they could find. Esen was terribly damaged by shell and small arms fire; buildings burned and many troops on both sides died in the vicinity. The worst was, however, yet to come.

During 19–21 October, with the area now in German hands and while the fighting moved on to Diksmuide and the Yser crossings, the church, nearby buildings and five windmills in Esen were deliberately burned or otherwise destroyed. Civilians took what shelter they could in the large buildings of the brewery and in cellars of houses nearby. For many it proved to be a fatal move. 161 Belgian civilians were murdered by troops of Reserve-Infanterie Regiments 203 and 204 (both Berlin units under the 43rd Reserve-Division) in Beerst, Handzame, Ledegem, Staden, Roeselare, Vladslo and Esen. Of these, forty-nine were killed in Esen and a further 275 deported from the village.

Esen witnessed some particularly notable German atrocities against its civilian population in 1914.

Those civilians found sheltering in cellars were ordered out and were searched for arms: it is said that bullets were found in the pockets of Julien Warmoes and Alois Couffez, neither of whom were heard of again. Another local man, Alberic Costenoble, already wounded in his back, was slow to move. A German, enraged by his alleged reluctance, killed him in cold blood and in sight of others, including women and children. Gradually more and more people were herded into the brewery cellar: without a supply of proper food, with little water or medication, they were held in hellish and unsanitary conditions for several weeks, until 15 November. Some died; it is said that a birth took place within. On that date, 522 people were finally released and force-marched to Zarren. It completed the civilian evacuation of Esen, which would remain as a desolate military garrison until 1918.

Esen is often barely mentioned in the list of atrocities carried out by the Germans in Belgium. Even by the time that the Uhlans arrived, its villagers would have read the news and heard horrible rumours of what was happening elsewhere. As early as 6 August, the Germans were expressing outrage at the unexpected resistance of the Belgian army and also civil resistance. With memories of the *francs-tireurs* of 1870,

The Grote Markt in Veurne, packed with horse transport columns of the Belgian army.

the German newspapers called for retribution. A selection of headlines in the *Kolnischer Zeitung* read: 'The beast in Belgium', 'From savage Belgium', 'Liège atrocities'. Retribution came quickly. Civilians old and young were murdered, hostages taken, towns and villages plundered and destroyed. In the province of Liège there were 1200 known victims, in that of Luxembourg, 842, Namur 2000, Brabant (where between 25 and 28 August the old town and library of Leuven were set aflame and left to burn, to the horror of the rest of Europe) 839. The soldiers of the Yser would, of course, have been well aware of the rumours if not the horrifying detail of what was taking place. Unfortunately for the Belgians, it was just a foretaste of years of severe treatment.

The Conclusion of the Battle of the Yser
As the waters began to rise, on 29 October 1914 the German III Reserve Corps continued its attacks in the area of Pervijze and along the railway to its north, even though the 6th Reserve Division had raised an objection to the order to do so. It reported that it was exhausted, time to prepare for further operations had been too short and the ground was beginning to saturate. Its task was to attack through the Pervijze-Booitshoeke area towards Veurne, while on its right the 5th Reserve Division would work with the 4th Ersatz Division to break the allied line south of Nieuwpoort, encircle the town and press on as far as possible towards Dunkirk.

The subsequent assault was not carried out with the accustomed intensity but, even so, the Belgian 3rd and 4th Line Regiments suffered heavy losses. It proved to be but a precursor. The Corps pressed its divisions for greater effort, for it appeared that the battle, not only on the Yser but down at Ypres, was reaching a crescendo: possession of at least the railway line was judged to be paramount.

30 October
The heaviest attack for several days commenced at 5am next day after a night of awful weather. The general water level had risen by one and a half metres or so, the ditches were filled and digging in was now an impracticality. Some German units were reporting that their men were standing knee deep in water and, to compound their difficulties, it was still raining heavily when the attack began at 5am. The greater success came on the front of the 5th Reserve Division, facing the Belgian 4th Division and especially the 5th Line Regiment holding the railway line east of Ramskapelle. Behind the 5th, the 6th and 7th Line Regiments were in reserve but the supporting field artillery was now down to a stock of only sixty rounds per gun. The attack cut through the Belgian defences at the railway between Ramskapelle Station and Violon Farm, 600 metres

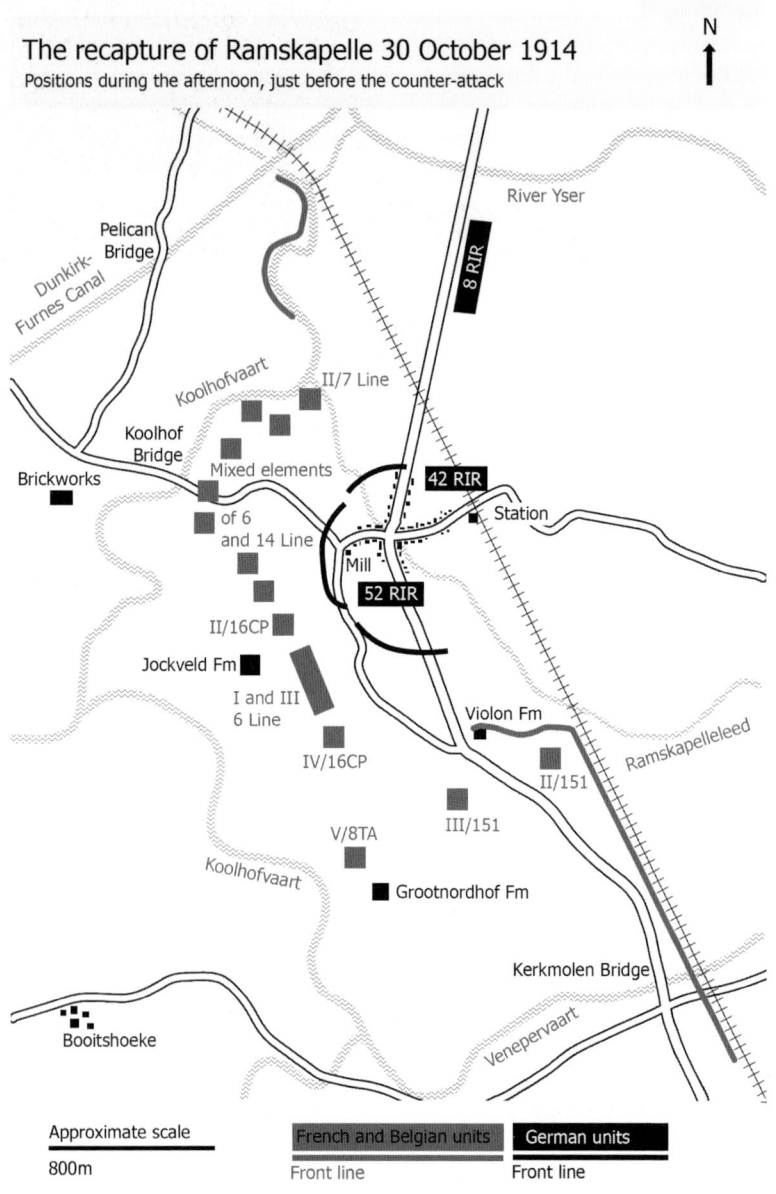

Ramskapelle Station became a front line position, protected by a broad expanse of flood water.

to the south, which had been held by the regiment's 1st Battalion. It was a considerable achievement by the Germans and physically exhausting, for some of the assault units had to wade through water in places. The German 48th and 52nd Reserve Infantry Regiments quickly pushed on into the village and beyond to its western outskirts. Belgian units on either side of the break-in, finding themselves outflanked, inevitably had to turn their own flank to face the enemy. The scattered remnants of the 5th Line fought brief rearguard actions as they were pushed back, but it was only once they had crossed the Koolhofvaart Stream that they could disengage and reorganise in the area of a brickworks.

German machine guns were soon set up around a windmill on the west side of Ramskapelle, dominating the approaches to the village from all directions. It was a moment of opportunity for a deep advance and potentially the rolling-up of the whole allied line in Flanders, if the Germans could maintain momentum. The 8th Reserve Infantry Regiment came up to reinforce the attackers, ready to continue the advance towards Wulpen. Yet the rising water level made this a fantasy and orders would very shortly be given for some units to withdraw across the Yser, just as an allied force was about to strike back. In retrospect the Battle of the Yser was over, but its last action would add to the battle honours of several units.

Dossin and Grossetti reacted to the German break-in with remarkable speed: even before it was daylight a counter-attack had been organised, although the force needed time to organise and it was timed for 4pm. It would be no easy task, for it required an advance of a kilometre over an open, completely flat area of increasingly saturated ground that was crossed by numerous ditches and streams now bursting their banks, exposed to fire, not least from the machine guns at the mill. They could now draw upon 76 Brigade of the French 38th Division, which had arrived at Lampernisse and Veurne only the previous day, bringing in hard and experienced North African units, the 5th Battalion of the 4th Régiment of Zouaves and the 4th and 5th Battalions of the 8th Regiment de Marche de Tirailleurs to the counter-attacking force, joining the 3rd Battalion of 151 Infantry Regiment and the 16th Chasseurs à Pied (all placed under the tactical command of Lieutenant Colonel Vallet of the Tirailleurs), along with the Belgian 6th and 14th Line Regiments. The latter would attack towards the north of Ramskapelle from the Koolhofvaart; the French from the west and south. At 11am the allied artillery opened fire on the village centre and railway and the counter-attacking units began to move across the Koolhofvaart to close in for the main assault.

The light failed well before 5pm and it proved to be a cloudy, very dark night. At 5.30pm the artillery fire intensified and ninety minutes later the first of three waves of attack commenced. It appears that the first element to reach the buildings of the village was a battalion of the 16th Chasseurs à Pied on the south side, but soon enough other units joined in the street fighting, pushing the enemy back at bayonet point. The recapture of Ramskapelle proved to be a hard and bloody affair and which continued through the night. There was heavy loss to both sides, including more than 300 Germans taken as prisoners of war; and inevitably the village centre stood in smoking ruin. By around 8.15am on 31 October the village and railway line were once again in allied hands. In many parts of the Yser Sector held by the Germans the forward troops were now in knee-deep water and within hours only outpost troops remained on the west bank. Jack Sheldon's book on the German Army here in 1914 sums up what must have been the thoughts of many on the Kaiser's side: 'After giving their all for twelve long days they found themselves forced back to the east bank of the Yser by a spreading lake of filthy water. It had all been for nothing.'

441 LA GRANDE GUERRE. — En Belgique. — Ramscapelle sous l'eau Une attaque allemande d'avant-poste repoussée par des soldats belges. In Belgium. — Ramscapelle under the water. — A German attack of out-posts is pushed back by Belgian soldiers. — LL.

A postcard illustration of a Belgian detachment beating off a German attack on an outpost at Ramskapelle.

A new German formation, a Marine division that would in 1915 be expanded and named the MarineKorps Flandern, now entered the arena. It was destined to play a key part in the Yser Sector, under its formidable commander, Admiral Ludwig von Schröder, for the rest of the war. Not unlike the Royal Naval Division, it was initially made up of naval and marine units. In later years it would develop into a versatile and noteworthy joint maritime, land and air force. At the same time 38th Landwehr Brigade arrived from Reims to relieve the tired 4th Ersatz Division. On 4 November the brigade, along with the 1st Seebataillon and 1st Matrosen Regiment, seized Lombardsijde, taking more than 200 Belgian prisoners of war in a short and wholly successful action.

3 November
An attack mounted by the Fusiliers-Marins and the Belgian 1st Grenadiers, the latter attempting to advance over the flat land of the west bank on Den Toren Farm, met with a terrible repulse from machine-gun and artillery fire. The Grenadiers, going into action only 260 strong, came out of the action with just fifty-nine, although some eighty wounded came in over the next two days. The rest were dead or missing, taken prisoner. Among the dead was a 19 years old Ghent University student and war volunteer, Pierre Pirenne, the brother of a noted historian.

5–16 November
General Bidon, the GOC of the 81st Territorial Division, took command of all French forces co-operating with the Belgian army in the Nieuwpoort area. He envisaged mounting a counter-attack to recapture Lombardsijde and the ground south of Westende, but knew that he could not count on

significant Belgian support. Colonel Félix Maximilien Eugène Wielemans, who had taken over as King Albert's Chief of Staff in September 1914 and had largely masterminded events since, said that 'for the moment' his army could not attack due to 'lack of artillery equipment on the one hand, artillery ammunition on the other hand'. However, he would arrange to push patrols towards and then across the river once the French had achieved their objective.

Bidon's group made their attack on 7 November 1914. His 81st Territorial Division achieved its objective and Belgian patrols, as promised, advanced into the inundated area, reaching Stuivekenskerke and Vicogne. The situation on the Yser Front settled down to a few days of uneasy calm, but not far south the Battle at Ypres was reaching what turned out to be its denouement, the German forces organising in preparation for what they hoped would be a breakthrough assault on the city.

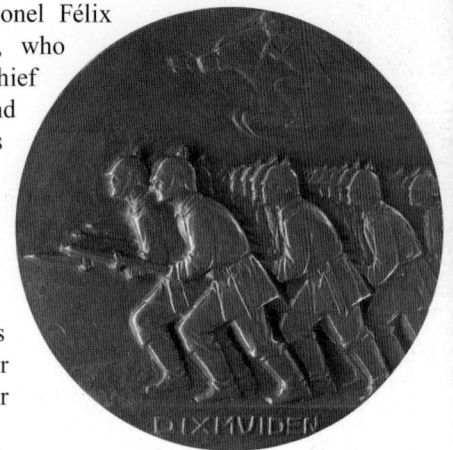

German commemorative plaque.

During the morning of 10 November a major attack was aimed against the French-held front from Diksmuide down towards Ypres. After bitter street fighting, Diksmuide was finally prised by the 43rd Reserve Division from the hands of the Fusiliers-Marins and the town and the east bank were occupied by German forces by mid-afternoon. In reality this was a major lost opportunity for the Germans; a failure to stick to a planned and co-ordinated attack with Prince Rupprecht's Army lying before Ypres meant that these two major blows, instead of being struck almost simultaneously and on the same day, were separated by a crucial twenty-four hours.

It would be years before the Germans would be dislodged from Diksmuide but, equally, they could advance no further. To the north, Lombardsijde once again changed hands and further south the Germans also reached the line of the Ypres Canal and at one point crossed it at Poesele (southwest of Merkem). Despite the evident pressure on Ypres, Foch sent reserve forces to ensure the enemy made no further progress on the Yser front. On 16 November the Fusiliers-Marins were finally relieved and moved out to the rear around Hoogstade before they went down to re-enter the line at Steenstraat, north of Ypres.

Although Veurne was not razed in the way of Diksmuide and Ypres, it came under frequent shell fire, causing medical units to relocate elsewhere.

From the beginning of the last stand battle on 18 October, when the total Belgian effective strength was 52,683 men, its army had sustained grievous losses. Within twelve days the number of effectives had fallen to 34,161, a loss of about one man in three killed, wounded or missing.

British and other volunteers with the Belgian forces

The reporting of the news and the characterisation of the country as 'Brave little Belgium' encouraged many private initiatives to raise relief funds and provide practical help from Britain. The War Office was especially wary of such initiatives, not least when it came to provision of medical care. It had long and bitter memory of such things during the Boer War.

The earliest notable example dates to 12 August 1914 when Millicent Sutherland-Leveson-Gower, the recently (1913) widowed Duchess of Sutherland, arrived in Brussels from Paris. She had enrolled into the French Red Cross just three days previously and was now on her way to work with the Belgian Secours de Blessés. She quickly established a fifty-bed unit in the salons of the Cercle Artistique, assisted by a Miss

Gavin and some eight French nurses (amongst whose number there was a countess and a marchioness), and soon telegraphed home for a Guy's Hospital surgeon, Oswald Morgan, and eight more nurses.

The Duchess certainly had an eventful war. After moving her 'ambulance' to Namur she became trapped in Brussels as the Germans overran it. She managed to escape to England and returned to France on 23 October 1914 (by which time she was known as Lady Millicent Fitzgerald, for she had found time to remarry), establishing another hospital. Her energy, contacts, skills of persuasion and organisation proved to be of enormous value.

The early rush of recruitment in Britain was not confined to the armed forces, for the Red Cross and Order of St. John were overwhelmed with volunteers for medical and support work. Many of the volunteers were of the middle class, some from very wealthy backgrounds. They included qualified surgeons and doctors, nurses, administrators, vehicle drivers and others with no specifically useful experience but much enthusiasm and courage. Several American nurses who found themselves stranded in Europe also joined in the clamour to help. On 16 August 1914 the Red Cross despatched its first 'Belgian Unit' and the original contingent was soon swelled by more arrivals during the month. Established in a number of buildings turned over for hospital use in Brussels, some detachments also went forward to Antwerp. The '2nd Belgian Unit' went overseas on 3 September. Large numbers of these early volunteers were taken prisoner as the German advance engulfed Brussels and then Antwerp. Some escaped that fate by crossing the border into the Netherlands. In most cases they were repatriated home fairly quickly, recognised as non-combatant.

While the Red Cross was getting these and many other operations in France and Belgium underway, a number of unofficial organisations began to develop: as one of their number was to recall, that they were 'splendidly freelance'. A report of an organised group going overseas from England appeared in the *British Journal of Nursing* on 12 September 1914.

> Miss M. Theresa Bryan left London on Monday in charge of the British Field Hospital for Belgium. She has with her eighteen fully-trained nurses, twelve doctors (of whom four are women) and several dressers, and equipment for forty beds. The nurses will sleep under canvas. Mrs. Congreve, wife of General Congreve, who is a trained nurse, has gone out to help with the nursing. Several ladies and gentlemen will accompany the expedition with their own motor cars, amongst whom are Mrs. Winterbottom, Mr. Somers

and Mr. Carr-Gomm. Lord Glenesk's niece, Miss Borthwick, has lent her yacht for the use of the Hospital. Two farmers' wives have gone with the Expedition, each taking a horse, and they are prepared to help with ambulance work, cooking, scrubbing, &c. Several motor caravans have been lent to the Hospital, and they are ready to be sent directly they are required. A staff of women has gone out to do the washing, cooking, &c., all of which help is entirely voluntary, and many have had to be refused, also doctors and nurses, but they will go out later if required. A telegram has been received by Lady Helena Acland-Hood, the Hon. Secretary, saying that the party had arrived safely as far as Ostend. Lady Helena was not at liberty to say what was their final destination. Col. The O'Gorman (Hon. Treasurer) received a gift of £350 on Tuesday for a motor lorry for the Hospital.'

Mrs. Cecelia Congreve, née La Touche, had long been active with the Red Cross. Her husband Walter held the Victoria Cross for actions at Colenso during the Second Boer War; her son William (Billy) would go on to earn a posthumous VC for his actions at Longueval (on the Somme) in the summer of 1916.

Gladys Winterbottom originated in Boston in the United States. There were numerous reports of her intrepid nature, driving an ambulance car around Antwerp. She continued to do that sort of work in supporting the Belgian 1st Division at later dates, earning herself the nickname 'Miss Cacao' for providing hot drinks, refreshments, stationary and other comforts at a tent she set up near the front line. One soldier of 24th Line Regiment reported seeing her going off to an exposed outpost at Oud-Stuivekenskerke.

The party was widely reported to have received an enthusiastic and cordial welcome at Ostend on 4 September, from which it moved to Antwerp to support the besieged Belgian force. It quickly established 150 beds in sixteen wards in a school building, along with a small motorised ambulance unit.

23 year old Jessica Borthwick, who had spent over a year at the Balkan war as a photographer and film maker, including six weeks at the cholera camp in Thrace, offered her 150-ton yacht *Grace Darling* to the Admiralty for carrying casualties across the Channel, paid for her captain and engineer and appealed for volunteers to crew it. It was reported to have brought over 1000 wounded from Antwerp to England and made outward journeys carrying Red Cross stores to Dunkirk, before being the last boat out from Ostend before it fell. Borthwick returned to Belgium to work with the 'Allies Field Ambulance Corps', attached to a

Belgian Field Hospital and was reportedly given a corporal's stripes by the Belgian colonel of a regiment of Karabiniers. She certainly served under fire at Diksmuide and was wounded by shell fire at Oudekapelle in mid-November 1914 but remained at duty. She later went to Serbia.

Another character with the hospital was Dr. Dorothea Clara Maude, a pioneering woman in the medical profession who had an Oxford First and had trained at the London Royal Free Hospital School of Medicine for Women. After Antwerp she left for France, joining a British army hospital at Calais as an anaesthetist and eventually established the first Maude Hospital with her husband at Dunkirk. Nursing sisters Marcia Isabella and Meta Elizabeth Stack came from County Tyrone; Meta was awarded the Croix Civique in 1916 for conspicuous courage and devotion to humanity.

After a period at Veurne from October 1914, which it was eventually forced to quit due to shellfire, the Belgian Field Hospital was established in the large building of the Gasthuis Clep at Hoogstade, where it continued to provide medical support for the Belgian, French (and on occasion British) units in the area.

Dr. Hector Munro's 'flying ambulance corps' landed on 15 September 1914. A former ship's surgeon and psychologist, Munro's energy and background in feminism and the suffragist movement soon brought together a remarkably intrepid group. He had made a short visit to Belgium and perceived a need for a fleet of light cars to ferry wounded from the field to hospitals (which at the time were in Antwerp and Ghent). He recommended the Ford model and projected operating costs of £275 per car per three months. An urgent appeal for funds and vehicles appeared in the British press and the Midland Autocar Company began collecting donations. On 4 September Munro asked the Women's Emergency Corps to supply twelve women who were *first-class nurses, able to ride and drive, and with nerves of iron*; it also reported that he advertised for *adventurous young women to equip an ambulance unit for service in Belgium*; of the 200 applications received, four were accepted. They were joined by one other, Mary St Clair (best known as the writer May Sinclair), who acted as commissariat, treasurer and secretary.

The group's initial contingent comprised Medical Officers Leslie N Reece, Donald Renton and Eric Hemingway Shaw; volunteer drivers Cecil Cooper, Mairi LC Gooden Chisholm, Lady Dorothie Feilding, Eustace Gurney, Elizabeth (Elsie) Blackhall Knocker, Jack Secker and Reverend S. F. Streatfield; stretcher bearers Arthur Gleeson and CS Wakefield; assistant Helen Gleeson and secretary May Sinclair. A married couple, John and Violet Clifton, arrived as reinforcements on 20 October.

Lady Dorothie Feilding (second left), with other members of Munro's Ambulance Corps and Belgian troops near Dendermonde in October 1914. (*Illustrated War News*)

Properly named as Munro's 'Motor Ambulance Volunteer Corps' the group moved from Dunkirk to the Flandria Hotel in Ghent and began its work in the area of Melle and Zwijnarde. It inevitably soon moved westwards as the Belgian Army withdrew and continued to support the Belgian forces thereafter. Most of its work was in ferrying casualties from the dressing stations to hospitals at Veurne and other locations. The drivers were exposed to very considerable hardships and hazards, often coming under fire, especially during the battle for Diksmuide. By December 1914 it had carried more than 1800 wounded and had grown to thirteen cars, eight motor ambulances and eight touring cars: the latter also acted as a postal service for the Belgian force. Its work was so appreciated that the Minister of War placed his son, Lieutenant Robert de Broqueville, in military charge of it, enabling unquestioned access to the front and secure areas. Munro's corps remained entirely voluntary and self-supporting. Appeals were made at home for supplies of all sorts, varying from cigarettes and chocolate to blankets, flannel shirts, mittens and socks, to lemonade and wine. Requests for morphia, feeding cups with spouts, bandages and other medical supplies underlined the seriousness of its endeavours. It was only gradually that the corps became recognised and then supported by the British and Belgian Red Cross.

Volunteer driver Mrs Hilda Wynne, who lent her private converted car for ambulance work, *hands smokes to a Belgian,* **according to** *The Sketch.*

Amongst the reinforcements that arrived to build up the corps was volunteer drive Mrs Hilda Wynne, who landed in France on 2 November 1914. She lent her private converted car to the cause and was the subject of fetching photographs that appeared in *The Sketch* in March 1915, noting how chic her uniform was! Georgiana Fyfe arrived on the same date, to work with the corps' commissariat. Newspaper reports of December 1914 reported that Labour politician, pacifist and future prime minister Ramsay MacDonald was working with the corps in Belgium.

Three of the original contingent went on to earn considerable fame and acclamation. Perhaps the first to emerge as newsworthy was Lady Dorothie Feilding – and little wonder, as she was a daughter of the Earl of Denbigh and from a wealthy establishment and military family. At the very outset of the war she had busied herself as a local representative of the Soldiers and Sailors Families' Association for the area round her family home at Newnham Paddox, near Rugby, and acquired some medical training. Despite her evident enthusiasm to go to war, Dorothie found herself debarred from going overseas by the Red Cross in 1914 as it insisted on three years of hospital experience, so she instead responded to Munro's recruitment campaign. Her fine and fearless work as a motor ambulance driver was recognised in a special order of the day issued on 31 December 1914 by Admiral Ronarc'h, who commanded the Fusiliers-Marins at Diksmuide. She was decorated by King Albert with the highest Belgian military decoration, the Order of Leopold II, Knights Cross (with palm) on 1 February 1915 and subsequently also received the French Croix de Guerre in bronze. Her exploits continued: in 1916, the officer commanding the Royal Naval siege guns, Commander Henry Halahan RN, commended her to Prince Alexander of Teck, then head of the British Military Mission in Belgium.

> 'I venture to submit that Lady Dorothie Feilding should in like manner be rewarded. The circumstances are peculiar in that, this being an isolated unit, no medical organization existed for clearing casualties other than this voluntary one and owing to indifferent means of communication etc, it was necessary for the Ambulance to be in close touch with the guns when in action. (She) was thus frequently exposed to risks which probably no other woman has undergone. She has always displayed a devotion to duty and contempt of danger, which has been a source of admiration to all. I speak only of her work with the Naval Siege Guns, but Your Serene Highness is also aware of her devoted services to the Belgian Army and to the French – notably to the Brigade des Marins.'

Lady Dorothie became one of first female recipients of the British Military Medal. She continued to serve with the Ambulance until June 1917 and died in 1935, tragically young, aged only 46.

One of the locations often on Dorothie Feilding's ambulance route was a forward medical post (*Poste de Secours Anglais*) established just a hundred metres from the front line at Pervijze by two of Munro's other originals, Elsie Knocker and Mairi Chisholm. The former was a trained nurse and a member of the Women's Motorcyclist Club at the outbreak of hostilities. Chisholm had first worked as a despatch rider for the Women's Emergency Corps, carrying messages through the London traffic on her motor bike. The two continued their gruelling medical work at Pervijze and then, from April 1915, at a hut established near Avekapelle, mainly in support of the Belgian 3rd Division. They were frequently under fire and at great personal risk, having to twice relocate their post due to enemy shelling. Queen Elisabeth took a particular interest in their work and on 2 March 1916 their post was honoured by a visit by King Albert. He had already, as early as February 1915, decorated all three ladies

Another image of Lady Dorothie Feilding, said to have been taken at Aalst. (*The Sketch*)

with the Order of Léopold II, Knights Cross with Palm. Elsie Knocker, née Shapter and also sometimes known as 'Gypsy', became a baroness when she married (her second marriage) Baron Harold de T'Serclaes, a Belgian officer of the flying services, in January 1916.

Novelist Sarah Broom Macnaughtan already had experience of work with the Red Cross in South Africa during the Boer War. Now aged 49, she joined the unit in Ostend. Her memoirs paint a wonderful picture.

> 'This evening Dr. Hector Munro came in from Ghent with his oddly-dressed ladies, and at first one was inclined to call them masqueraders in their knickerbockers and puttees and caps, but I believe they have done excellent work. It is a queer side of war to see young, pretty English girls in khaki and thick boots,

coming in from the trenches, where they have been picking up wounded men within a hundred yards of the enemy's lines, and carrying them away on stretchers. "Wonderful little Walküres in knickerbockers, I lift my hat to you!"

'.... Dr. Munro asked me to come on to his convoy, and I gladly did so: he sent home a lady whose nerves were gone, and I was put in her place. ... I began to make out of whom our party consists. There is Lady Dorothy Fielding – probably 22, but capable of taking command of a ship, and speaking French like a native; Mrs. Decker, an Australian, plucky and efficient; Miss Chisholm, a blue-eyed Scottish girl, with a thick coat strapped around her waist and a haversack slung from her shoulder; a tall American, whose name I do not yet know, whose husband is a journalist; three young surgeons, and Dr. Munro. It is all so quaint. The girls rule the company, carry maps and find roads, see about provisions and carry wounded.

... Mrs. Knocker came into Dunkirk for a night's rest while I was staying there. She had been out all the previous day in a storm of wind and rain driving an ambulance. It was heavy with wounded, and shells were dropping very near. She – the most courageous woman that ever lived – was quite unnerved at last. The glass of the car she was driving was dim with rain and she could carry no lights, and with this swaying load of injured men behind her on the rutty road she had to stick to her wheel and go on.'

Mrs Madelon 'Glory' Hancock: American by birth; a British army officer's wife; and a volunteer nurse, whose work at Gasthuis Clep was recognised by three nations. (*North Carolina Museum of History*)

Mrs Madelon Hancock, née Battle, an American citizen born in Florida in 1881, daughter of a physician and a qualified nurse, married a British officer, Mortimer Pawson Hancock, in 1904. He commanded the 2nd Royal Fusiliers on the Western Front on two occasions. The intrepid Madelon landed in Belgium on 6 October 1914 and went to Antwerp under her own

Geraaert (left), Georgiana Fyfe of Munro's Ambulance Corps and Robert Thys (right) of the Sapeurs-Pontonniers, Christmas 1914. (*Thys*)

steam. Later she would work in Paris at the American Ambulance, one of many Americans to toil in support of the French. Madelon, who acquired the nickname 'Glory Hancock', also worked at the Belgian Field Hospital at Gasthuis Clep. She was eventually decorated by the Belgians, French and British, a feat which was said to make her not only the most decorated nurse of the war, but the most decorated woman in history at that time. In 1928, after her divorce, she changed her surname by deed poll to Hellancourt. Sadly, she died quite young (in Nice) in 1930. Her medals are held in the North Carolina Museum of History.

Munro's unit was broken up in November 1915, but by then a number of medical units, soup kitchens and other facilities were being manned by extraordinary, memorable volunteers such as those of 1914.

Chapter Four

The Northernmost Part of the Western Front 1915–1918

Recovery and Renewal
Although Belgium was now largely under a most repressive and hostile occupation and what little that remained free was a war zone, it managed a remarkable feat of recovery. Through the army's high command and the government in exile in France, it implemented a relentless effort to recruit men for the army. In all, it brought the remarkable figure of another 120,000 men to arms during the war. Some 25,000 had evaded the Germans and crossed, at enormous personal risk, into the neutral Netherlands. Others were domiciled or otherwise away from Belgium when war broke out, including those who had been in the country's colonies in Africa. Many had fled to Great Britain, Ireland, France or elsewhere in the first weeks of the war. Men began to enlist voluntarily, but from March 1915 a royal decree conscripted those aged below 25. From July 1916, all men aged under 40 were liable for service.

The rising numbers of recruits enabled the Belgians to raise the size of the field army to 130,000 in 1916 and 150,000 the following year. By 1918 the army on the Yser had been reorganised into ten divisions, along with the necessary lines of communication and support services units. Under the pressure of repeated request from the allies, the Belgian-held front was extended from twenty-one to thirty-eight kilometres

Alfons Stuckens, of the Belgian 7th Line Regiment, during training in France.

in the face of the series of major German offensives in the spring of that year.

During the first months after the line stabilised, the Belgians were largely supplied by France and Great Britain; armaments, munitions, equipment, rations, forage and all manner of other supplies arrived in bewildering variety. Gradually, the Belgian population overseas was mobilised to support the war effort. An appeal was made in April 1915 for Belgian engineers and skilled men to organise and work in national factories, to ensure that the nation would 'only ask from the allies what they could not manufacture themselves'. Such facilities developed in France (for example, a major munitions works at Graville Ste. Honorine, near Le Havre; it suffered a huge explosion during 1915) and in Britain. The huge 'Elisabethville' shell factory at Birtley, County Durham, employed 4000 Belgians, with a family community totalling 6000 accommodated nearby. By 1917 some 22,000 were employed in producing material for the army, including artillery pieces, rifles, mortars and ammunition with the exception of the heaviest calibres. Belgian troops were supplied with a standardised khaki uniform produced in Belgian workshops.

By early October 1914 an army training centre had already been established at Granville, France, and under the leadership of de Selliers de Moranville it became part of a comprehensive network for training officers and men in the fast-evolving tactical, organisational and armament developments emerging from the Front.

Camille Emile Jules Pintelon, sixth of a family of twelve from Ostend. He was killed, aged 22, by a bullet to the head while in the trenches with the 22nd Line Regiment at Kaaskerke, facing Diksmuide, on 9 July 1917. Originally buried at Adinkerke, he was later reinterred at his home town. The photograph, taken in De Panne by his brother Eduard, is now in the Archief van Oostende. Further family information was supplied by Eduard's grandson, Eddy Pintelon. (*Kusterfgoed*)

A unique battlefield

The Yser sector became unlike any other along the 600 kilometres length of the Western Front. The depth and breadth of the inundation, which continued to demand careful hydrological management by the Belgian engineers, ensured that neither side could contemplate a major

The work of maintaining and managing the flood levels was continuous.

offensive in the area. The remaining actions that are described in this book, and the final allied offensive of late September 1918, took place on its flanks: at the narrow dune land bridgehead at the Yser Estuary and on the northern edge of the Ypres Salient.

Over time both sides adapted to the unusual situation and developed their defences. Digging soon met with water even where the ground was dry so, as elsewhere in other parts of Flanders, the front line 'trenches' and 'dugouts' were built up ramparts of sandbags, earth and timber, i.e. effectively a form of breastworks. In most places there was no discernible parados. So vast were the number of sandbags filled and piled up that the Belgians joked that if the war lasted they would need to dig up the whole country: the Flemish called the bags *Vaderlandjes* (a diminitive equating to 'fatherland sacks'). In the 3rd Division's sector, in front of Pervijze and Oostkerke, more than 150,000 of them were used in constructing a trench line of just over a kilometre. Both sides constructed concrete shelters at later dates and also reinforced the ruins of existing buildings for similar purposes. Both also deepened their defensive systems over time, constructing secondary and in places tertiary lines, separated from the front line and linked mainly by wooden plank paths and roads.

The main Belgian secondary defence ran about 1500 metres west of the Yser Front and the basics of a third line were constructed along the Loo Canal, south of Veurne. The German system of defence in depth also eventually incorporated the Flandern I Stellung line, but that was so

British transport wagon on partly flooded roads near 'Au Lion Belge'. *Communauté Urbaine de Dunkerque*

A Belgian casualty being carried along the duckboard tracks on the Yser Front. The army developed a sophisticated medical chain of evacuation.

German troops at Schoorbakke.

far to the east of the area described in this book that it does not feature. Behind the lines an increasingly comprehensive network of broad gauge and light railways brought men and materials to the gun positions and trenches.

For much of the war the allied front line snaked around from the North Sea beach and the east side of the Yser Estuary, past the Goose Foot complex of canals at Nieuwpoort. It then continued along the railway embankment past Ramskapelle and Pervijze. As the line neared Diksmuide it departed from the railway and curved around on higher ground to meet the west bank of the Yser. At that point it came nearest to the German front line, which was established on the west bank from Schoorbakke southwards. South of Diksmuide the two front lines diverged, to face each other across another wide stretch of inundated land. South of Drie-Grachten the geography became more complex, with two peninsulas of slightly higher ground separating some deep streams flowing northwards. Until September 1917 the allied line lay to the west of these peninsulas, running down past Reninge towards Zuydschoote and the Ypres Salient. During that month, in conjunction with the British offensive at Ypres, French forces advanced across the peninsulas, capturing Merkem. The line remained in that position; taken once more by the Germans, it was quickly recaptured by a notable Belgian counter-attack in April 1918 and then held until the final breakout offensive in September of that year.

Belgian front line trenches dug into the Yser Dyke. (*Debeer*)

Between the end of the Battle of the Yser and before the final offensive, Belgian losses on the Yser amounted to another 40,000 killed, wounded or missing; its dead in the years 1915 to 1917 inclusive were less than the totals of 1914 and 1918.

The royal couple
King Albert and Queen Elisabeth came to be a central part of the legends and myths of the war on the Yser. Their personalities and roles were quite unlike those of any other monarch involved in the conflict; and certainly they played a much more direct, front line part.

Born Albert Léopold Clément Marie Meinrad Saxe-Coburg-Gotha in April 1875 at the Palais de la Régence in Place Royale, Brussels, fifth child of Prince Philippe, Count of Flanders and of Princess Marie de Hohenzollern-Sigmaringen, he was the grandson of the first King of the Belgians, Leopold I. His mother was a relative of Germany's Kaiser Wilhelm II. Albert succeeded his elder brother Baudouin, who died in an influenza epidemic in 1891, as the next in line to the throne after his uncle, who however died in 1905. Albert then became the Heir Apparent to King Leopold II and came to the throne in 1909. He was educated at the École Militaire, where one of his teachers was General

Gérard Leman (of the 1914 defence of Liège fame), and in 1892 he was commissioned in the Regiment of Grenadiers. Before he became King, in June 1900 Albert had married Princess Elisabeth Gabrielle Valérie Marie, Duchess of Bavaria. By 1906 they had three children: Léopold, Charles and Marie-José.

On 2 August 1914 Albert formally took command of the armed forces in accordance with Article 68 of the Belgian constitution. During the conflict the couple were based at a villa at De Panne but travelled frequently within the area of operations and as such were rarely out of range of enemy shell fire. Elisabeth's work as patron of hospitals and schools, and serving in a nursing role, and Albert's presence not only at army headquarters but also in the dugouts of brigades, battalions and in the trenches, are well documented and remembered in diaries and memoirs. The couple are believed to have paid personally for supplies and equipment of all kinds, including 5000 gun-metal watches as an award to men who had carried out distinguished acts. The couple's impact on morale and the great regard in which they were held was palpable. It is noteworthy that there are no accusations of the 'lions led

Many seaside villas in de Panne were turned over for military and medical use.

by donkeys' type, for men knew that the royal couple were sharing the burden and not shying from their work and dangers.

On 8 April 1915, young Prince Léopold was enlisted as a private into the 12th Line Regiment in a ceremony conducted on the beach at De Panne. It was an unprecedented gesture. As a young teenager, Léopold was not committed to the front line and about six months later he was sent to continue his education at Eton.

Albert rarely left the fighting zone but did go to France and later Italy for short visits and also went briefly to England in 1918. Elisabeth also crossed the English Channel on a number of occasions, ostensibly to visit her children.

Actions on the flanks of the inundated area

Lombardsijde: the seaward flank of the Western Front.
In the latter stages of the Battle of the Yser, the German Marine Division (soon to be the MarineKorps Flandern) had established itself in the dune land, leaving the French holding only a narrow bridgehead east of the Yser Estuary. It was a precarious position for the occupying infantry, for

The exposed plank 'passarelles' linked the allied front line with the outposts across the water.

A pontoon bridge near Pelican Bridge, crossing the Dunkirk-Veurne Canal. (*Thys*)

the bridgehead could only be reached by a number of plank walkways constructed across the estuary or via the Goose Foot and the old earthwork fort known as the Palingbrug or Grand Redan.

Trenches dug in the dune sand would tend to collapse at the slightest tremor unless they were strongly revetted – and every inch of timber for the purpose would need to be man-handled across the bridges. Artillery and most medical and support service remained on the west bank. The Germans held high dunes near the coast, notably the 'Grand Dune', which the Germans called Affenberg (Ape Hill), Höhe 17 and the Hexenkessel (Witches' Cauldron), which gave excellent observation across all of the bridgehead.

Foch, in his *Mémoires: pour servir l'histoire de la guerre de 1914–1918*, recalled in December 1914 considering with General de Mitry, commanding the French II Cavalry Corps, an offensive designed to push out from the bridgehead and ultimately along the coast past Westende. The governor of Dunkirk could provide boats and bridging materials necessary to pass and support a force across the estuary, but only field artillery would be available and none of any great calibre. Agreement reached, operations began on 15 December, with some progress being made and the first houses in Lombardsijde were reached and on the polder between there and the high dunes near the coast. Overcoming local counter-attacks, within four days the French had secured an advance: shallow in depth; overlooked and under fire from the dunes; in the very difficult sandy and waterlogged ground; but just about tenable.

The 7th Regiment de Marche de Tirailleurs Algériens, veterans of the Marne and Ypres, arrived in the area on 20 December and were ordered to carry out an attack two days later. It was quickly brought to a standstill by small arms fire and provoked a serious artillery retaliation. A second attempt on 24 December gained a small section of German trenches in the high dunes but no more, and continued firing caused numerous casualties to the French unit. Over the next month preparations were made for another assault. The miseries resulting from the wet winter along the North Sea coast lashing the rudimentary trench network in the sand included the discovery that no platoon could physically withstand the strain and exposure of more than two days in the front line.

The renewed attack eventually took place on 27 January 1915 and made no significant progress against a determined defence and at a heavy human cost. The Tirailleurs Algériens lost 121 killed, 206 wounded and forty-six missing. Amongst those killed was 26 year old Lieutenant Pierre Thuret, who had returned to duty after being wounded in September 1914. His body was never found but at a later date a memorial headstone was erected by his family. Renovated in 2007, it still stands and is the most northerly remaining physical representation of the old Western Front.

Belgian troops during mobilisation in August 1914, according to 'The Sphere'. The army's uniforms had rather archaic designs.

Although bogged down in entrenched positions, fighting continued in the dune land and flared up at frequent intervals. In June 1915 French Zoauves attempted to capture the Hexenkessel, without success. In the December another French attack failed. During the following month, the first action of 1916 saw a German attack into the polder area meet with similar results. As with most other areas of the Western Front in Flanders, the dune land came to be a wilderness of trenches, half-destroyed dugouts, festoons of rusting barbed wire and all the attendant squalors and miseries of life in such a desolate landscape.

British ambitions and the German Operation Strandfest
The strategic importance of the Belgian coast was never lost on Britain. It had long been known as the 'dagger pointed at the heart of England' and by early 1917 the dagger came mainly in the form of the U-boat fleet based at Bruges and its port of Zeebrugge.

The nightmare prospect of Germany continuing to hold the coast when the war was over nagged at the British until it was finally eliminated in the very last days of the war. As early as 26 October 1914 Sir Winston Churchill, then First Lord of the Admiralty, was pressing Field Marshal Sir John French to eject the enemy: 'we must have him off the Belgian coast'. French simply did not have the resources to achieve it and his allies did not see it as a priority, but as the British Expeditionary Force expanded and naval nervousness escalated, Haig began to mull over the possibilities.

On 26 December 1915 Rear-Admiral Sir Reginald Bacon, commanding the Dover Patrol, suggested landing a force at Ostend. Haig appointed Lieutenant General Sir Aylmer Hunter-Weston, recently returned from Gallipoli, to assess the situation and advise him. Bacon's plan was ready by March 1916 and had some innovative ideas, but exposed the force to the threat of annihilation within the harbour. Hunter-Weston was critical of it and the idea was shelved. The German expansion of naval capacity in Ostend during 1916 and early 1917 forced the British to reconsider the possibility of action against the harbour and its facilities: the destroyer fleet at Ostend had grown from four to twenty-one ships; the Germans had installed forty-two coastal batteries, including several with 12-inch guns that would be a very considerable nuisance to British naval interests; and the U-boat menace against sea-borne trade had escalated to the point where British defeat could not be discounted. The Royal Navy was also nervous of a potential German landing west of Dunkirk.

Thus a new plan emerged, which eventually became an integral part of the thinking for what became the Third Battle of Ypres. As early as 18 September 1916, just three days after their battlefield debut on the

Somme, Bacon suggested landing tanks on the coast. The idea was a simple one: the British would take over the northernmost part of the Western Front at Nieuwpoort and would attack along the coast. The attack would link up with a force landed from the sea west of Ostend in the area of Middelkerke. The operation would begin once a major attack from Ypres had made headway (and ultimately it was the failure to advance deep enough from Ypres in July and August 1917 that caused the plan's cancellation). The German line facing Nieuwpoort would be outflanked, opening up the possibility of rolling up their entire position in Flanders.

The plan was simple in concept but technically demanding. To land the tanks, specialised pontoon craft would be employed. Three of these were to be built, each pushed onto the beach by two monitors. The pontoons would have a draft of just eighteen inches at their 'sharp' end. Monitors needed fourteen feet of water, so that determined the length of each pontoon, which would need to be 550 feet long and would land a line of several tanks. They were duly built at Chatham and trialled in great secrecy in the Thames estuary. The pontoons would demand excellent seamanship, would need to land in a smoke screen (to protect them from shore batteries) and had to be precisely located. Therefore it would be necessary to lay out, without giving the game away, a grid of light buoys off the Belgian coast to guide them into position.

Landing the tanks on the beach was one thing, enabling them to proceed inland was quite another. In addition to enemy resistance, they faced the problem of a steep wall. The architect of this relatively new sea defence was traced – he was a refugee in France. Including the curved coping at the top of the wall, a tank would need to climb at 60 degrees, which was well beyond its capability. A replica of a section of the sea wall was built at Merlimont, near Le Touquet. Trials there led to development of the tanks' engine and the addition of 'spades' on the tracks to provide grip. By May 1917 tests had shown that the tanks were able to climb the wall.

The next task was to assemble a suitable force, which came under the experienced General Sir Henry Rawlinson. XV Corps was quietly moved from the Somme to a secure training area camp at Le Clipon (near Dunkirk) and on 12 June 1917 set up its headquarters at the casino at Malo-les-Bains. Men practised embarking and landing from the sea. Every step was taken to keep the activity as secret as possible: some called it 'Hush Camp' and the whole enterprise has come to be called 'Operation Hush', although it is not clear whether this phrase was ever in contemporary use. At the same time, XV Corps took over the front line at Nieuwpoort and the Lombardsijde bridgehead.

The arrival of the British in the Nieuwpoort sector became known to Admiral Ludwig von Schröder and the MarineKorps Flandern within a day or so. On 19 June, even while much of the force was still on its way to Le Clipon, 3rd Marine Division captured eleven prisoners from the British 32nd Division, which had just taken over part of the front line. Whatever information they knew and gave away is not known, but with aerial observation and the evident build-up of force behind Ypres (not to mention the successful British attack on Messines Ridge earlier that month) it appeared that an offensive was imminent. It was enough for von Schröder to authorise a surprise blow, to be called Unternehmen Strandfest (Operation Beach Party – who says that the Germans have no sense of humour?).

The British found the coastal sector to be as dangerous as any on the Western Front, principally because of continuous long range shelling that fell on the camps, dumps, roads and artillery positions and on the port installations at Dunkirk. Corps headquarters suffered a direct hit on 27 June 1917. A single 750kg shell from the 380mm Lange Max gun at Leugenboom killed ten clerks and orderlies and wounded fifteen more. Rawlinson's office and those of all of his key staff were wrecked. It was a minor miracle that the casualties were not greater. It was thought to be the first shell fired in anger by the gun, whose huge concrete emplacement, forty-two kilometres from where the shell fell, had first been observed from the air on 7 May. The Leugenboom gun represented a severe threat to the allied rear and regularly fired on Dunkirk, Veurne, Koksijde, Alveringem and Fortem until it was finally captured in October 1918. In this role it effectively replaced a marine 380mm gun that had been installed near In de Predikboom Cabaret, south-east of Diksmuide, near Klerken, firing with great effect from late April 1915 until silenced by aerial bombing in August that year.

German field artillery began a slow bombardment of the Lombardsijde and Nieuwpoort area on 6 July 1917, continuing for the next three days. Fog and low cloud prevented detection of troop movement behind the MarineKorps Flandern's front. Holding the dune land trenches at Lombardsijde after crossing the Yser by plank bridges, the newly-arrived 1st Northamptonshire Regiment and 2nd King's Royal Rifle Corps of the 1st Division began to familiarise themselves with the curious landscape from Affenburg High Dune down to the old Palingbrug Redan and the canal complex beyond.

The German onslaught virtually destroyed the two battalions. It was designed as an attack on a narrow front with a definite and limited objective, employing a combination of tactics that would become all too familiar to the allies when facing the Germans in the spring offensives of

1918. At 5.30am on 10 July the massed German artillery, including three 24cm naval guns in shore batteries and fifty-eight artillery batteries, opened up on the British position in the bridgehead and on artillery and communications across the river. The bombardment included the use of tear and Green Cross (Diphosgene) gas; another new gas agent was used for the first time as well, wholly unforeseen by the defenders. This is often mistakenly reported as being mustard gas, which was developed at around the same time, but it was in fact Blue Cross gas (Diphenyl Chloroarsine). This was not a gas but a very fine particulate that penetrated gas respirators and caused choking, forcing men to remove the masks and expose themselves to the poisonous Green Cross.

The shell fire demolished all but one of the fragile Yser bridges, isolating the two battalions from reinforcement or escape: some of the few survivors eventually swam the river. Telephone communication was also cut, making co-ordination with supporting artillery almost impossible. The German bombardment continued throughout the day. British artillery attempted counter-preparation fire but several guns were knocked out and the German infantry were held back in well protected dugouts. Hand-picked men, lightly armed with grenades and machine guns, and with instructions to penetrate gaps and infiltrate behind the British front, might be characterised as storm troopers. At 8pm, the 3rd Marine Division finally launched the main infantry assault, by which time the two British battalions had already suffered 70–80% casualties. The storm troopers, provided with air support, attacked in most strength near the coast, outflanking the British and then turning inward. Their attack was then followed by waves of marines, supported by flamethrower teams to mop up dugouts. After a gallant defence, the Northamptons and King's Royal Rifle Corps were overwhelmed. Only four officers and sixty-four other ranks managed to reach the west bank of the Yser. Fifty officers and 1,253 other ranks were killed, wounded or missing, with most of the latter being taken as prisoners of war.

The German attack extended to the front held by 97 Brigade, 32nd Division, further to the east, but was less successful. Although there was some penetration into its line, a counter-attack that night by the 11th Border Regiment, supported by two companies of the 17th Highland Light Infantry, restored all but 500 yards of the front line but at a very considerable cost in casualties. A general counter-attack was initially ordered for 11 July but the order was soon rescinded. The British casualties suffered during Strandfest amounted to approximately 3,126 all ranks, killed, wounded and missing.

The situation in the area remained very active, with a continued significant use of artillery and gas by both sides and with local trench

British wounded at Nieuwpoort. (*Thys*)

raids and fighting in the 32nd Division's area. The 49th (West Riding) and 66th (2nd East Lancashire) divisions were later brought into action. While the sector paled in significance when contrasted with the scale of the fighting associated with the Third Battle of Ypres, for the men who fought at Nieuwpoort it was a nightmare experience. XV Corps continued to hold the sector until 19 November 1917 when it was relieved by the French XXXVI Corps. The French corps was soon replaced by the Belgian 6th Division after a proposal made by King Albert, whose force had grown and could now hold a length of thirty-eight kilometres of front. By 27 March 1918 the Belgians held the whole front from the North Sea down to Langemark, north east of Ypres. They would continue to do so until the final offensive of September 1918 broke the German position in Flanders.

On the edge of the Ypres Salient
For the purposes of this guide, the village of Steenstraat and the nearby hamlet of Lizerne can be considered as the boundary between the Yser and Ypres sectors. From Steenstraat, the Ypres Canal leads down to

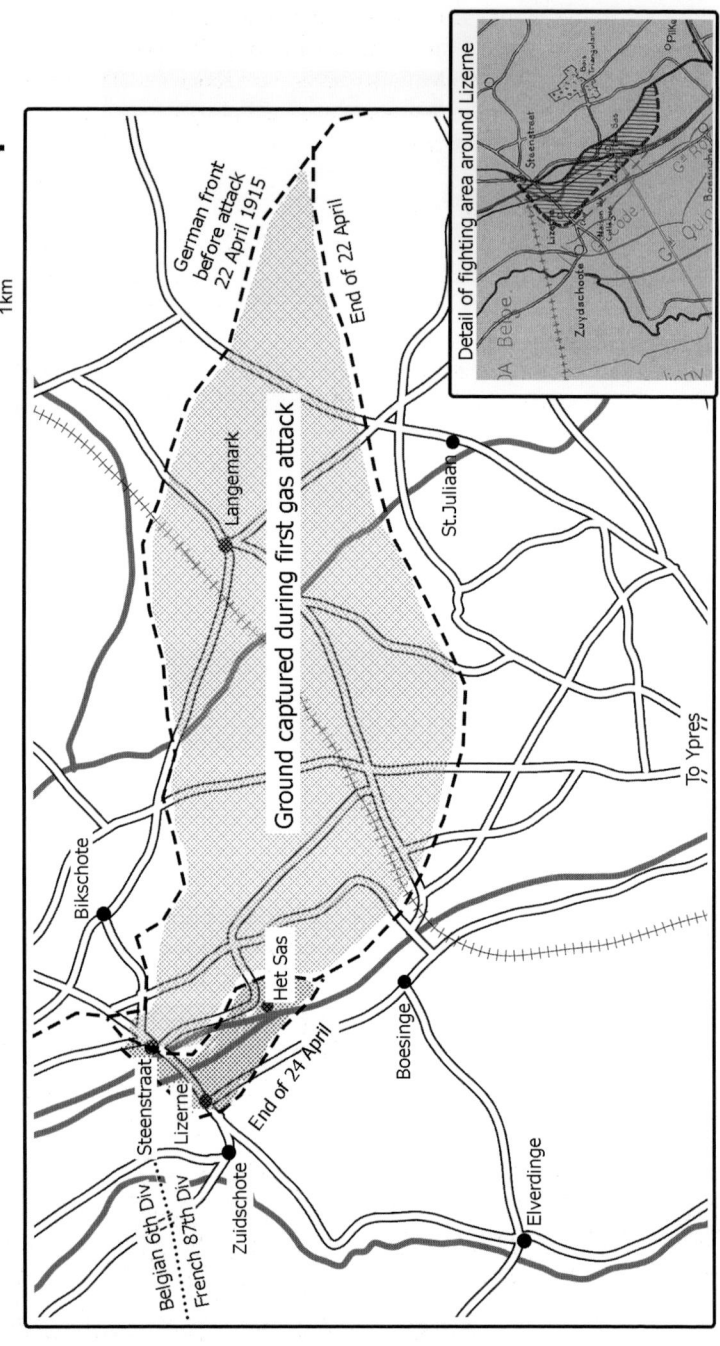

The Second Battle of Ypres, April–May 1915.

the city, passing by or through Boesinghe and Brielen. The two most significant periods of action in this area during the war in the period 1915 to early 1918, known to the British as the Second and Third Battles of Ypres, are covered in numerous works, including several volumes in the Battleground Europe series.

The Second Battle of Ypres, April-May 1915
On 22 April 1915, the area was held by the French 87th Territorial Division. On its right was the 45th Division d'Afrique. Steenstraat lay just inside the French front line, which bent there from a north-south to a west-east orientation. The village had been captured in December 1914 by the brigade of Fusiliers-Marins, which had moved to this sector after its epic fight for Diksmuide. Immediately on the left of the French came the Belgian 6th Division (under General Armand de Ceuninck), with the boundary between the two forces a short way north of the village. The Belgian formation was thinly stretched, holding some six kilometres of front as far north as Drie-Grachten. The German XXIII Reserve Corps faced the Belgians and the 45th Division.

Drie-Grachten. (*Thys*)

Inundated land on the outskirts of new Stuivekenskerke.

The battle commenced in the afternoon with the release of chlorine gas from cylinders installed in the German lines. Drifting into the French lines, the gas caused severe loss and mayhem amongst the defenceless and suffocating men. Fortunately for the Belgians, the wind took the gas in a more southerly direction and not directly across their position. By day's end the 46th Reserve Division (the German formation on the extreme right of the front being attacked) had advanced through the French line and reached the canal. To counter the advance, the Belgian 6th Division used its artillery in support of the French and turned to create a flank defence, including placing machine gun detachments to cover the canal bridge at Steenstraat. Its right-hand element was the Regiment of Grenadiers under Colonel Gustave Lotz, who placed his battalions under Captains Donies and Borriemans in position between the canal and in front of Lizerne Mill to face south. For a while, under continuing artillery fire and with gas still lingering in places, the position was held. German efforts to cross the canal were brought to a standstill and an infantry attack against the Belgian right was beaten off. Next day the Belgians made contact again with the French Territorials and extended their line to Lizerne, where they turned to face east. Behind them, the French 4th Regiment of Zouaves came into a reserve position at Zuydschote.

During the night of 23–24 April a renewed German attack prised Lizerne from Belgian and French hands and the defenders were obliged to withdraw north-westwards to link up with the main Belgian line. The attack, made by the German XXIII Reserve Corps, pushed on against the Belgian right and Zuydschote but was repulsed. While the battle widened and grew in intensity in front of Ypres – ultimately with great loss of life and the British being obliged to withdraw to a much tighter salient line around Ypres, the situation in the Lizerne and Steenstraat area did not fundamentally change. Lizerne was recaptured and the front line at the battle's conclusion ran through Steenstraat.

The Stampkot raid

This local action took place during the night of 25–26 March 1917 but was to have significant consequences in that it provided a basis for legend and mythology. On 12 March 1917, the Belgian 1st Division took over the front of the Steenstraat sector and five days later issued orders: the 24th Line Regiment would carry out a raid against the German front line at the Stampkot, a position alongside the Ieperlee (Ypres Canal). The regiment ordered its 6 Company to make the attack, with the raiding party comprising a lieutenant and four sections, each commanded by a sergeant. Two of the latter were the Van Raemdonck brothers, Eduard Jan Lodewijk and Frans Emiel Joseph. Originating from Temsche (now Temse), on the River Scheldt, near Sint-Niklaas in the province of East Flanders, they had volunteered in August 1914. The two were by 1917 experienced men, each having been wounded and returned to action. They had been members of the Catholic Flemish Student Association Temsche Voorwaarts (Forwards). As the war progressed, mainly led by Frans, they became involved with the trench newspaper *Onze Temschenaars* (Our Boys from Temsche) and the Frontbeweging (Front Movement), with individuals agitating for increased recognition of the Flemish (see a later discussion in the book).

Exactly what happened to them is now clouded by layers of propaganda. It appears that when the raiding parties were returning Frans was found to be missing. Edward went out to locate him, but he too did not return. It was not for another eighteen days that a patrol found them in No Man's Land, together with the body of Corporal Amé Louis Joseph Fiévez. He came from Calonne, coincidentally also on the Scheldt but near Tournai, in a French-speaking area. The three, the only men not to return from the raid, were buried where they were found.

Legend and myth began on 12 April 1917 with an article included in *Ons Vaderland* (Our Fatherland), the journal of the Frontbeweging. Written by comrade Oscar Dambre, it included a passage that translates approximately as: *They would not return one without the other, even if they had to die in another's arms.* It referred solely to Eduard and

Frans and was but the first mention of the notion of perfect Flemish brotherhood dying in each other's arms. Other pragmatic versions suggest that if anyone died in anyone's arms it would have been Frans and Fiévez, for Eduard died after going out to find Frans. In a sense it no longer mattered, for the seeds had been sewn which led to the brothers becoming a symbol of the entire Flemish battle on the Yser.

In 1924 the remains of the three were transferred to the Belgian military cemetery at Westvleteren, despite an objection raised by the Van Raemdonck family. The remains were in a single coffin that was placed below the centre of three headstones. In 1932 it was exhumed and reburied in the crypt of the Yser Tower Memorial.

The Third Battle of Ypres
On several occasions the French and British suggested – demanded would perhaps be more accurate but it was couched in diplomatic language – that the Belgian force be subordinated to their command. King Albert, while remaining co-operative, stoutly refused. Never was the situation more acute than during discussions about the July 1917 offensive that became the Third Battle of Ypres. Haig was planning a very large-scale break-out attack and requested French and Belgian forces on his left to participate and broaden the front. Not for the first time, Albert demurred and was on this occasion forthright in his response. He stated that he considered *that the operation has no chance of success* and that *the invasion of the greatest part of Belgian territory and the lack of reserves resulting from it, besides the King's duty to prevent any useless losses among his men, would compel him to decline all participation in an operation which, in his opinion, is bound to fail.*

French forces did participate, successfully, on the left of the attack, which began on 31 July, driving the enemy from Bikschote and towards the St. Jansbeek at Langewaade. As with the British Guards Division south of Steenstraat, their attack was assisted by an earlier German withdrawal. On 27 July, even as the allied guns were roaring out the preliminary bombardment, patrols discovered that the German front line had been abandoned. The Guards and the French took advantage of this and crossed over the canal.

Luigem and Merkem
Drie-Grachten lies 4.6 kilometres along the Ieperlee north of Steenstraat. It remained in German hands until the French advance during Third Ypres, which enabled the Belgian force then holding the line at Noordschote to move forward to seize it. By 20 September 1917 the French and Belgian line faced the next significant waterway, the

The rather bucolic Drie-Grachten in more peaceful days. (*Geneanet*)

Maartjevaart (called the St. Jansbeek south of Langewaade). On the far side the Germans held the slightly higher ground of a peninsula on which stood the ruins of the hamlet of Luigem and the village of Merkem. They had been incorporated into the second and third German defensive systems in Flanders; lines which ran southwards towards Pilkem and Langemark respectively and which had, south of Merkem, been captured in the allied advance. In the rear of Merkem was the Ypres-Diksmuide road and the crossroads at Kippe; beyond that was Houthulst Forest. The German Merkem and Bultehoek artillery groups had been stripped from the area to reinforce the zone facing British forces and only the Houthulst group remained.

On the night of 15–16 October 1917, the French 51st Infantry Division of XXXVI Corps relieved another division and took over the Bikschote-Drie-Grachten sector. With the British continuing to push not far to the south and now menacing Houthulst Forest, it immediately began to send offensive patrols across the St. Jansbeek and generally adopted an aggressive stance. It faced the 19th Landwehr Division, a mediocre formation that had been in Flanders for some time but which would soon be sent to the Eastern Front. The patrols found only patchy resistance,

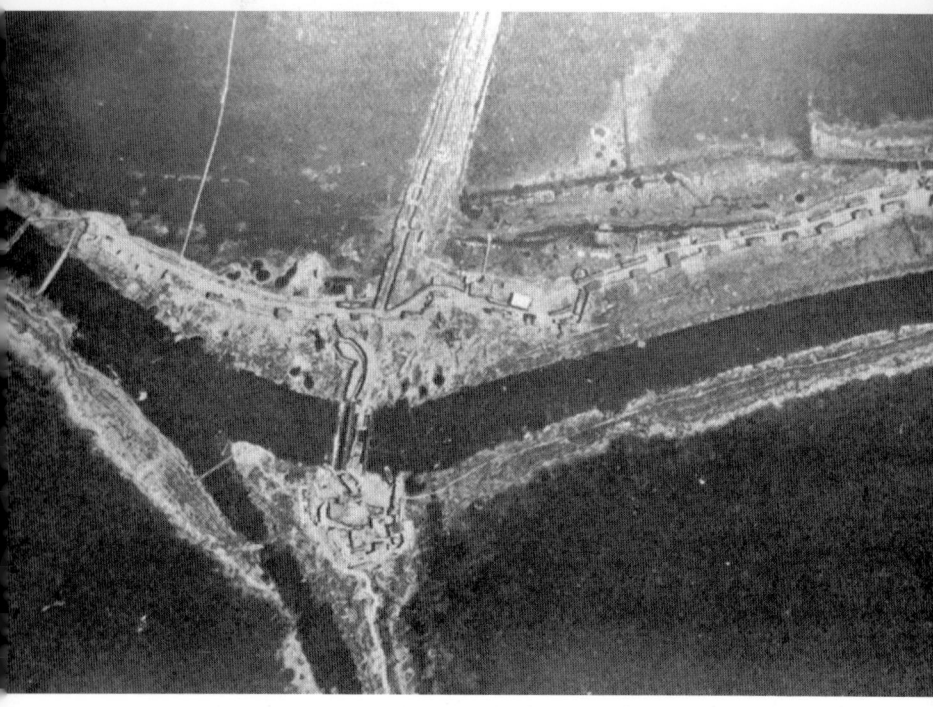

German defences at Drie-Grachten before the French advance in 1917. (*Thys*)

which encouraged plans for a larger scale attack designed to capture the higher ground. It was easier ordered than executed. The Maartjevaart, while normally only about three to four metres across, was artificially widened by the management of the inundations north of Drie-Grachten and presented a considerable barrier to any further advance. With the rains of October, the extent of water had broadened even further. The journalist and author Philip Gibbs described it as swirling round a peninsula of mud.

The old bridge at Langewaade having long since been destroyed, the only foot crossing was by a nearby ford. Two battalions – the 6th and 4th of the 273rd Infantry Regiment – were selected to make the attack, supported by machine-gun detachments of the Fusiliers-Marins, along with the Belgian 2nd Karabiniers. Its objective was to capture the higher ground and push on as far as possible to reach a position from which Houthulst Forest might then be encircled. French artillery fired an extraordinary bombardment of some 160,000 shells during the attack, which commenced at 11.45am on 27 October. It played the key part in protecting the advancing infantry – plodding might be more accurate,

The Maison de Passeur Outpost provided good observation across the Maartjevaart towards Luigem and Merkem.

for the two battalions had to move in single file, wading at waist-deep height through Langewaade Ford – and enabling them to get onto the higher land and rout the German posts. The advance reached Kippe Crossroads. Forty-six Germans, from the 388th Landwehr Regiment, found themselves going the other way into captivity, along with large numbers of mortars and machine guns. The French delighted in clearing a large number of concrete bunkers and described the desolate peninsula as *the prettiest sector one could dream of*. It had been an entirely successful and surprisingly cheap tactical victory, especially when put into context: the day before, British divisions had suffered appalling casualties floundering in the mud before Passchendaele and Gheluvelt. On 11 November 1917 the Belgian 4th Division relieved the French XXXVI Corps and took over the newly-captured front.

From the Merkem area, allied guns could enfilade Houthulst Forest and they became a decided nuisance to the occupants. There were several German attempts to counter-attack and regain the peninsula during the period November to early March 1918, but all were repulsed

Belgian troops at Drie-Grachten on 15 November 1917.

and the Belgians worked to improve the defences and create a deeper system. On 27 March the Belgian front was extended southwards as far as Langemark, in the northern part of the Ypres salient.

Tannenberg

The strategic situation changed most significantly in late 1917, when Bolshevik Russia pulled out of the war. Germany was able to consider redeploying large numbers of troops from the Eastern Front and would enjoy a distinct manpower advantage on the Western Front until American soldiers arrived in adequate numbers on the allied side. My book, *The Battle for Flanders: German defeat on the Lys, 1918* (Barnsley: Pen & Sword, 2011), describes Operation Georgette, the third German offensive undertaken against the British armies in the spring of 1918 and the following description of Merkem's part in it is summarised from the book.

The attack began in French Flanders on 9 April and was extended to the Messines Ridge the next day. It made alarming progress towards the vital railway junction town of Hazebrouck, with potentially dire consequences for the British Second Army and the Belgians. If the Germans made sufficient progress and cut railway supply to the Ypres area and the main roads coming in behind the city, it would oblige both armies to retire westwards to avoid encirclement. On 9 April King Albert agreed with his Chief of Staff that the army would retire on the

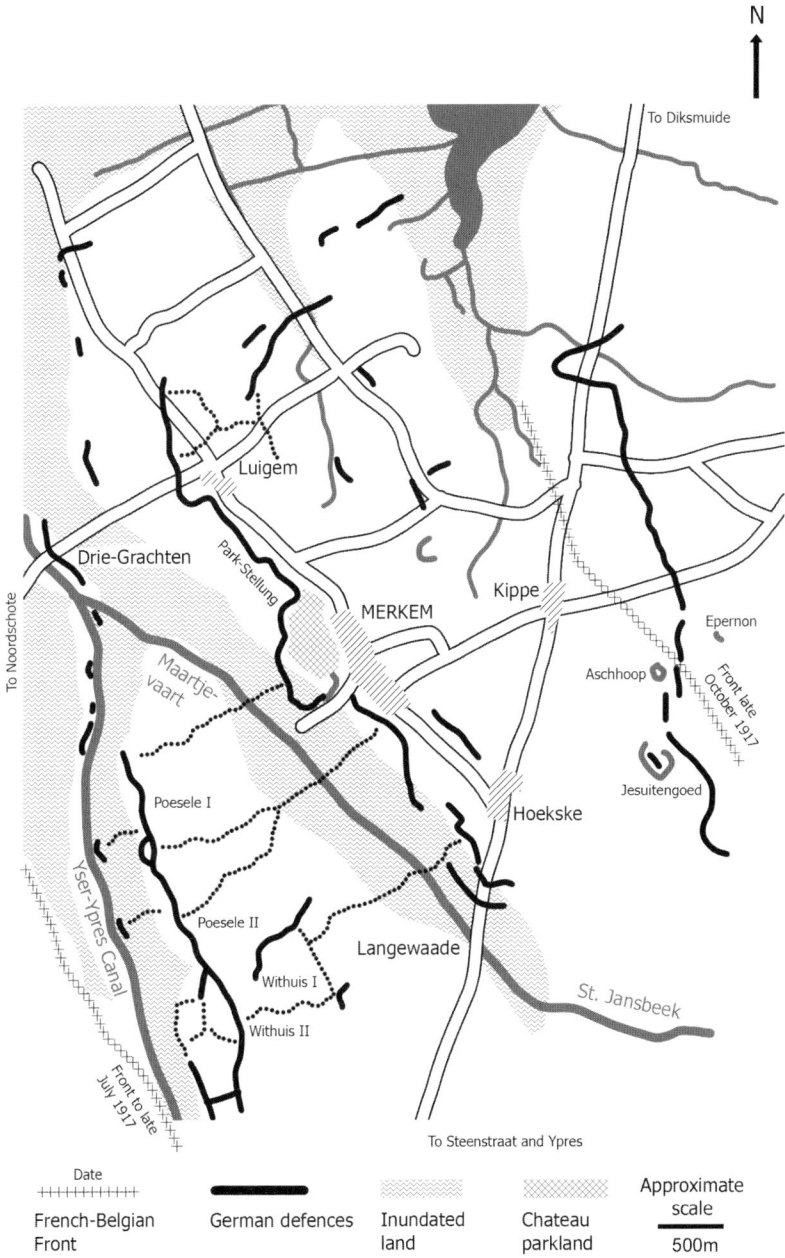

Drie-Grachten, Luigem and Merkem.

Loo Canal if absolutely necessary; but the general principle should be to hang on to Belgian territory. To stem the assault in France, Second Army withdrew its line towards Ypres – giving up the blood-saturated ground of Passchendaele and much other hard won ground from the offensive of the previous year – which enabled some divisions to be redeployed.

Although it falls geographically outside the area of the main German thrust, a subsidiary operation, known as Operation Tannenberg, was launched against the Belgians holding seven kilometres of the front west of Houthulst Forest, stretching from the Kippe Crossroads down to Langemark, on 17 April 1918. The 6th Bavarian, 1st Landwehr and 58th Divisions made the attack, together with a regiment of the MarineKorps Flandern on the left at Kippe: altogether it was a force of uneven quality. Facing the onslaught were, from left to right, the 9th (partially), 3rd and 10th Belgian Divisions.

The 3rd Division occupied two parallel lines of posts with a third entrenched line down to the Corverbeek. The forward posts – Kippe, Aschoop, Jesuitengoed, Honoré and Poitiers – were trench works

The colours of the Belgian 11th Line Regiment, decorated with the Order of Leopold in 1918.

Le drapeau du 11ᵉ de ligne, décoré de l'Ordre de Léopold.

grouped around captured German bunkers. The second line – Britannia, Verbrande Smis and de l'Hermine, Obusiers, Hibou and Mazeppa Farms – were not so strong. Each of its regiments holding the front (9th, 11th and 12th Line) placed a battalion in the posts, with another behind it in counter-attack positions by the canal. Beyond, the 10th Division's area was in a much less developed state of preparation, with a single chain of posts. Behind them was the Steenbeek Stream, flowing northwards from the British area, joining the Broenbeek in the 10th Division's area and the Loobeek just north of the Diksmuide road.

The German attack began earlier on the left than elsewhere, with 103rd and 106th Infantry Regiments of the 58th Division advancing at 5.45am. As they crossed the Broenbeek they were met by a hail of fire from the Belgian posts at Denain, Montmirail and Champaubert. A second attempt at 10.30am met with similar resistance. Only at a few places did German troops get into the Belgian posts, where counter attack parties ejected them. No lasting inroads were made; a battalion each of 13th and 19th Line defended themselves with complete success against concerted effort by seven German battalions.

The attack on the German right and centre began at 7.30am with heavy shellfire and gas aimed at the Belgian batteries across the Ypres Canal, and concentrated trench mortar fire against the forward posts. German infantry of the 1st Landwehr and 6th Bavarian Divisions rose to attack half an hour later. On their left, the 31st and 84th Landwehr Battalions met a similar fate to their comrades of the 58th Division, being cut down by fire from Mondovi, Gourbi and Poitiers posts. The right of the 84th Landwehr, with 5th MarineKorps on their right, managed to break through and in between Honoré and Jesuitengoed posts, and were quickly followed by two more battalions that overwhelmed the next posts and pressed on through to the trench line. The 33rd Landwehr also broke past Kippe and captured Britannia Post. Orders were given by the Belgian 3rd Division at 11.50am to prepare to blow the bridges over the Steenbeek but in the event this was not required. The reserve battalions manning the trench line (known as the Bretelle at the north end and the Crête de Draaibank at the south) held firm and poured fire onto the German detachments that emerged. The enemy got in places to within ten yards of the line, but no further.

The Belgians soon regained their composure, reorganising on and behind the trench line to launch a series of counter attacks. As early as 9.45am, 1st Foot Jager were pressing the Germans back and, in conjunction with 9th Line Regiment, recaptured Britannia later in the morning, taking a hundred prisoners and ten machine guns. Local counter attacks went on through the day until by about 7pm the

Merkem, a proud Belgian battle honour from April 1918.

entire position was back in Belgian hands. In this extraordinary and determined fightback, twenty German officers and 759 men were taken prisoner by the Belgians. The British Official Historian would comment that *the palm of honour of this day must be awarded to the Belgians.* The northern element of Tannenberg, conceived in the German strategic reappraisal of the situation in Flanders in late 1917, had been utterly defeated. The defence of Merkem became one of the proudest of Belgian battle honours.

War across the water
War continued to be waged across the inundated area, although operations were clearly limited in scope and needed a certain amount of ingenuity. Both sides remained in possession of certain buildings, farms and village centres that stood proud of the water but were isolated by it and completely exposed to observation. They became outposts, connected back to the front lines only by fragile and exposed plank walkways or by boat. Their names gained notoriety and a place in history: the reader can only imagine the emotions and anxieties of a detachment going out

to garrison one of these posts. In many areas, the breadth of water was so considerable that the two sides could barely see the other's front line; the outposts provided an early warning of any potential offensive action and provided the only ground level possibility of spotting for the allied artillery and observing enemy activity. The posts inevitably attracted shellfire. Near Diksmuide the front lines converged and the two sides glowered at each other across the river banks. At one notorious spot – not for nothing did the Belgians call it *The Trench of Dea*th - the two lines were on the same river bank and separated only by barricades.

From north to south, the four key Belgian outposts were called the Grote Wacht (the Great Guard). They were numbered: 4 at Berkelhof Farm, 3 on a patch of higher ground on the Kleine Beverdijkvaart, 2 at a farm east of Reigersvliet Stream (the British called it Newt Farm) and 1 at Oud-Stuivekenskerke. This was the vestige of a village that had long been abandoned before the war, but where its church tower remained as a valuable observation post. From south to north, the Germans held Den Toren Farm, Vandenwoude Farm, Kloosterhoek, Vicogne Chateau and the hamlet at its gates, New Stuivekenskerke and a series of smaller farms in the bend of the river. They were not only linked by bridges to the main front line on the river bank but also to each other.

A Belgian advanced post in the Yser inundations. Such positions were terribly exposed to enemy observation. (*Bart Debeer*)

The defences of the advanced post at Oud-Stuivekenskerke.

May 1915

Despite the general adoption of a policy of defence, the Belgians played a part in supporting British and French offensives by undertaking local tactical actions. They had already done this in the form of the sorties from Antwerp and were to do so again in May 1915. The French Tenth Army began its offensive in the Lorette and Vimy ridge area on 9 May, and on the same date the British First Army carried out its disastrous supporting attack against Aubers Ridge. On the Yser, the Belgians also carried out a number of supporting actions.

The 4th Division sent its 8th and 13th Line Regiments into action against the German outposts at Ter Stille and Violette Farms, north east and east of Ramskapelle and south of Union Bridge. The two farms lay some 600 metres from the Belgian posts and close to the Noordvaart, the raising of which had created the inundations. They had been subjected to a costly and fruitless Belgian attack by the 1st Division in January 1915; and on this occasion the results were no better. German artillery stopped much of the advance. In the centre some initial progress was made but the advance was then cut down by machine-gun crossfire from detachments of the 3rd Matrosen Regiment of the MarineKorps Flandern.

The circumstances of the action, which began with a bugle call, defy imagination. War Volunteer Florimond Pynaert of the 13th Line Regiment recalled that the plodding advance on foot through the water proceeded well at first, but then met uncut barbed wire in front of the farm (he was in the attack on Violette). German machine guns opened up, cutting an officer in half and killing and wounding large numbers of his comrades, to which nightmare was added hand grenades and flares that lit up the gruesome scene. *We lay there, without cover, bobbing on the water.* When the remnant of the assault party was forced to withdraw, it had no choice but to leave its dead hanging on the wire. Many of these men were never traced and have no known grave today. The farms, raided again, most notably in November 1917, remained in German hands until 1918.

Down near Diksmuide, the 3rd Division (under General Jacques) held the Pervijze-Oostkerke Front from December 1914 until April 1916. They knew every centimetre of the ground and exactly where the trouble spots were. A key feature was a German outpost position at two tall cylindrical steel petroleum tanks which stood on the west bank of the Yser near the Sixteen Kilometre Post. They had been set on fire by the Germans in October 1914 and one had partially collapsed, left tilting at an angle. Both were riddled with damage from shellfire. They were a distinct hazard to the Belgian position, for from the tanks the Germans enjoyed good observation across the trenches and water towards Kaaskerke and the road bridge into Diksmuide. Jacques ordered an attack to remove the post.

During the night of 9–10 May, Colonel A. Ledoseray's 1st Foot Jagers carried out an attack against the tanks, supported by a heavy bombardment by the divisional artillery. Progress was made and after about an hour the lead of three companies had reached a position about

The bells of the Sint-Pieterskerk in Lo (near Reninge) were removed to safety by the Belgian 2nd Engineers before they blew up the church's tower. They were taken to be buried in an area behind Gasthuis Clep Hospital, in Hoogstade. (*Renneboog collection in Aalst Stadsarchief*)

Pervijze Station was a Belgian front line post for much of the war. (*University of Ghent*)

sixty metres east of the tanks, right on the river bank. But they were now in a flooded area and Belgian shell fire was falling short. In the dark, men could not tell whether they were about to step and sink in a ditch or a flooded shellhole. They had no choice but to withdraw. A second company, south of the tanks, came under heavy machine-gun fire and was also compelled to fall back but held on to a position about thirty metres from the tanks. Further attempts over the next two nights came to the same outcome. The dead were lost in the flood water. The regiment lost a total of thirty-six dead and about 120 wounded of the 500 or so who had participated, gaining nothing but the realisation that the Germans did not actually hold the ruined tanks but a position slightly to the north of them, on the Reigersvliet Ditch. In his after-action report, Jacques ascribed the failure to the state of the ground and, in his opinion, that the attack had not been carried out with the necessary vigour, blaming certain officers and NCOs. Colonel A. Bernard, commanding the brigade, was dismissed on 15 May: he had predicted that without heavy artillery support and given the difficult terrain, the attack would fail.

It is said to have been on the King's intervention that a decision was to taken to call off any further assaults. The 9th Line Regiment came in to relieve the shattered Foot Jagers during the night of 12–13 May and set about the dangerous and exposed task of erecting at least the basis of a parapet to protect the ground that had been won. They did so among the dead of both sides and while stretcher bearers continued to evacuate the wounded Jagers who had been lying out on the ground for three days. A new approach was now decided upon: to sap out from the Sixteen Kilometre Post along the broad dyke and create a communication trench to link up various fragmentary

A typical contemporary postcard. It is doubtful that the ordinary soldiers of the Yser saw much glory in their work.

trenches (in reality most were no more than mud-filled scratches of the surface) that now faced the tanks. It was to be called the Boyau de communication de la borne 16 de l'Yser; it was more often known as Boyau de l'Yser and before long would become the Boyau de la Mort – the *Dodengang*, the trench of death. Work began on 18 May. It proceeded at satisfying rate, although was initially only about seventy centimetres deep, hardly a trench at all, giving no protection for the digging teams from the machine-gun and mortar fire that rained upon them. During the night of 27–28 May it was discovered the Germans were engaged in the same task, sapping from the tanks towards the Belgians.

The Minoterie Raids

The Belgian position opposite Diksmuide proved to be a most difficult and dangerous one. To a great extent this was due to German possession of a riverside complex of buildings known as the Minoterie. It was situated between the road and railway bridges that led into the town from the

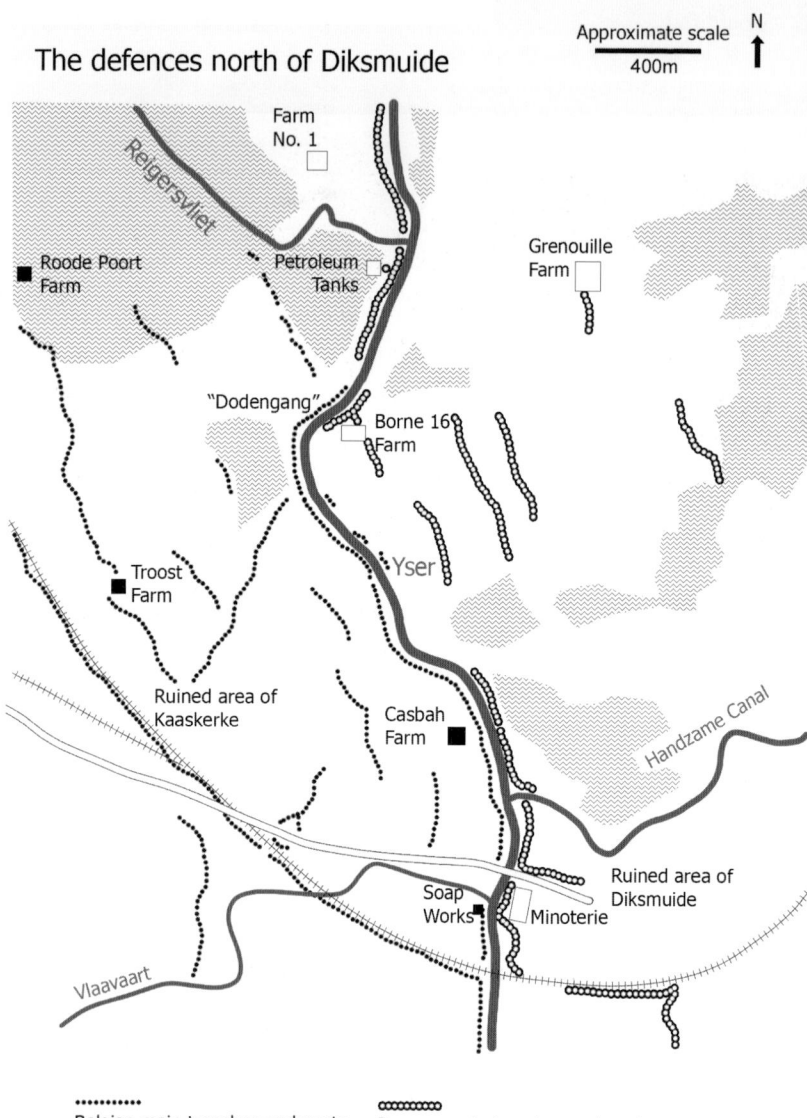

The Minoterie and, in front of it, the road bridge into Diksmuide, taken before the war.

west. In 1891 local engineer Eugène Devos-Quatannens had purchased a redundant beet sugar factory and had invested in modernising the plant into a modern steam mill. Contemporary photographs show a tall but squat central brick built tower, chimneys and outbuildings. The site fell into the hands of the 43rd Reserve Division on 10 November 1914 and remained in German hands until late 1918. The Minoterie dominated a wide swathe of the Belgian front. Directly in front of it, Belgian trenches along the river bank were barely twenty-five metres distant. There was excellent observation and fields of fire along the river in both directions and over the flat, inundated hinterland between the railway and the river. One Belgian would say of it: *Mythology speaks of the Minotaur, a bloody monster. The Minoterie must surely be his sister.*

The Germans made huge efforts into creating an impregnable defensive position out of it. An initial sandbag barricade was soon dwarfed by the concrete and steel that turned the mill into a fortress, protected on all sides by entrenchments and barbed wire defences. German engineers and transport established a *pioneerpark* on the

La Minoterie et les Abris à Dixmude.
De Bloemmolen en onderstanden te Dixmude.
The Flourmills and shelters at Dixmude.

The Minoterie site became riddled with trenches and dugouts.

Handzame Canal, north of town, bringing in metalwork, cement and timber by barge. The 20th Landwehr Division occupied the Diksmuide front from October 1916 (it had arrived very soon after it was formed) and wasted no time in strengthening the position.

Nowhere felt the sting of sniper and machine gun fire from the Minoterie and the defences in front of Diksmuide more than the *Dodengang*. Both sides had sapped out along the dyke and their trenches now ended in barricades separated only by a short expanse of water, for Belgian engineers had breached the dyke to create flooded ground between the two cul-de-sac trenches. German trenches also lay on the far bank of the river, whilst from the tower of the Minoterie shots could be fired into the Dodengang from the rear. The position remained static for many months. Both sides reinforced saps and trenches, strengthened the barbed wire, and on the Belgian side ran a light railway right up to the entrance near the Sixteen Kilometre Post. It remained a deadly spot, with a constant and morale-sapping drip, drip of casualties.

On 14 March 1917 Major-General Honoré Drubbel, commanding the Belgian 2nd Division, submitted an appreciation that considered offensive operations against enemy forces at Diksmuide. In it he argued that the devastated yet strongly fortified and defended town could

Part of the complex of light railways that brought ammunition and supplies directly into the Dodengang position. (*Debeer*)

King Albert in conversation with General Drubbel in Belgian trenches. (*Europeana*)

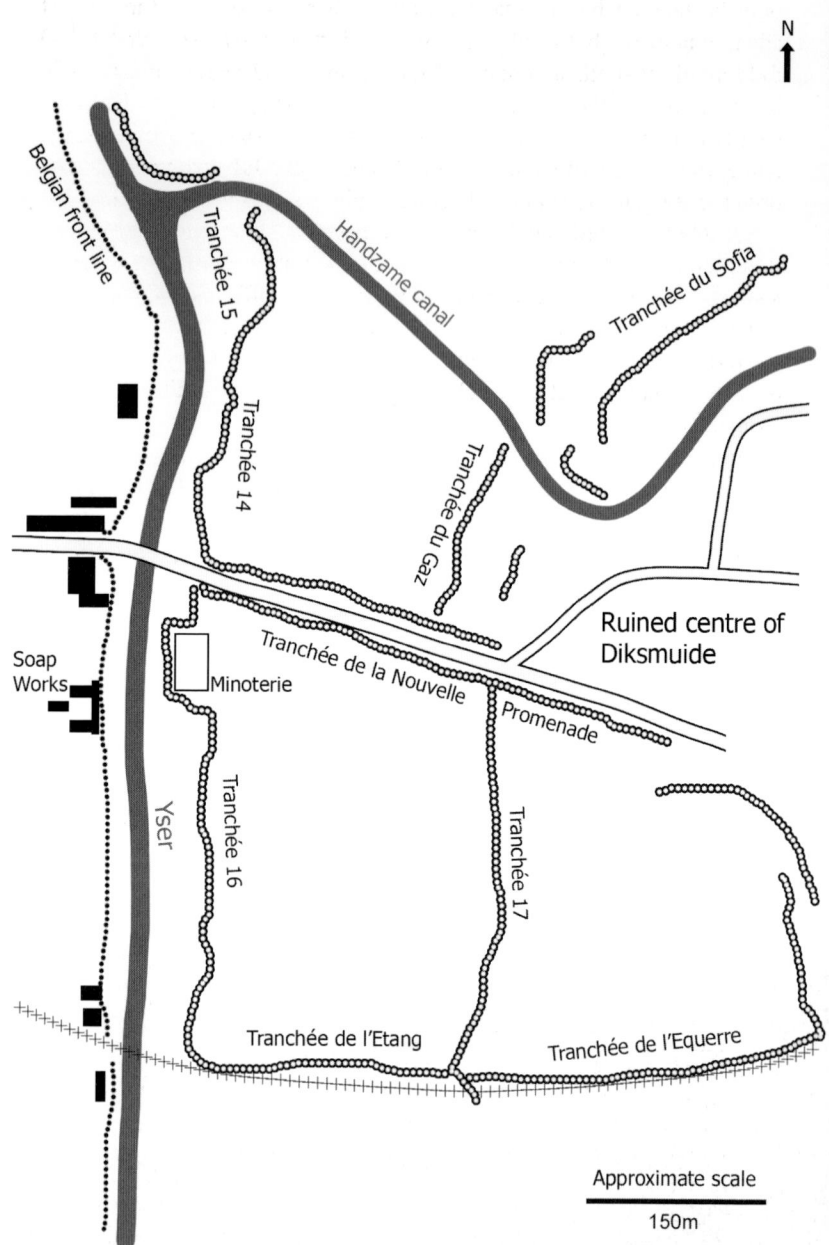

German defences of Diksmuide and the Minoterie.

only be tackled by encirclement, although at some point the task of advancing through it would have to be undertaken. An estimated 27000 field artillery shells and some 17600 medium and heavy shells would be required for the operation. At a normal firing rate, the Belgians simply did not have the artillery resources to undertake it. However, the launching of the British offensive at Ypres in late July brought pressure onto the Belgians to support that and Drubbel's idea was revisited.

Drubbel ordered the formation of a special operations group on 9 September and began to reconsider the operation, scaling it down to a short and explosive raid on the Minoterie. The officers and men were to be young, fit, intelligent and keen and would be taken from normal operations for special training. Each battalion and brigade would provide a small, selected detachment: typically, each battalion provided twelve men.

Fourteen siege batteries of the Royal Garrison Artillery and Royal Marine Artillery, organised as a group under XIX Corps Heavy Artillery, would work with the Belgians and moved into the area from 7 October. They included guns of every heavy calibre up to the huge

The ruins of the Belgian position facing the Minoterie.

15-inch weapons of numbers 3 and 5 Batteries of the Royal Marine Artillery, which had both been in action in the Nieuwpoort sector. Before it could move to its allotted position, 5 Battery RMA had to wait for the bridge at Oostkerke to be strengthened to bear its 94-ton weight. The gun was damaged three times by enemy fire during the period 31 October to 7 November and a decision was taken to dismount it and take it to a repair workshop. While this activity was underway during the night 8–9 November, another German shell struck, killing Lieutenant Charles Comyns and six men and wounding another eleven.

A detachment of the British Special Brigade of Royal Engineers (i.e. those responsible for the deployment of gas other than by shell) was also formed and sent to support the forthcoming operation. On 9 October M and N Special Companies moved by bus and lorry from Philosophe and Beuvry respectively to Fortem, where they came under the temporary orders of the Belgian 2nd Division. Over the next few days they began the task of moving their equipment and armaments to the dump at Kaaskerke and then into the front line area. The highest level of discipline had to be observed: all the men had to wear Belgian helmets, maintain absolute secrecy and generally be as quiet and inconspicuous as possible. Livens projector tubes, base plates, oil drums, gas cylinders and pipework were moved by trench tramway but the moves into their final position all had to be done manually, whilst all material and dumps had to be camouflaged. Heavy rain made the work arduous, only clearing up a few days before the raid. M Special Company alone dug in 1000 projectors but its work was halted at times due to enemy artillery firing in response to Belgian trench mortar activity. Once they were in place the company installed an additional 250 4-foot projectors: weapons which gave the maximum firing range of some 1500m. The two companies reconnoitred positions and agreed with the Belgians those dugouts which could be taken over and which spaces could be used for dumps and installation of the weapons. N Special Company was positioned on the left of the raid front, opposite the Handzame Canal; M Company was on its right.

On 22 October P Special Company and a section of Z also moved to Fortem and received instructions. They began moving gas cylinders containing a mix of Phosgene and Chlorine known as "White Star" forward by trench tramway and were assisted by a Belgian working party of an officer and 60 men who hauled a total of 998 cylinders. On 25 October – deliberately late in order to maintain secrecy – they began installing pipework and taking the cylinders to their allotted front line position. They were spread along the line, organised into four sections, each under a second lieutenant. The placing of the final cylinders and connecting up the pipework did not take place until the last few hours preceding the raid. Z Special Company's secret weapon was an enormous static flamethrower, which was installed in a position to throw its jet of burning fuel across the river and into the trench system south of the Minoterie. These devices had been used ten times during the Battle of the Somme but not at all for over a year. Finally, a section of 2 (Mortar) Special Company arrived at Fortem on 23 October. Its war diary reports that its Stokes guns fired 300 Phosgene and 150 Thermit rounds into Diksmuide the next day.

Colonel-Commandant Evrard issued the final orders from 6 Brigade to Captain Devijver, who was to lead the raid, and to the units of the brigade. The purpose of the operation was to observe the effects of gas, take prisoners and bring back war material. The raiding party would reach Trench 16 (south of the Minoterie) and go on to Nouvelle Promenade Trench (a communication trench running alongside the main bridge road towards the town centre). It was to be organised into three sections, each under a lieutenant (Lieutenants Goethals, Baudouin and Verhaegen) and consisting of twelve to fifteen men, accompanied by three or four engineers equipped with explosives. A section under Second Lieutenant Maurice Dupont of 16th Line Regiment would provide medical and communications support and Devijver would also have a twelve-man reserve at hand. The operation would begin with a gas bombardment at midnight; flamethrowers would fire for a few minutes at 2.40am and then the mortars would join in. Machine guns would fire on the trenches on the river dyke and indirectly on the bridgehead, particularly focusing on any attempt by German reserves to advance from the south, and artillery would fire a six hours' long barrage to box Diksmuide off to prevent any escape or the arrival of German reinforcements.

The raiding parties had no option but to cross the river by raft or hastily erected plank bridge. Just south of the Minoterie, a small boat would land several men of the *pontonniers* who would then haul across a bridge. Lieutenant Baudouin's dozen men of 6th Line Regiment and the few engineers attached would then cross. Lieutenant Verhaege's men of 16th Line Regiment would then proceed to reach Equerre Trench. Lieutenant Goethals and his section of the same unit would come after, heading for Etang Trench and a tunnel that was known to lead towards the town.

The operation began on time, midnight, with the gas and oil drum bombardment. P Special Company had seven of its own men gassed: they may well have been the only gas casualties of the raid, for the poison worked upwards along the river but quickly cleared on the high parapet of the opposite bank. When the raiders returned they reported that the Germans held their position and had not even bothered to wear their respirators. The artillery opened up what appeared to be a fearful bombardment, but too few heavy calibre shells fell on the key Trench 16 (this was, after all, a precise fire mission, for the German trench was remarkably close to the Belgian front line parapet) to destroy or even significantly suppress the enemy garrison there. German shell fire opened up in retaliation, but the raiding parties, accompanied by Second Lieutenant Lock of P Special Company, soon crossed the river and deployed into the swampy, cratered, chaotic ground of Etang and Equerre Trenches.

At about 1.50am, artillery fire aimed at the area they were entering appeared to wake the enemy up and from that time resistance greatly increased. By 2am the raiding parties were in position, and no doubt ducked as at 2.40am the huge British flamethrower fired two bursts, accompanied by 150 Thermit mortar shells. The first burst was stopped when a German shell exploded in the river and the cascade of water doused the flame. Burning oil gushed back into the Belgian and British trenches. Across the water, the hellish night-time scene at the southern corner of the Minoterie defences can scarcely be imagined, with mortars and shells exploding, black jets from the flamethrower, poison gas drifting up river and small arms fire opening up as the raid progressed. Verhaege's men managed to advance some fifty metres east from their point of entry; but they could go no further as the Belgian artillery was firing short and they also came across a bunker that had not been previously identified. They found it recently unoccupied but with a stock of grenades. But it was no use: on the left the fight got bogged down by resistance in Trench 16 and the raiding parties were recalled. They were back across the Yser by 4am. Among the casualties of the raid was Maurice Dupont, who died of wounds at 7.15am, having been evacuated to the field hospital at Gasthuis Clep, near Hoogstade. Aged 21, he had already been commended for his part in a raid on the Maison du Passeur outpost near Noordschote in June 1916.

Over the next two days P and Z Special Companies attempted to disconnect their pipework and dismantle their equipment, but were hampered by enemy shellfire on their position and the damage it did to the trench tramway leading back to Kaaskerke. Three men were gassed in spite of them wearing respirators. Empty gas cylinders were salvaged and returned to the railhead for re-use. Full ones were rolled into the river.

The raid had clearly failed in its objectives and the Belgians came away with a decidedly negative view of the efficacy of the gas. Even

The Maison de Passeur Post on the Yser-Ypres canal.

so, Drubbel ordered a second attempt. This time, the 2nd Division's 5 Brigade would take their turn. The Brigade ordered 5th and 15th Line Regiments, together with a company of engineers, to make preparations for a raid that would commence at 2am on 29 October. The approach dispensed with any use of gas but incorporated a heavier and more sophisticated artillery fire plan. It relied on the construction, under a protective bombardment, of four plank bridges across the river: one on either side of the Minoterie and two near the railway bridge.

The operation went wrong from the start, in that it proved to be so difficult to bring the bridging material to the river – under fire, across a morass of destroyed and now bogged ground – that construction was delayed. The sappers then found themselves under machine-gun and artillery fire as they built the span across the Yser. Orders had to be given for the mortar fire that would box off Trench 16 to begin half an hour later than planned, and even by 2.05am only the northerly of the Minoterie bridges was in place. Inevitably this restricted the number of raiders that could cross. Twenty minutes later, the southerly bridge was completed and men began to cross, but the raid was by now incoherent and fragmented. Grenade and hand to hand fighting took place within the ruins and trenches of the Minoterie and close by. A shouted order to retire was heard at one point, causing further confusion, and eventually the order to withdraw was given. Despite one of the bridges being damaged by a German shell, the raiding party managed to slip back, even bringing with them its dead and wounded, with the loss of just three men missing. That the loss was so small was a minor miracle.

Despite the disappointing results, the raids contributed to the 20th Landwehr Division being relieved and moved elsewhere for the first time. In its place came the 54th Reserve Division. This was a more experienced *eingriff* (assault) formation but one needing recuperation after recent fighting at Ypres. It soon learned that Belgian prisoners under interrogation had stated that another attack was to be made on 31 October to support the British, who were now nearing Houthulst Forest.

Activity meanwhile continued on the Diksmuide Front, with another gas release of over 1400 cylinders, but things went suspiciously quiet on the German side, with barely a shot being fired and very few men to be seen. On 31 October, Drubbel ordered all his brigade commanders to prepare fresh raid plans for their respective fronts and called for heavier artillery support, particularly from the French 370mm (15-inch) railway-mounted guns. In the end, it was 6 Brigade which was once again ordered to mount a further raid on the Minoterie.

The plan was in effect a scaled down version of the raid of 29 October and met with much the same result, although with more serious losses. The raid was timed to commence just before dark on 4 November, the time at which the Germans were known to reinforce the posts at the Minoterie. Once again, the engineers had a terrible time in even bringing materials forward across the cratered ground and the river dyke, but had everything fully in place by 4.30pm. Despite the noise and little by way of a support bombardment, it was not hindered by the enemy. Neither was the raiding party, led by Lieutenant Cyrille Baudouin. Once across, it again found the destroyed ground of Trench 16 hard going but was unmolested as it split into two groups in order to pass the centre of the Minoterie on either side. They had in fact fallen into a trap, for the Germans had deliberately removed the garrison along the front line on the river. As soon as the groups emerged into the space behind the Minoterie they came under heavy grenade and small arms fire from intact bunkers and dugouts. Baudouin and Corporal Theophile Bauwens were killed, along with another man; Sergeant Bontinck was missing and fourteen others were wounded, all within seconds. The remainder of the party promptly withdrew across the bridge, covered by a Belgian artillery barrage that ensured there were no further losses or German pursuit.

As if in a final defiant flourish before they left to rejoin the British force at Ypres, the Special Companies launched heavy gas attacks on the Minoterie on 6 and 9 November.

During March 1918, a month which saw many large German raids on the Belgian front, the 2nd Bavarian Reserve Infantry Regiment carried out one every bit as hazardous and difficult as those described above but with rather greater success. Around 235 troops took part and for the most part engaged the Belgian 3rd Foot Jager of the 5th Division. At 3.45am on 18 March a heavy artillery and gas bombardment fell on the Belgian position in front of the Minoterie, drawing only a weak response. Trench mortars joined in at 5.40am and soon enough a thick, whitish fog formed on the river, a deadly mix of smoke and gas that cloaked the raiding parties as they emerged. Twelve minutes later, a machine gun barrage came down on the Belgian river bank and the mortar fire lifted to box off the trenches from the rear. Five flat-bottomed boats set off from the Handzame Canal, carrying detachments of assault troops. The leading boats were hit by Belgian machine gun fire; shell explosions caused casualties in others and the casualties on the water were severe. Even so, enough men completed the crossing to be able to storm the enemy's position. A bridge was also constructed, but damage and machine gun fire meant that it could not be made to span the entire river and men had to wade the last stretch. A short fight with grenades and small arms took place, but by 6.45am the attacking troops were back on their own side with eighty-four prisoners and seven machine guns. Twenty-six Belgians lost their lives and a further sixty were wounded or gassed. It was a considerable feat, despite German losses believed to be about sixty in all.

Wilhelm Schmidt of 248 Reserve Infantry Regiment participated in a boat raid across the Yser at Diksmuide in January 1918, an act of bravery for which he was decorated. He was killed five months later. (*Europeana*)

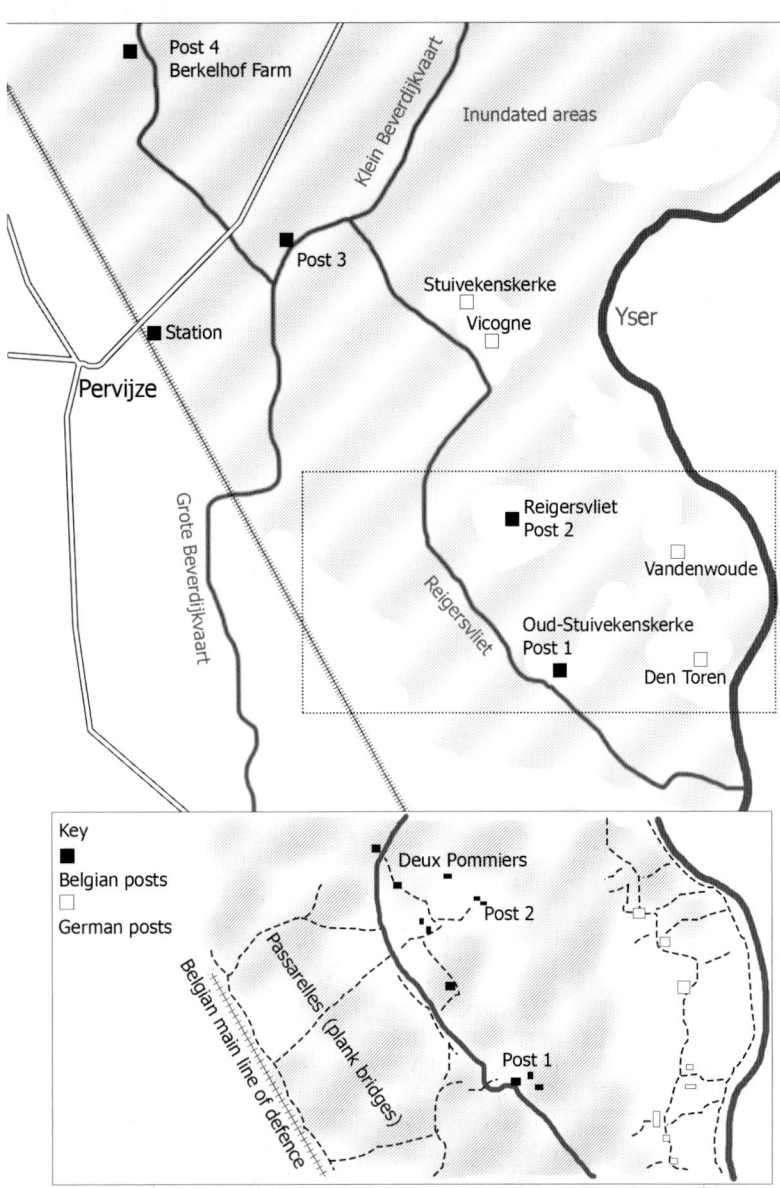

The defences of the Grote Wacht.

March 1918 attacks on the Reigersvliet
Flowing towards the petroleum tanks on the Yser bank near the Dodengang, the Reigersvliet Ditch comes down in a curve past Stuivekenskerke and its long-abandoned origin at Oud-Stuivekenskerke and the four Belgian outposts of the Grote Wacht. Almost all of the area was under water, with the outposts being established on the few islands of higher ground. By 1918, although their situation remained precarious simply because of their forward and isolated nature, the outposts had been reinforced, furnished with concrete shelters and listening posts, surrounded by barbed wire defences and heavily armed with machine guns and mortars. Plank bridges connected them to a number of smaller posts, back to a lateral bridge along the Reigersvliet and ultimately to the main line of defence on the railway embankment. The posts were frequently subjected to shell fire and relief of the garrison could only be carried out in the hours of darkness. Between 6 and 18 March, the Grote Wacht was subjected to three German attacks (the last being at the same time as the boat raid in front of the Minoterie).

On 6 March 1918, 210 men of a company of the dismounted 5th Lansiers of the Belgian 2nd Cavalry Division provided the garrison of Post 2 and its nearby satellite, Poste de Deux Pommiers, while two companies of the 2nd Battalion of Karabiniers-Cyclists were holding Post 1 at Oud-Stuivekenskerke. After a reportedly quiet night, at 5am

Germans captured on the Reigersvliet in spring 1918.

artillery of the German 214th Infantry Division commenced a very heavy bombardment of both posts. Infantry advanced under its protection and reached the barbed wire defences, which it proceeded to cut. Both posts were then attacked. While the Karabiniers-Cyclists fended off the assault, mainly by machine-gun fire, Post 2 and its satellite quickly fell to the enemy and the survivors withdrew over the plank bridge to the Reigersvliet Line.

A counter-attack was quickly organised, employing two squadrons of the dismounted 1st and 2nd Horse Jagers and reinforcements from other units. Supported by the artillery of the 2nd Cavalry Division, it successfully ejected the Germans from the post.

Three days later both posts were once again bombarded, this time including poison gas, but all attempts by German infantry to approach them were repelled by machine gun fire. On 18 March the Germans tried again against both posts, once more employing gas. On this occasion, Post 2 held while Post 1, at Oud-Stuivekenskerke, fell to the enemy. It was held by a company of the 1st Karabiniers-Cyclists. A counter attack was organised and carried out by the regiment's 2nd Company.

Losses to both sides were heavy in this series of localised and ultimately fruitless actions. The casualties of the 5th Lansiers are a case in point: just thirty-nine men who had been holding the post when first attacked were left to continue at duty. Among the dead was Camille Cyriel Bollaert, a private who came from Boesinghe, near Ypres. Later reports of him being seen at a German prison camp proved to be false and, as with many others of this fighting, he has no known grave.

Failure to achieve anything against the Grote Wacht Posts, taken together with the remarkable Belgian success at Merkem in April 1918, served notice to the Germans. The Belgian army they were now facing had developed from the courageous but ramshackle and doomed force of 1914 into a well drilled, well organised and capable force. In late September 1918 the lesson would be reinforced in some style.

Chapter Five

Politics and the Shaping of Memory

The British War Office's *Handbook of the Belgian Army, 1914* observed:

> 'The Belgian nation, and Belgian regiments, are composed of two different races – the Walloons, who speak a sort of French, and the Flemings, who speak a sort of Dutch. Many Walloons can only talk French; many Flemings can only talk Flemish. On the outbreak of a Franco-German war public opinion in Walloon districts is likely to be actively pro-French, whilst in Flemish districts, though hardly pro-French, is not likely to be actively pro-German. Both are Belgians first and foremost; Walloons and Flemings only in second place. Belgian country people generally, and especially the Flemings, are very religious, and the large majority are Roman Catholics.'

Of the nation's population of 7.4m (1910 figures), 45% were Flemish-speaking only and 40% French-speaking only.

The troops were *Belgians first and foremost* perhaps, but any tour of the battlefields of the Yser exposes a fracturing of the sites, symbols and practices of remembrance on cultural lines that cannot be ignored if they are to be understood. These things have their roots in an increasingly active Flemish nationalist agitation within the Belgian armed forces during the war, and it drew inspiration from a movement that had already existed for decades.

The Blauwvoeterij, Catholic Flemish student movements and the Frontbeweging
The fortunes in the economic and cultural development of Belgium in the nineteenth century swung sharply in the direction of Wallonia. It could be argued that Flanders had the greater history over the centuries, with the cities of Antwerp, Bruges, Ghent, Leuven (Louvain), Kortrijk (Courtrai) and Ypres having prospered on their wool and flax trades, agriculture and, certainly as far as Antwerp was concerned, seaborne traffic and international business. Industrialisation, however, left them behind: coal, iron and steel industries grew rapidly in the south,

particularly around Brussels, Liège, Charleroi and Mons. Employment and wages there overtook those in Flanders and the French language and culture assumed dominance in all public affairs.

The Belgian Constitution guaranteed freedom of private use of language, but the nation's aristocracy, central government, system of justice and other important areas of life were dominated by French and the culture that went with it. Brussels, the capital city within the Flemish-speaking area, adopted French in all but some of its working class suburbs. All education was delivered in French in the early decades of the new nation's history, despite the fact that at least half of the nation did not speak French as their natural language. Inevitably, a sense of bias and alienation led to calls for change. It was not until 1878 that government communications in Flanders had to be Flemish or bilingual, and five years later school education in Flanders was allowed in the local language. Higher education remained in French, leading to the universities in Flemish-speaking Ghent and Leuven as natural focus points for grievance and activism. Power and authority remained strongly French dominated – and its use within the armed forces would play a core part in how Belgium came to remember its Great War.

The seminary at Roeselare, where influential Flemish writer, poet and priest Guido Gezelle taught, became an epicentre of the movement for greater recognition of the language in the mid and late 1800s. Gezelle's pupils, perhaps the most important and visionary being Hugo Verriest, developed the notion of a romantic, idealised struggle for linguistic and cultural independence. Late in 1875, the movement began to be recognised as *De Blauwvoeterij* (after the title of a song by Albrecht Rodenbach, often described as a battle hymn for Flanders) and spread throughout the Flemish Catholic student population through the journal *De Vlaamsche Vlagge* (The Flemish Flag). From student thought and agitation developed a wider Flemish movement, driven by the intelligentsia but gradually broadening in its appeal.

The question of language used by the army became a notable source of internal conflict during the Great War but was by no means a new subject. In early 1913 the Belgian Parliament – already assailed by general strikes and demands for electoral reform in a turbulent year for Europe - debated a Military Bill in which substantial commitments to the expansion and modernisation of the armed forces were proposed in the teeth of resistance. Prime Minister (and also Minister for War) Charles de Broqueville needed to employ every political tool to enable the bill's passage; the question of language came into the debate mainly as a means to encourage Flemish factions to support it.

Pushed by the Flemish movements, pressure had been growing for some time for the creation of separate Flemish and Walloon regiments in which officers and other ranks would as a matter of right communicate with each other in the respective languages. Future officer cadets would need to be bilingual and training would be in both languages. The Walloon factions rejected the possibility of a bilingual army: rather than submit to it, said Member of Parliament and Walloon separatist Jules Destrée, his people would rather prefer to be severed from Belgium. Broqueville's statesmanship steered the bill through but the matter of language within the army had not begun to be addressed when the war came.

At the outset of the war, King Albert's proclamation ended with what he intended as a unifying paragraph, recalling key moments in the mediaeval history of the two peoples:

> 'Glory to you, Army of the Belgian people! Remember in the face of the enemy that you are fighting for your Fatherland and for your menaced homes. Remember, men of Flanders, the battle of the Golden Spurs! And you, Walloons of Liège, who are at the place of honour at present, remember the six hundred men of Franchimont!'

During October 1914 the army journal *De Legerbode* began to carry the masthead, *This sheet is meant for soldiers: every company, squadron and battery receives ten French and ten Dutch copies.*

It is beyond the scope of this book to discuss Flemish nationalism within German-occupied Belgium; but its development within the army (and indeed amongst the refugees that fled to France and Great Britain in 1914) is of importance for it led to the concepts that formed part, or even much, of how the war is remembered in the Yserland. The specific recognition of Flemish heroes; the erection of special grave headstones; the establishment of an annual pilgrimage; and the building of the Yser Tower Memorial all have their roots in a movement that crystallised in 1917 as the political *Frontbeweging* and turned in 1919 into the *Frontpartij* (Front Party). The theme of agitation was based on a notion of unfair sacrifice - that Flemish troops were shouldering more than their share of the burden – and of official discrimination.

Activism spread and was encouraged within the army through the circulation of newspapers and journals of which *De Belgische Standaard* (Belgian Standard), *Stem uit Belgie* (Voice from Belgium, also named *L'Echo de Belgique*), *Ons Vaderland* (Our Fatherland) and *Vlaamsche Stem* (Flemish Voice) were perhaps most significant but alongside them were many other locally-focused productions, such as *De Poperingsche Keikop* (Poperinge Pebblehead) and *Onze Temschenaars* (Our Temse Boys). Bringing news from the government in exile, from refugees, from occupied Belgium and the wider world, they passed free of censorship, despite containing an element of dissatisfaction, criticism and calls for independence. The larger circulations numbered in their thousands. For a considerable time the existence of this material was ignored by the authorities, but in 1916 and 1917 there were crackdowns that resulted in bans and many titles ceasing to print.

Symbols, controversy and conflict: Heldenhuldezerkjes
In accordance with the use of French in the army, Belgian troops were buried and notified as *Mort pour la Patrie*. On 15 August 1916 an organisation known as the *Vlaamsgezinde Comité voor Heldenhulde op van Studenten, Oud-studenten, Hoogstudenten en Oud-Hoogstudenten* (The Flemish-minded committee for a tribute to heroes of students and former students) was formed under the leadership of Father Cyriel Verschaeve. Its manifesto included the notion of replacing wooden crosses by erecting a *zerk* (headstone) at the grave of each former student, incorporating the credo AVV-VVK (*Alle voor Vlaanderen – Vlaanderen voor Kristus* – All (or Everything) for Flanders – Flanders for Christ). This was an existing concept that had stemmed from the

Heldenhuldezerkes in the churchyard at Watou.

Ruines de Caeskerke-lez-Dixmude 1914-18 La Place, l'Eglise et les tranchées
The ruins at Caeskerke-near-Dixmude 1914-18 The Place, the Church and the trenches.

Kaaskerke, a village on the road to Diksmuide, became a key support and logistics area behind the Belgian front lines and consequently paid a heavy price for it.

A typical heldenhuldezerkje headstone that has been allowed to remain in the military cemetery. This is to Sapper Alfons Deleu, killed near Reninge on 10 January 1916.

Catholic Student Movement and was an expression of moral rather than explicitly political thought and intent. The original design of the stone was produced by a soldier, Joe English: topped by a celtic cross, the stones were made locally in concrete and bore the AVV-VVK text and an image of the blauwvoet bird.

The erection of the stones was controversial but generally tolerated by the authorities, although there were instances of vandalism and destruction both in wartime and afterwards. In particular, on 27 May 1925, by order of the Minister of Defence, Albert Hellebaut, a very large number of such stones at Adinkerke were destroyed, crushed to use as material for road laying.

The zerkjes that exist today can be viewed as falling into four categories: those erected at soldiers' graves during or shortly after the war; those erected (before 1925) and after 1925, for example the zerkjes in the churchyard at Watou; those that were placed on post-war graves of veterans; and finally some stones that resemble the originals, such as that on the grave of Father Verschaeve in his churchyard at Alveringem.

The Yser Tower

The site on which now stand the two Yser Towers lay in an area of the Belgian front line between the Kaaskerke road and the Veurne railway. Facing Diksmuide and the high buildings of the Minoterie mill on the German-occupied right bank, the Belgian fire trench ran along the river dyke and connected with the defences of the railway embankment. A small soap factory had been here in 1914 and was subsumed into the front line works. This ravaged land was acquired in 1924, originally intended for a Flemish cemetery that would be created by bringing in the remains of those men who had been buried below the *Heldenhuldezerkje* headstones. When in May 1925 hundreds of these headstones were crushed to build a road leading to the military cemetery at Adinkerke (such stones at Oeren having already been destroyed), it provoked much indignation and inspired the alternative idea of erecting a tower memorial. It would be designed as a symbol of remembrance of the Belgian Great War dead and the promotion of peace but also as a strong symbol for Flemish independence: a potent and provocative mixture of themes.

Construction of the original tower, fifty-two metres high, began in 1928 and was opened during the eleventh annual *Ijzerbedevaart* pilgrimage on 24 August 1930, by which time additional adjacent land had been purchased to receive the huge numbers of visitors. The tower was inscribed with the motto *No more war* at its inauguration. More than a hundred *Heldenhuldezerkjes* were moved from their original locations and transferred to the tower between 1932 and 1937, by which year nine men considered and symbolised as Flemish heroes and martyrs had been reburied within the crypt: Firmin Deprez, Joe English, Frans Kusters, Frans Van Der Linden, Renaat De Rudder, Bert Willems, Juul De Winde and the Van Raemdonck brothers. The Walloon corporal Amé Fiévez was buried with the brothers.

Diksmuide suffered some damage during the fighting of May 1940 and the tower sustained a serious hit half-way up one side from a British aerial bomb on 30 May. Flemish nationalist militancy before and during the war, encouraged by Nazi Germany, and in some cases local collaboration with the enemy, caused many Belgian patriots and those on the political left to regard the tower site increasingly with suspicion and as a symbol of wrong. The *Ijzerbedevaart* pilgrimages continued during the occupation. In 1942 the organising committee added large AVV-VVK lettering to the sides of the tower, intending to make it resemble more a giant *heldenhuldezerkje* and, as such, further strengthened its Flemish rather than Belgian symbolism.

On 16 June 1945 and, to finalise the destruction, on the night of 15–16 March 1946, the tower was blown up with dynamite: on the second occasion the tower collapsed, leaving the ruins that now remain. The argument was put forward to leave the ruin as its own memorial, not unlike that in the early twenties regarding devasted Ypres. Eventually, of course, that city was reconstructed largely in its original design. A white cross bearing the AVV-VVK text was constructed above the ruin in 1948: it also incorporated the text of Cyriel Verschaeve's poem: *Here their bodies lie like seeds in the sand; hope for the harvest, O Flanders land.* During 1948 the *Paxpoort* (peace gate) was constructed in front of the ruined tower, using its debris as core material.

Debate about the treatment of the site eventually turned into an agreement to build a new, higher but similar in style, tower some a hundred metres behind the original. At eight-four metres in height and with twenty-two floors, it now dominates the area and can be seen for many miles around. Even so, it would have been dwarfed by the 250 metres high tower that was one of the proposed alternatives: it would have made the new Yser Tower one of the tallest buildings in the world at the time.

One of the original architects, Robert Van Averbeke, produced the design and construction of the reinforced concrete and brick structure that was begun in 1951. The first stone was laid symbolically during the 1952 pilgrimage. A crypt was opened on Armistice Day in 1958 but the tower was not completed and inaugurated until 22 August 1965. It has long since included a museum within, which was renamed the *Museum aan de Ijzer* after its renovation in 2014. The original tower area was renovated in 1997.

The site is certainly one that visitors to the Yser battlefields should take the time to see. Parking nearby is free of charge (although it can be very busy on public holidays, at weekends and whenever any remembrance events are taking place). There is a modest entrance fee. The site has been modelled to encourage the visitors to see the old tower ruin before proceeding past various memorials and symbols to the new. They include reference to the *heldenhuldezerkjes* that were destroyed at Oeren and Adinkerke. A very fast lift takes visitors to the top of the tower, from which there are excellent views across Diksmuide and much of the area. The museum floors below tell the story of the Belgians at war and contain many interesting artefacts. The downward journey can be done on foot or by taking the lift, although it does not stop on all floors. The tapered nature of the tower does make the interior feel a little claustrophobic, particularly on the higher floors, but increasingly less so as the floor plan widens at each level. At the ground floor are refreshment and toilet facilities, meeting rooms and a small bookshop; it is located at: Ijzerdijk 49, 8600 Diksmuide. Website www.aandeijzer.be (with an English language option).

Ijzerbedevaart

An annual *Bedevaart naar de graven van den Yzer* (Pilgrimage to the Graves of the Yser) soon began to the locations of the graves of certain Flemish heroes: in 1920 Joe English in Steenkerke, in 1921 the Van Raemdonck brothers near Steenstraat, and in 1922 Renaat De Rudder in Westvleteren. In 1923 it was held at Oeren and from 1924 at what became the tower site. Contemporary records show large numbers in attendance.

The 1930s saw a growth of nationalism across Europe and during that turbulent decade the Yser Tower site became the focus for much propaganda and agitation for Flemish national independence, particularly under the influence of *Vlaamsebeweging* and *IJzerbedevaartcomité* organiser Clemens De Landtsheer. The latter was also a successful film producer, including news documentaries of the annual pilgrimages. One of the films of the pilgrimages shows more than 120,000 people streaming through Diksmuide, across the river to the site and the partially completed tower in 1929: priests conducted services in the town square, flags flew, bands played. De Landstheer's film, *With our boys on the Yser*, (1928 and re-edited partly in colour in 1933), an embittered indictment of war and of the perceived ill-treatment of the Flemings, proved to be a popular and successful fundraiser. In 1935 the secretariat of the Yser pilgrimage committee was transferred from Temse to Diksmuide; and in the following year the pacifist slogan, *No more War!*, was introduced.

The 13th Ijzerbedevaart in 1932 focused on the memory of Joe English.

Ruines de Dixmude, 1914-18 L'Yser
The ruins at Dixmude, The Yser.

Years of shellfire had razed Diksmuide and the Minoterie by the end of the war.

More scenes of devastation: this time the area of Diksmuide's Railway Station.

Ruines de Dixmude
1914-18
Le quartier de la gare et le jardin botanique.

The Ijzerbedavaart pilgrimages drew huge crowds in the inter-war years.

The *Ijzerbedevaart* continued as an annual event throughout the German occupation and after the liberation of this area in 1944, with the Yser Tower site as its focus. The pilgrimage increasingly attracted political extremists of the far right from across Europe. By the mid-1990s the organising committee was trying to incorporate a message of a free, peaceful and tolerant Flanders; but the events of 1995 and 1996 were marked by violence and an air of menace as the extreme nationalists protested against the adoption of this position. The reputation and attraction of the event suffered severely. By 2012 the attending crowd had dwindled to as few as a thousand people. That year was also notable as being the first on which a Walloon delegation officially attended. A decision was taken to move the event to 11 November each year. Much effort has been made since then to ensure that the focus is on remembrance and peace, to the extent that in 2018 the message was that the *Ijzerbedevaart* should no longer be considered a pilgrimage but a day of peace, *Vredesdag*. Since 2003 the more radical right wing of Flemish nationalism has promoted an alternative event, the *Ijzerwake*, in late August, held near the Van Raemdonck memorial.

Father Cyriel Verschaeve
Born in Aardoie in 1874, Verschaeve was ordained as a Roman Catholic priest in 1897. In the early 1890s he studied at the seminary at Roeselare and came into contact with the Flemish student movement and the Blauwvoet. After continuing his studies at Jena, during which his exposure to Flemish nationalism increasingly merged with an appreciation of the Germanic values and way of life, he returned to his native Belgium in 1911 and became the parish priest at Alveringem. In addition to his parochial work, he was a busy author and playwright

During the Great War Verschaeve was a leading figure in the development of the *Frontbeweging*. In 1917 he wrote two open letters that demanded improved rights for Flemish servicemen; the second, in August, included criticism of King Albert for failing to respond to the first. Verschaeve had already led efforts to commemorate the Flemings with a memorial; the first steps to what eventually became the IJzertoren Memorial, at which he laid the first stone in 1928.

During the 1930s Verschaeve was a vociferous supporter of the National Socialists in Germany, and once Belgium was under occupation, was appointed to the Nazi-sponsored Flemish Culture Council. He also became involved with recruitment to the German forces of the Flemish Legion and Waffen-SS. Verschaeve fled to Austria in 1945 and, condemned to death in absentia by a Belgian court, lived there until 1949, when he died at Solbad Hall (Tirol), where he was also buried. In 1973 a nationalist organisation, known as the *Vlaamse Militanten Orde*, exhumed him and returned him to Alveringem, where he rests today below a heldenhuldzerkje headstone. Despite having various streets and, rather unusually, a rose named after him, Verschaeve's story remains one of great controversy.

Joe English
Born Joseph Alphonse Marie English in Bruges in 1882, Joe was the son of an Irish father and Belgian mother. He became a naturalised Belgian and undertook military service in 1901–02. A talented and prize-winning professional artist and draughtsman who worked and studied in Antwerp, he came into contact with the radical student movement centred at the university at Leuven (Louvain). This led him to design a cover for the *De Vlaamsche Vlagge* journal and to work for other student publications. It placed him in a network that was central to the development of the Flemish nationalist movement during the Great War.

Married in 1910, English was mobilised from the reserve in 1914 and saw service during the siege and retreat from Antwerp. Meanwhile, his wife and children found themselves under German occupation at Bruges

The Belgian L'Océan II Field Hospital at Vinkem.

and never saw him again. He continued his artistic work while serving at Veurne and in the front line with the 7th Line Regiment. Amongst his achievements were the original design of the heldenhuldezerkje headstones and the illustration of the *Mass and Prayer Book of the Flemish Soldier*. He died of appendicitis at a field hospital, L'Océan II, near Vinkem, on 31 August 1918 and was buried in the Belgian military cemetery at Steenkerke. English's reputation caused him to be lionised as a Flemish hero and his grave was used as the focal point of the first *Ijzerbedevaart* pilgrimage in 1920. Twelve years later his remains were reinterred in the crypt of the Yser Tower. A monument that was erected at Steenkerke and unveiled in 1920 is now located on the tower site. English's widow Elisa Goedemé died in Bruges in 1926 and, as much for her work in founding the Yser Tower as her relationship with Joe, is also recognised by an AVV-VVK headstone.

Chapter Six

The Tours

The area is well covered by marked cycling and walking routes: this one is named in honour of the heroes of the inundations.

The battlefield area is generally easy to tour and the following suggestions are designed for travelling by car or cycle. Please note that you should make a preliminary trip if you plan to follow the routes in anything much larger than a car; in most cases a medium-sized minibus is practicable.

The road network is excellent, although in the more remote spots the roads tend to be single carriageway, often narrow and with ditches on either side. This can cause issues when stopping for any length of time at some of the sites and you must always be aware of other road users in the more rustic parts agricultural vehicles in particular.

Driving is on the right. Care is required and drivers should be alert at junctions and to oncoming traffic and be willing to find sensible passing places. Signposting is generally good, although not all of the smaller lanes have name signs. Flanders has a maddening habit of closing the entire width of a road when work is needed, sometimes leading to lengthy diversions: they are usually signposted in orange with the text *wegomlegging*; it has been known for these diversions signs just to stop, so always come armed with a map of a reasonable scale. It might also be added that road works are often frequent and can continue for lengthy periods of time – by that is meant, literally, years.

The tours include a small amount of walking, mainly for closer access to specific sites. Many people in the area speak English well. My advice is, unless you have some command of Dutch, that it is preferable to use English rather than try French.

Dienst der Verwoeste Gewesten or Office des Régions dévastées

The 'Service for the Destroyed Region' was established in 1919 by the Belgian Ministry of the Interior to oversee and advise on reclamation and reconstruction. By law, reconstruction was a matter for the national government rather than regional or local councils or a matter of an individual enterprise or initiative. The service ensured the application of the law, audited the financial resources allocated and acted as an intermediary between the administrative authorities and the various private and official groups involved in reconstruction work. Initially the scheme had the promise of being rather visionary, projecting large scale housing projects, including garden cities, and experimental speedy building through pre-fabrication. Political instability, competing visions and financial constraints soon refocused the work of the service onto the more mundane technical and administrative issues of planning and building regulations.

Belgian military cemeteries

There are eight cemeteries within the geographic scope of this book (Adinkerke, Hoogstade, Keiem, Oeren, De Panne, Ramskapelle, Steenkerke and Westvleteren), with the large Houthulst Cemetery not far away. Although they have their origins as war time burial plots, all were expanded by the post-1918 concentration of remains from scattered cemeteries and graves, including many that had been buried in parish churchyards. This was carried out under the supervision of the graves registration service of the army. The cemeteries are now under the management of the Belgian War Graves Service, a section of the War Heritage Institute, with day to day maintenance carried out by private firms funded by the Belgian Ministry of Defence.

To be considered a war death, the serviceman must have died within the period 4 August 1914 to 30 September 1919 inclusive. Standard headstones designed to promote national unity and equality in death by the Brussels architect Fernand Simons were erected. The headstones bear no reference to the soldier's religion. They have a solid but ornate classical Greco-Roman design in concrete, bearing a bronze plaque

Belgian troops at Drie-Grachten on 15 November 1917.

The enamel marker identifying the grave of a Belgian military veteran.

with the soldier's name, rank, unit, date and place of birth and date on which he died. Above the plaque is a small, tri-coloured enamelled roundel in the colours of the Belgian flag. Some of them have a Flemish lion or a cross above the central stripe, but the application of this is not consistent. They were included at the family's choice but when being replaced in recent times these additions have been omitted.

The plaque also incorporates information about the casualty's medals, the selection of which varies by individual. Typically placed on the left is a facsimile of the *Kruis van Ridder in de Orde van Leopold II* (an award for bravery or meritorious service) and on the right is the *Oorlogskruis* (Croix de Guerre). Between them are text symbols: V is for the *Overwinningsteken* (Victory Medal), Y for the *Yser medal or Yser Cross* and a circled '14' for the *Herinneringsmedaille van de oorlog 1914–1918* (the commemorative Great War medal).

A standard Belgian headstone.   The headstone of an unknown Belgian soldier has text in both of the country's two main official languages.

Amongst the standard stones visitors will see numbers of the AVV-VVK heldenhuldezerkjes. This, it appears, was at the family's choice if the man had originally been buried below such a stone.

From 1921 the government permitted the exhumation and removal of remains for burial nearer to home. This appears to have been implemented in order to overcome the practice of illegal exhumations. The government paid only for railway transport to the closest point to the chosen place of burial, while other costs would need to be paid by the family: inevitably this created a division that was based on the ability to pay. About half of the Belgian casualties were eventually transferred under this system.

Churchyards and other public cemeteries
Visitors to these cemeteries may spot some graves marked with a round enamel badge with the text *Hier rust een oud-strijder – Voorbijganger gedenk hem*: Here lies a veteran – passer-by remember him. These badges are often on the graves of men who died at any time after the Great War. At the entrance to some cemeteries is a rectangular green plate on which is written: *Belgische Oorlogsgraven – Sépultures du Guerre Belge*. This symbolises that at least one man's remains were

repatriated from his war time place of burial into the cemetery, which usually means he was local to this community and that his family had requested that he be returned. His grave will be marked with tricolour roundel plate with the text '14–18 Pro Patria'. Note that there are often restricted – but not particularly onerous, i.e. daylight hours would be usual – opening hours in town/communal cemeteries.

Local village or other war memorials can often be found in these places as well.

French, British and German military cemeteries

The existence, design and architectural treatment of the cemeteries follows the practice applied elsewhere. Many French remains were repatriated in the post-war period; those that remained in Belgium were concentrated into fewer plots. The British did not repatriate, but some who had been buried in the area or who were found in later years were moved considerable distances for burials in 'open' cemeteries. German burials have been subjected to waves of concentration and in the area covered by this book there is now only one, at Vladslo.

Indicators of the presence in a cemetery of military graves of the three allied nations.

Demarcation stones

Nineteen of these stones now stand on Belgian soil but only a few fall within the area of the tours described in this book. They are part of what began as an ambitious 1920s project to mark every kilometre of the 650 kilometres of the Western Front. The Touring Club de France and its equivalent in Belgium were instrumental in the original funding, but it is also known that the Ypres League erected a small number in the Ypres Salient area and that Portuguese funds added some others in the Lys valley. The stones have a common format in that they have text equivalent to: 'Here the invader was brought to a standstill' and mark the position of the deepest German penetration in France and Belgium; but odd placement and subsequent relocations have left some in inaccurate locations. Each is topped by a facsimile of the steel helmet worn by the troops of the nation that held the enemy at that spot, but even some of those choices can be suspect. Nonetheless they are of historical interest and are pointed out within these tours.

Albertina Memorials
These diamond shaped memorials mark sites of particular interest around the battlefields of West Flanders and many are featured in these tours. They were erected in three phases in the mid-1980s. The main face is of white natural stone, mounted on a base of concrete. Each bears an inscription to name the spot. Above it is an aluminium plate illustrating the coat of arms of the province and at the bottom is the monogram of King Albert I (hence their name).

Tour A

Nieuwpoort, Lombardsijde and Ramskapelle

Starting point: park near the large *King Albert I Monument*, situated on the N34 in Nieuwpoort on the north side of the river estuary.

The tall, circular memorial is unmissable but has very little parking immediately adjacent to it except for holders of blue disabled parking badges. It is suggested that tourists use the large free car park that is on the town side of the estuary, and then walk the few hundred metres across the river to the site. The car park is accessed from the large traffic roundabout on the N34.

Walk at first to the **Nieuwpoort British Memorial to the Missing**. This is situated adjacent to the King Albert I Monument site, across a paved area before the N318 road to Lombardsijde. The British memorial commemorates 566 officers and men who were killed in operations on the Belgian coast during the First World War and who have no known

King Albert's Monument, seen from the British Memorial at Nieuwpoort.

Tour A Route Map.

The British Memorial to the Missing at Nieuwpoort.

grave. The earliest deaths commemorated are those of seventeen men of the Royal Navy and Royal Marine Light Infantry of the Royal Naval Division that was committed to Antwerp and who lost their lives in the area of Lier on 5–9 October 1914.

Among them was Norwich man Colour Sergeant 5896 Edward Albert Churchard of Chatham Battalion RMLI. He had completed twenty-one years of service in 1911 and re-enrolled into the reserve. He left a widow and two children. Described at the time as the eldest naval officer afloat, Lieutenant Commander Henry Thomas Gartside-Tipping, at the age of 67, was commanding the armed yacht *Sanda* when it was sunk by German gunfire from a battery near Blankenberg on 25 September 1915. Unusually, his widow was also killed during the war. Mary Stuart Gartside-Tipping, after working for nearly a year at the Munitions Workers' Canteen at Woolwich, moved in January 1917 to join the Women's Emergency Canteens at Compiègne, operated by the London Committee of the French Red Cross. Mary was accidentally shot by a reportedly deranged French soldier on 4 March 1917. The French military authorities did everything possible to express their sympathy. The Croix de Guerre, which had been withheld from women since November 1916, was awarded to her and she was buried with full military honours. Mrs. Gartside-Tipping lies in Vauxbuin French National Cemetery.

Six days before *Sanda* went down, Arthur Pearson RN, a member of the crew of the monitor HMS *Marshal Ney* was drowned. A Rotherham lad, he had enrolled in the Royal Navy as a boy of seventeen in 1909 and had been with the ship since 14 August. *Marshal Ney* was rather unusual in the Royal Navy in being named after a foreign individual, along with the similar *Marshal Soult*. She suffered from numerous technical difficulties during her period off the Belgian coast, with poor engines and instability due to her high centre of gravity as a result of the weight of a turret with two 15-inch guns. Official records give no clues as to how exactly Pearson met his death.

Most of the others listed lost their lives in the Nieuwpoort sector in in the summer of 1917. Of these, 240 died on 10 July, the day of the German offensive Operation Strandfest at Lombardsijde, within sight of the memorial.

Three men of 604 (Mechanical Transport) Company of the Army Service Corps, attached to the heavy artillery of XV Corps, died on 10 July when long-range German shell fire hit the railhead at St. Idesbald. Six of the company's lorries were destroyed and several others damaged, whilst eight men were killed and twenty severely wounded. Privates Arthur Bradford, Howard Carter and John Gillespie have no known graves and are commemorated on the memorial. Their comrades lie in Plot I of Coxyde Military Cemetery.

It is unsurprising to find that the 1st Northamptonshire Regiment and 2nd King's Royal Rifle Corps, which suffered such losses on 10 July 1917, are represented in great number. To them can be added the fifty-three names of men of the 11th Border Regiment. By the end of that terrible day, the battalion reported the loss of eight officers and 350 men killed, wounded or missing. A further forty-eight named are of the 15th Highland Light Infantry, killed when their battalion was ordered to counter-attack in the early hours of 15 July and regain ground lost five days previously. German machine gun fire accounted for some 200 casualties, all within a matter of minutes.

Constructed of Euville limestone, with the names on affixed bronze panels, the memorial was designed by William Bryce Binnie MC, an Imperial War Graves Commission architect and a former officer of the Royal Highlanders (Black Watch), who had twice been wounded in action. The lions standing at each point of the triangular platform were designed by Charles Sergeant Jagger MC, a celebrated British sculptor and a Worcestershire Regiment veteran of the Western Front. The memorial was officially unveiled in July 1928.

Optional detour to Lombardsijde
A short walk of some 150 metres from the British Memorial along the N318 Lombardsijde road brings you to a **demarcation stone**. Beware: this can be a very busy road and there is no footpath, although it is possible to walk with care along the grass verge. One of a chain of such monuments erected along the Western Front, the stones aimed to represent the positions where, as the inscription says, 'Here the invader was brought to standstill'. The original text was obliterated during German occupation in the Second World War but restored in 1991. This stone is the second most northerly of the chain; there is one in Nieuwpoort-Bad but which is in a very odd location as it is on land that German troops never reached until 1940. It marks the final extent of the German advance in 1914. Directly across the road was the site of the Grand Redan of the Palingbrug defences; but of them there is now no trace.

The village of Lombardsijde lies ahead down the straight N318 road. Should you wish to visit, beware that a walk along this road is hazardous and a car or cycle is recommended. 740 metres beyond the demarcation stone is a small supermarket, with Weststraat going off to the right. The German front line ran through this junction and it was from this position that the Strandfest attack was launched on 10 July 1917. Further on, the large Onze-Lieve-Vrouw-Bezoekingkerk church has eleven CWGC graves from the Second World War in its grounds, and there are a number of *heldenhuldezerk* grave headstones bearing the 'AVV-VVK' motto. Those aside, there are no traces of the village's warlike past.

The duneland between Lombardsijde and the estuary has been greatly altered by the construction of a yacht harbour that occupies much of the area of the trenches that were held by the allies. Much of the rest is inaccessible, being covered by the Ijzermonding Nature Reservation and a military facility. Should you wish to see the area in which the British battalions were destroyed in *Strandfest*, the nearest approach can be made by turning back from the church in the direction of Nieuwpoort, but very soon taking the right turn across the tram line into *Schoolstraat*. On reaching the main N34 turn left, and after 290m turn right onto *Halvemaanstraat*. Keep right when the road splits off to the left and follow it to the end, where there is a free car park next to the yacht harbour. Near the car park, a small lane (signposted as a dead end) can be followed: the estuary is on the left and the lighthouse can be seen ahead. The lane is on the line of the support trench of the

Lombardsijde bridgehead, and the front line was only a matter of yards away on the right, more or less parallel to the estuary. Note how narrow the bridgehead was: it is easy and sobering to reflect on how little protection the troops holding this sector had and how slim their chances were of withdrawing across plank bridges to Nieuwpoort if they came under attack.

The Goose Foot

Now return to the thirty metres diameter, circular **King Albert I Monument**, which was erected in 1938 on the initiative of the veterans' associations and was renovated in 1973–74 and again for the centenary of the Great War. In the centre of the circle is an impressive equestrian sculpture of the King. He is surrounded by twenty brick columns supporting a ring walkway a hundred metres in circumference. Recently constructed below the monument is Westfront, a relatively new museum and educational facility that tells the story of the Goose Foot and the inundations of 1914.

The walkway above the monument may be accessed by lift from within Westfront. The view of the Goose Foot, of canal and waterway locks and sluices and across the flat Yser land, is well worth seeing. There are orientation tables arranged around the walkway. Of added interest is the graffiti of names, symbols and text scratched by visitors into the stone and metalwork of the walkway: some of it dates to the Second World War.

A national tribute to the King and heroes of the Yser is held at the monument every first Sunday in August.

The next part of this tour – around the Goose Foot at the head of the estuary – can be done by car, although, as parking is generally difficult in the area and not possible at all close to the various points of interest, it is suggested if possible that you leave the car where it is and make the route on foot. There is some limited parking along the northern bank of the Yser, about halfway round the complex.

Six waterways come together. Although there has been much recent development, particularly of an inner harbour along the Yser, the pattern at the

The Memorial to the French 81st Territorial Division.

Goose Foot is essentially as it was constructed in 1876–78 and when it played such a crucial role in 1914. The N380, which runs alongside the King Albert I Monument, crosses the six waterways with footpaths on both sides, although visitors need to remain vigilant for their safety in traffic. Note that it is now a one-way road for vehicles; it is only possible to drive it in a north to south direction.

After crossing the Gravensluis, the **memorial to the French Territorial 81st Division** is in trees on the right, opposite the road going out to Leffinge. After crossing the Ieperbrug across the Yser, on the right is the **Yser Memorial** by Pieter Braecke, unveiled in 1930. It represents a woman who, turned away from the enemy, holds the Belgian crown in her hands. The four figures around the memorial represent resistance and are represented by a blind, a hurt, a sick and a resilient soldier. In front of it stands the memorial plaque *to* **lieutenant du génie Belge Léopold Calberg**, an officer of the Sapeurs-Pontonniers killed here on 16 October 1917.

Walking across the Veurne-Ambacht, immediately on the right you will see the **Albertina Memorial Onderwaterzetting (Inundation) 29 October 1914**. A few metres further on, but across the other side of the road, is the **bronze plaque memorial** marking the site of shelter used by the Sapeurs-Pontonniers. It was responsible for the maintenance of the locks and hydraulic equipment on the Belgian front and which, once established, set up its base and workshops in Veurne.

Lieutenant of Engineers Léopold Calberg is remembered by a memorial at the Goose Foot.

This Albertina marker reminds us of the inundation and is appropriately situated at the Goose Foot.

One platoon worked continuously thereafter at the locks in Nieuwpoort, with others at Wulpen and Veurne. The Company suffered the loss of twenty-seven men dead, fifty wounded and 143 gassed during the war. This memorial, along with several others described below, was unveiled on 1 September 1957.

Nieuwpoort Town
It is possible to continue this tour on foot if you have the time and energy, but you may alternatively chose to return to your vehicle and move it. A good choice is to drive across the Goose Foot, turning left onto Pieter Deswartelaan after crossing the last waterway, the Veurnevaart. There is free parking along the northern bank. A trench, Tranchée de le Sardinerie (Sardine Works Trench, although in 1917 the British called it Novel Trench), ran along this road; on the opposite bank were more trenches and much barbed wire.

Walk along Pieter Deswartelaan and turn onto the straight Langestraat. This was one of the main thoroughfares of the Nieuwpoort of 1914 but was completely devastated by war's end. It is now rather nondescript; but several memorials hint at its history. On the facade of Number 5, on the right, is another **Sapeurs-Pontonniers memorial**, marking the location of a shelter for twenty men. Take the first left turn into Willem de Roollaan and immediately on the left is a similar **memorial** to the company's cooks.

Continue for 150 metres and, as the road bends, see a ruined tower on the right: **Saint Laurentius Tower** is a remnant of a site of much history. The original church, dating back to 1281, was destroyed and then in 1383 converted into a fortified moated castle. From 1400, Philip the Bold, Duke of Burgundy, further fortified it and in the sixteenth century it became a military garrison during the Spanish occupation. During the Great War the tower was used for observation towards Lombardsijde and Ramskapelle, until in 1916 German artillery reduced it to the ruin that exists today. The tower is

The Devil's Tower in Nieuwpoort, one of the town's few constructions that pre-dates the Great War.

popularly called in local dialect the Duvetorre, as it said that Jeanne Panne, the witch of Nieuwpoort, kept her assignations with the devil here. It was also known as the Tour des Templiers during the war. The main **memorial to the Sapeurs-Pontonniers** is on the face of the tower. A communication trench (Boyau des Templiers, for the British, Novel Lane) ran along the road in front.

Continue another 150 metres along Willem de Roollaan and then turn right into Schoolstraat (which is signposted as a dead end). In less than a hundred metres, on your right, you come to the Bommenvrij. This building is in disrepair and not well signposted – a pity, as it is the oldest surviving structure in the town and the last remnant here of Dutch military architecture, constructed in 1818–22. The Bommenvrij originated as a powder magazine and munitions store and was one of the very few buildings in the town to remain standing after the German shelling of the Great War. Its site backs on to that of Saint Laurentius tower.

Return to the end of Schoolstraat, turn right onto Willem de Roollaan and then first right onto Arsenaalstraat. Continue to its crossroads junction with Langestraat.

It is possible at this point to take a short detour: turning left onto Langestraat, in two blocks (about 150 metres) see on the right the former town hall, now a court. A bronze memorial plaque to the *Belgian Artillery Survey Service* is on its facade. Inside the building, an information panel recalls how the rich archive of Nieuwpoort was saved in 1914. Return to the Arsenaalstraat crossroads and turn left: it has now become Ieperstraat. When nearing its end, on the right is another memorial to the **Sapeurs-Pontonniers**, this time marking the billet used by two of its captains, Thys and Umé.

At the end of Ieperstraat, turn right and follow the road around to Pieter Deswartelaan along the Veurne Canal. Across the road on the left there are two memorials: a bronze plaque naming members of the Belgian resistance (*Belgische Militaire Weerstandsorganisatie*) killed or tortured to death by the Nazis in the Second World War, and a modern brick pillar memorial to Belgian friendship with French North African troops that fought in this area in the Great War. The former includes a sombre reminder of the role played by the Goose Foot in the later war: 'Thanks to the initiative of Roose Léopold, conductor of bridges and roads, resistance fighter, the locks of the inner harbour were demined on 7 Sept 1944 and the destroyed bridge repaired during the night of 9 Sept, which allowed the passage of the allied troops as from 10 Sept 1944'. Note, high on the front of house number 3 on the right, a plaque in memory of **Hendrik Geeraert**. At the first floor windowsill of house 9 (a café) is a bust of Geeraert, which presumably was originally installed in the niche at number 3. Return to your vehicle.

Before leaving Nieuwpoort's centre, note that the unusual **town war memorial** stands at the corner of Willem de Roollaan and Onze-Lieve-Vrouwestraat, in front of the church. It can be reached by car by following the instructions for the Saint Laurentuis Tower (above) and carrying on for 580 metres along Willem de Roollaan. The memorial, by Karel Loppens, was inaugurated in 1925 in memory of all local victims of the Great War. In 1949 the names of the military and civilian victims of the Second World War were added to the bluestone edges; on 11 November 1969 an urn was buried at the front of it with the ashes of fellow townspeople who had died in Neuengamme Concentration Camp, in Germany.

The Bruges Road Sector
The next phase of the tour starts from Nieuwpoort and visits the area of Ramskapelle, a hotly disputed sector during the Battle of the Yser.

Leaving the Goose Foot by the N367 Brugsesteenweg, signposted for Diksmuide and Sint-Joris (which, if leaving from Nieuwpoort, first means circumnavigating the King Albert I Monument, as the road over the Goose Foot is one-way only).

Just 215 metres after the turn, where the road crosses a waterway by the **Wittebrug Bridge** (named as Willebrug on the maps of the Great War), on the right hand side stands a **demarcation stone**. Designated as stone number 13, it is topped by a Belgian helmet and stands at the site of a Belgian front line trench: across the road the trench followed the line of the drainage channel; on this side it turned sharply to head towards Nieuwpoort. There is good access to this stone, with parking on the left hand side of the road. Its location is a stark reminder of how close German forces were to the Goose Foot before the rising inundation drove them back in 1914. The waterway is technically a syphon between the Nieuwendamme Creek and the Veurne-Ambacht.

Continue along the N367 for 500 metres, to the entrance of **Nieuwpoort Communal Cemetery**. This is now much expanded from the smaller cemetery that was on this site before the Great War. The Belgian front line trench ran alongside the road in what is now the front of the cemetery. It was used for sixty-seven British burials in the period June to early August 1917, mainly from the 2nd Manchester Regiment and 16th Lancashire Fusiliers. The British burials increased in the Second World War, with twenty-five buried here in May 1940. It also contains two Canadian victims of the Raid on Dieppe in 1942. Note that the cemetery is not permanently open and visitors are advised to consult its opening hours before travelling.

Some 250 metres further along the road, on the right-hand side, is **Ramskapelle Road Military Cemetery**. Most of Plot I was made in

Ramskapelle Road British Military Cemetery.

July and August 1917, but the cemetery was considerably enlarged after the Armistice when graves were brought in from the battlefields and smaller burial grounds: some of these were in an area that had been in German occupation, at Middelkerke and Gistel. Others were from around Nieuwpoort and Oostduinkerke.

There are now 841 Commonwealth casualties of the First World War buried or commemorated in the cemetery. Most relate to the period in 1917 when the British XV Corps held the front line in this area. 312 of them are unidentified, but special memorials commemorate two casualties known or believed to be buried among them. Also within this number are twenty-six special memorials to casualties originally buried in the Nieuwpoort area whose graves were destroyed by shell fire. There are an additional two unidentified foreign national burials. The cemetery was designed by Sir Edwin Lutyens.

The earliest casualty commemorated here is Lieutenant Edward Selby Wise RN of HMS *Severn*, whose work in the fighting for Groote Bamberg Farm on 20 October 1914 is described earlier in this book. The second was also a naval officer, twenty years old Flight Lieutenant David Keith-Johnston of the Royal Naval Air Service. He had taken off from Dunkirk in a Farman aeroplane on 10 August 1915 on a mission to drop bombs on a Zeppelin at Ostend. He was not heard of again. Tragically, a month later his younger brother, Macfie, perished in a flying accident at

RNAS Eastchurch. David was brought into Ramscapelle Road (VI.B.27) from the German military cemetery at Middelkerke.

Continue on the N367 for 690 metres and turn left onto the narrow St-Jorisplein. At time of writing there is no street sign to identify it, but there is a direction sign to the Hotel Gemeente Huis: this was the old town hall of the village of Sint-Joris (Saint-Georges in French). Very soon the street opens out on to a grassed square in front of the parish church. Turn right to approach the church and park. Situated next to the church is the grave of **Lieutenant General Baron Émile Dossin de Saint-Georges**.

Born in Liège in 1854, Dossin married Émilie Delfosse in 1893: their daughter Renée became the wife of future Belgian prime minister Paul van Zeeland. He had a distinguished military career, having at times commanded the Belgian War School and been Director General of the Cabinet of the Minister of War. Dossin was appointed to command the 2nd Division and led it through the fighting of 1914, including the defence of Antwerp and the Battle of the Yser. It was under his responsibility that the inundations were carried out. From 1915 until the war's end he acted as military envoy of the Belgian Government in exile in Le Havre. In the latter role he did much work in connection with the many Belgian troops who had been interned in the Netherlands. He added the Saint-Georges (after the Yser village of that name) in 1932 and was made Baron by King Albert I two years later. Amongst many foreign orders and decorations, Dossin was made a Commander of the Order of the British Empire. A large monument was erected at Ixelles in Brussels two years after his death in 1936; an avenue there was also named in his honour. The former Hof van Habsburg barracks in Mechelen was renamed as Kazerne Dossin; sadly, this later became a place of evil memory, for it was used by the German occupiers as a transit camp for shipments of people to Auschwitz.

Leaving your vehicle for a few minutes, walk back out to the main road by the short street that leads from the grave and turn left. Within a few metres, on the corner of General Baron Dossinstraat, is a **memorial to the Belgian 3rd Karabiniers**. It commemorates the regiment's defence of this area in late March and April 1918.

Return to your vehicle, go back onto the N367 *Brugsesteenweg* and turn left. In 830 metres, arrive at the small village **Communal Cemetery of Old Sint-Joris**. In an adjacent plot are the graves of nine Commonwealth airmen of the Second World War, but it features in this tour because of its importance to the Great War: the cemetery was very close behind the Belgian front line, from the period when the line stabilised at the end of the Battle of the Yser until 1918. A long communication trench

The Memorial to the 3rd Karabiniers at Sint-Joris.

ran along the northern side of the N367; at this junction two others branched off it to north and south. The front line, with posts beyond it, lay in the field that is between the cemetery and the motorway embankment and bridge that can be seen to the east. The motorway cuts across what had been No Man's Land. The land to the south was inundated during the battle.

Continue on the main road under the motorway; in 700 metres, as the road begins to rise to cross a bridge over the Yser, slow to find somewhere safe to park. Unfortunately this is very difficult. In particular, the right-hand slip road before the bridge leads onto a narrow riverside lane with no easy turning for a considerable distance, although it is usually possible to pull off the road onto the grass verge (beware that it is not disguising a ditch). The situation is slightly better by going over the river to the other side: there is roadside space on the right, and some limited space near the restaurant building on the left. The bridge is the *Uniebrug* (Union Bridge). There are two memorials of significance here, on either side of the N367 on the Nieuwpoort side of the river. Near the start of the slip-road is the **memorial to the Belgian 14th Line Regiment** and on the opposite side is the **memorial to the 7th Line Regiment**.

Into the inundated area
Return to your vehicle. If not already there, go down the slip road next to the 14th Line Memorial and take the river bank road heading to the south. For the first few hundred metres a German front line trench occupied this road, facing the Belgians across fields to the right, but for the most part their front line was across on the other side of the Yser. The entire area on the right was under water, held back by the embankment of this dyke road.

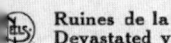
Ruines de la Vallée de l'Yser.   Schoorbakke-lez-Pervyse   1914-18   Première ligne boche sur l'Yser
Devastated valley of the Yser.   Schoorbakke-near-Pervyse   The 1st German line on the Yser

A postcard of late 1918 illustrating the former German line at Schoorbakke.

After 3.5 kilometres you will come to the first right hand turn, into Violettestraat. A German strongpoint was constructed around this junction, protecting the river crossing at Schoorbakke, a short distance away to the south, and encompassing the buildings of the Deystere Brewery. There is no trace of it today. In front, the sheet of water stretched for several kilometres, with only trees and abandoned buildings visible. Continue along Violettestraat – beware that it is a very narrow lane and the situation is not easy when being confronted by agricultural machines – to cross the inundated area towards the Belgian front. When what appears to be a t-junction is reached, turn left (although the right turn does indicate a dead end): this is still called Violettestraat. Eventually a second t-junction is reached. Turn right onto Hemmestraat but, just before doing so, look across to the fields to your left front. Some 300 metres from the road was Groote Hemme Farm, one of the places where buildings sticking up from the water continued to be held by a German garrison as an outpost. It was reached only by wooden plank walkways stretching all the way from the Yser or even by boat: consider how exposed the troops must have felt in making the journey. The farm was never rebuilt and there is now no remaining trace of it.

Some 800 metres after turning onto Hemmestraat, and just before the bridge over the (unsignposted) Beverdijkvaart Channel, the road crosses the Belgian outpost position facing Groote Hemme Farm. This was about 1600 metres in front of the main Belgian line of resistance along the Nieuwpoort-Diksmuide railway embankment. It too was only reached by plank walkway, although maps suggest that it was only very slightly higher ground and may not have been completely flooded. Continuing the drive, several of the farms on the right hand side of the road were also used as a basis for outposts in the inundated zone.

Ramskapelle village
Eventually the outskirts of Ramskapelle are reached. There is easy roadside parking. The village name sign has been erected alongside the line of the old railway, laid in 1868 and now a straight walking and cycle path that cuts across the road. This was the vital main line of Belgian resistance and is now known as the *Frontzate*. Steps had been taken to plug the twenty-two culverts and other means by which water might escape from the east, and the embanked railway (which is shallow in places, including at Ramskapelle) became an effective barrier to the flood waters going any further westwards. Next to the railway is an **Albertina Memorial** marked **'Slag aan de Ijzer [Battle of the Yser] 18–31 Oktober 1914'**.

Walk down the path on the left (south) side of the road, reaching in a few metres one of the key sites of the battle: **Ramskapelle Station**,

Ruins of Ramskapelle Station.

opened in 1886. The original buildings of the station were gradually destroyed during the war, but some of what remained has been preserved on this site. A concrete observation post, looking out towards the Yser, was constructed in the ruins and still stands. Some concrete slabs, now used as a garden path, bear the following dates: 3, 11 and 22 November 1917. A **memorial to the 14th Line Regiment** is also on the site. On returning to Hemmestraat it is worth a short walk of a few metres towards Ramskapelle, for on the left, outside number 39, is **another memorial to the 14th Line Regiment**.

Return to your vehicle and continue on Hemmestraat into Ramskapelle village. Several lines of trenches and belts of barbed wire protected the centre which, despite being well within range of German artillery, was used for billeting troops, as a headquarters, for medical posts and for supply. On reaching the central square, although it is intended to turn right and then immediately left into Molenstraat, stop for a moment to see the **joint memorial to the 6th Line Regiment and the 16th French Battalion of chasseurs à pied**. They were the two units that successfully counter-attacked and regained the village on 30–31 October 1914 after it had been briefly occupied by the advancing German forces. It stands in front of Sint-Laurentiuskerk church.

Note also the **plaque to the 6th Line Regiment** on the wall of the presbytery the large building on the right just as the square is entered. The **village war memorial**, topped by a statue of Christ, is also on the square.

Some 250 metres after turning into Molenstraat, just as the end of the built-up area is reached and the road begins to bend to the right, becoming Zesde Liniestraat [6th Line Regiment Street], stop. On the corner is a small construction of a windmill: it is a **memorial of the 16th French Battalion of chasseurs à pied**. In front of it stands a demarcation stone, number 3, marking the furthest point of German penetration. The site is close to that of the site of the village windmill, which stood on the opposite side of Molenstraat. It was reached by the counter attack of the 1st Company of the *chasseurs à pied* under Captain Wauthier in the late hours of 30 October, soon after which a bayonet charge by the French and Belgian units carried the advance as far as the main square. By 7.30am next morning Ramskapelle had been cleared of enemy and the allies had reached the railway. It would never again fall into enemy hands during the war.

Return to the main square and turn left onto N356 Ramskapellestraat. In 485 metres, on the right hand side, stop at the **Belgian Military Cemetery**. A post-war site for the concentration of graves and remains found in the area (mainly at Nieuwpoort, Westende, Lombardsijde,

It is perhaps not much of a memorial, but this model windmill at Ramskapelle stands at a vital spot on the 1914 battlefield, with the demarcation stone alongside as a reminder that German troops once reached the spot.

St-Joris, Mannekensvere and Ramskapelle) it now contains 632 headstones, of which about 400 are unnamed.

Just to the left (north) of the site, the road crosses the Frontzate railway line. An **Albertina Memorial**, inscribed similarly to the one at Ramskapelle Station, stands in memory of the battle. Two plank walkways set off for the outposts from the railway from just behind the cemetery site.

It is possible to stop the tour at this point and return to Nieuwpoort by continuing on the N356 but there remains a rather more remote site to visit should you have the time and energy. The approach route has been made a little complicated by the construction of the motorway that runs across the area. Continue on the N356, and just past the old railway crossing turn left onto Zesde Liniestraat. Follow it until you arrive at a traffic roundabout (having almost reached the windmill site again): take the first right, the N355, signposted for Nieuwpoort and the E40 motorway. Cross the motorway just a few hundred metres further on.

Take the second left turn into Koolhofstraat (NB! Be aware that it is only a few metres after the first left, which gives access to the motorway). Drive 1000 metres, including crossing the Kohlhofvaart Channel, which ultimately feeds the Verne-Ambacht at the Goose Foot, until reaching, on the left, a ruined chimney stack with an **Albertina Memorial** in front of it. The memorial is marked **'Observatiepost Steenbakkerij'**: the chimney and other buildings further away once formed part of a large pre-war Dutch-owned brick works. Internally reinforced with concrete, the stacks provided valuable height for observing the ground across to the east. In former times, the 'Café de la Grande Brique' stood close to the last farm just passed en route and houses built for the workers were also located in the area. A complex of concrete bunkers and shelters that once occupied this site is unfortunately no longer in existence. There used to be a number of ponds, part of the brick works, now filled in: there are stories of troops supplementing their rations with frogs they could catch here. And now return to Nieuwpoort.

Tour B

Diksmuide

The starting point of this tour is the village of Esen, which lies three kilometres to the east of Diksmuide. It could, alternatively, be visited at the end of the tour or stand as a special trip in its own right, not least as the Dolle Brouwers Brewery, a place of dreadful significance to the village's Great War story, still operates today and offers an interesting and flavoursome tour of the facilities.

Park in Esenplein Square, near Sint-Pieterskerk Church on Roeselarestraat. It is a pleasant and typical Flanders village, with shops, cafés and other facilities, which can date its existence as far back as 961 but is now a wholly post-1918 reconstruction that hides its grim past.

Esen
On Esenplain, adjacent to the hedge separating it from the church grounds, is a pillar **war memorial**, surmounted by a figure of Christ. Amongst the nineteen military dead of the Great War are brothers Médard and Cyrille Pollet, killed while serving with the 3rd and 15th Line respectively. Médard was amongst the early casualties of the war, dying at Hoegaarden in the defence of the River Gete line on 18 August 1914. His younger brother, Cyrille, did not enlist until July 1915 and lost his life during the German attack of

The village memorial at Esen remembers its civilian and military victims.

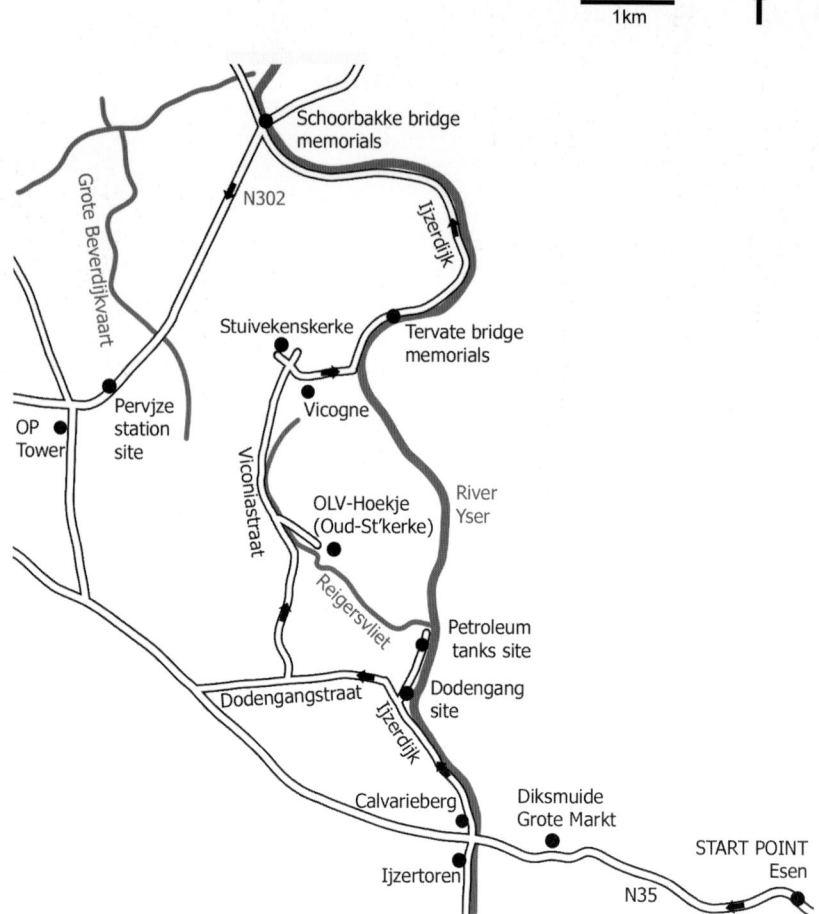

Tour B Route Map.

6 March 1918. Impressive stained glass windows inside the church are also a memorial to Esen's military and civilian dead. Some of the glass commemorates the brutal reprisal execution of a number of civilians by the Germans and there is (2020) an interesting, possibly permanent, exhibition in one of the transepts.

Walk away from the church for some hundred metres along Roeselarestraat (going in the direction in which the Christ figure is facing), reaching the entrance to the **Dolle Brouwers Brewery** on the right. The original building housing the brewery is believed to date from 1835 and has a long history since it was started by a local

The village centre of Esen, seen from just outside the brewery that witnessed such cruelty against civilians in 1914.

doctor, Louis Nevejan. It became the Costenoble Brewery in around 1882 and remained in the family for three generations. It was no longer operational when it was purchased and restored as a brewery in 1980. The large house to the left of the entrance has been rebuilt as it was in 1914. It is somewhat surprising that there appears to be no memorial to the terrible, tragic events of 1914, nor is it mentioned (at the time of writing) in the brewery's publicity material.

Return to Esenplein and drive to Diksmuide by following the N35 Esenweg. In 860 metres you will reach a roundabout, the junction with the N301 for Ieper. Once the fighting stabilised on the Yser on the far side of Diksmuide in 1914, the Germans began to develop their second line of defence in this area. The junction was the location of the rearmost reserve trenches. Continue towards the town: the perimeter of the allied defensive line (held here by Senegalese troops on your left and Belgians on your right) when the serious German push on Diksmuide began on 7 October 1914 was approximately where the town boundary sign is passed (a petrol station lies a hundred metres ahead of it, on the left hand side of the road). Modern development has obliterated any remaining signs of the conflict here.

Follow the signs for centrum (town centre) and park on King Albertstraat, just before the Grote Markt, on the square itself or one of the other nearby streets. There is plenty of on-street parking, mostly requiring modest payment. The square itself is often used for markets or fairs and so is not always accessible by vehicle.

Diksmuide was of central importance in the fighting of 1914 and the scene of much activity over the following years. It was completely razed by artillery fire. The centre has been sympathetically reconstructed and resembles its former state; but much of the battlefield to the east, and some of the key sites of the period of entrenched warfare, have been consumed by recent commercial and housing development. The centre is well worth exploring on foot.

Diksmuide town centre

Many of the sites of interest are in or clustered around the **Grote Markt**. It includes a 1930 statue monument to **General Jacques** or, to give him his full name and title, General Jules Marie Alphonse Jacques, 1st Baron Jacques of Diksmuide; remarkably it is just one of seven memorials to him that are scattered across Belgium. Already aged 56 when the war began and a veteran of the Congo, he commanded the 12th Line Regiment; he took over command of the Diksmuide bridgehead when the fighting was at its worst; and was given the 3rd Division in 1917. Jacques initially had his headquarters in the town hall but moved it to Ijzerlaan when the centre became untenable. He was slightly wounded during the battle. The monument is one of

The Jacques Memorial in Diksmuide.

the many legally protected sites of the Great War but is not without controversy. It suffered damage in 1950, presumed to have been at the hands of Flemish nationalists, who assigned to Jacques all the negative connotations of being a French speaking commander; but it also brings with it embarrassment at his part in colonial Belgium's treatment of the people of the Congo. There have been debates about removing the monument altogether or at least adding an information board to put his full story into context.

The splendid town hall, originally from 1428, was somewhat remodelled to become a neo-gothic town hall around 1880. It was completely destroyed during the war and rebuilt in 1923 in regional Flemish Renaissance style. It is free to enter and has a museum of local history. Visitors will note that artillery shell casings form part of the front steps. The large and impressive church of Sint-Niklaas, also devastated and rebuilt, lies just behind it. Many visitors who are familiar with Ypres will see similarities in the layout and fates of these buildings with their counterparts there.

To reach the **Ijzertoren** (Yser Tower), leave the Grote Markt by Kiekenstraat (on the left of the town hall as you look at it), continue as it bends into Vismarkt and then immediately crosses the Handzame Canal. Turn left onto Kleine Dijk and follow it, eventually re-crossing the canal, into Vaartstraat. Turn right onto the N35, signposted for Nieuwpoort. Drive across the bridge over the Yser, then turn left onto Ijzerdijk. Continue until you reach the car park on the right.

At the far end of the car park is the embankment of the railway line coming down from Nieuwpoort that formed the Belgian main line of resistance and for much of its length the barrier against the flood waters of the Yser inundations. Walk back along the road in the direction from which you have just come: the Belgian front line trench ran along this road and through the buildings of a soap works that were approximately on the site of the museum's ticket office.

The Yser Towers
Before proceeding to view the towers, look across the river to the Portus Dixmuda boat mooring and the very pleasant houses that line the southern bank. They stand on the site of the former flour mill (**Minoterie**) that featured so strongly in the fighting and the German defences of this stretch of the river. There is now no trace of the mill save the name of the lane, Bloemmolenkaai (flour mill quay), along which the houses stand. This is because in 1922 the Ministry of Defence's classification of the ground as a *site de guerre* prevented its reconstruction. A new mill site was developed in the north of Diksmuide, at the confluence of the Yser and the Handzame Canal.

Visit first the **ruin of the original tower** which stands nearest to the road. On land purchased in 1924, it was constructed in 1928–30 and was opened during the eleventh annual Ijzerbedevaart Pilgrimage. It had originally been intended to make the site into a cemetery by bringing in those men who had been buried below the heldenhuldezerkje Flemish heroes' headstones. When in May 1925 hundreds of the headstones were crushed to build a road around the cemetery at Adinkerke near the coast (such stones at Oeren having already been destroyed), it provoked much indignation and thus inspired the alternative idea of creating the great tower. It was designed to act both as a symbol of remembrance of the Great War dead and a rejection of war; but also to represent a desire for Flemish independence: inevitably deeply controversial in terms of Belgium's history and future.

The grave marker to the Van Raemdonck brothers in the destroyed crypt of the original tower.

The original tower stood fifty-two metres high. More than a hundred heldenhuldezerkjes were moved from their original locations and transferred to the crypt between 1932 and 1937, by which year nine men who were considered and symbolised as Flemish heroes and martyrs had been reburied within the crypt: Firmin Deprez, Frans Kusters, Joe English, Frans Van Der Linden, Bert Willems, Renaat De Rudder, Juul De Winde and the Van Raemdonck brothers. The Walloon corporal Amé Fiévez was buried with the brothers. Diksmuide suffered damage during the fighting of 1940 and the tower sustained a serious hit from a British aerial bomb on 30 May.

The complex, symbolic and almost mystic quality of the site was enhanced during the Second World War. It was by the time of the liberation in 1944 all too raw a memory that some Flemish nationalists had collaborated with the Nazi occupiers or fought with the German forces. The potent combination of nationalist Flemish militancy and collaboration with the enemy caused many Belgian patriots, as well as those on the political left, to see the tower as a focus of much that was detestable. In 1945 and 1946 the tower was twice damaged by bombs; on the second occasion the tower collapsed, leaving ruins and the edifice that now remains. It was surmounted by the white cross bearing the "AVV-VVK" text in 1948: it also bears words from Cyriel Verschaeve's poem, translated as *Here their bodies lie like seeds in the sand, hope for the harvest of Flanders land.*

The mighty and rather mystical Yser Tower.

A wonderful view of the Yser valley and Diksmuide from the top of the new tower.

Two years later the *Paxpoort* (Peace Gate) was constructed in front of the ruin, using debris from the original tower. Beginning in 1951, the new and much larger 'eighty-four metres' high, twenty-two-floor tower began to be constructed: it was eventually inaugurated in 1965. It had long since included a museum within, which was renamed after renovation in 2014 the **Museum aan de Ijzer**. The museum itself is of course of considerable interest, but the views across the Yser land are simply unmissable. Visitors are advised to check opening times and current prices in advance. The site certainly makes for a thought-provoking and unusual experience.

The Yser Front
Return to the crossroads near the Yser bridge and go straight on into Ijzerdijk, which follows the river on the right hand side of the road. The two opposing front line trenches continued to hug each bank of the river, although the continuous German front only ran to a point opposite the Diksmuide town exit sign. Flood water from that point northwards caused it to be made up of isolated forward outposts, with trenches in places further from the river.

Just 230 metres from the junction, on the left stands a white-painted *crucifix* atop the **Calverieberg Memorial Chapel**. It is not at an easy place to stop (you may even wish to walk to it from the Yser Tower car park), so beware of traffic. Built in 1924 and inaugurated in 1928, it pre-dates the original tower and became an early place of pilgrimage. The text on the façade translates as 'Sanctify the cross, our only hope'. The Belgian front line here was known as Casbah Trench.

The Calvarieberg Memorial, situated just outside Diksmuide, not long after its inauguration.

Going north from this spot, a number of small Belgian outposts were established on the opposite bank of the river.

Continue 1400 metres along the Ijzerdijk. The Belgian front line trench was continuous along your route. Pull into the car park of the Dodengang (Trench of Death).

The Trench of Death
This notable site is the only preserved trench system on the Yser Front. Access to the site is usually unmanned and requires use of a payment card: cash is not taken. The entrance fee for adults is (2021) currently €5. Most importantly, visitors are advised to check opening times and prices by checking on the internet or at local tourist offices.

Just as at Vimy Ridge and other locations, some visitors may find that the replacement of original trench materials with concrete detracts from its appeal and interest but it obviously makes maintenance less of an issue. When walking through the preserved defences, the complexity and nature of the trench system becomes clear, as does its exposed position. The cul-de-sac head of the trench is overlooked from enemy positions on both sides of the river, with German machine guns near the ruins of the petroleum tanks further along the Ijzerdijk being able to fire in enfilade along the Belgian trenches.

The site has been recently completely renovated to coincide with the centenary of the war and there are good displays in the reception building as well as a viewing area, whilst 'then' photographs along the trench system do much to provide atmosphere and understanding to this site.

The next stop is within walking distance of the Trench of Death site; beware of traffic on the narrow dyke road. It could be driven: on leaving the car park turn immediately right to continue along the Ijzerdijk. In about 400 metres you will reach an **Albertina Memorial**

The Dodengang Trench Complex is preserved in concrete.

The view along the Yser from the 'Dodengang' towards Diksmuide. German guns directed from the Minoterie dominated this area.

marked **'Petroleum tanks 1914–1918'**, with behind it in the field a half size representation of this important battlefield site. The dominating views that the Germans once had from this site are now, sadly, usually obscured by tree and hedge growth.

Turn to head back to the junction of the Dodengang and turn right onto Dodengangstraat. This takes us through an area of Belgian

The reminders of the notorious position at the 'Petroleum Tanks'.

communication trenches and reserve positions. In 1300 metres you will see the right turn onto Viconiastraat, signposted for Stuivekenskerke. First go on another hundred metres to the railway line and another **Albertina Memorial** marked **'Slag aan der Ijzer'**. This was the main Belgian defensive line that ran all the way between Diksmuide and Nieuwpoort: the *frontzate*. Now turn to go up Viconiastraat and follow it for 1500 metres, then turn sharp right onto the narrow Oud Stuivekens. At the time of writing it is marked by a brown tourist sign for *O. L. Vrouwhoekje* (Our Lady's Corner). Follow the very narrow dyke road until you reach a small car park on the left, by a cluster of houses, the reinforced stump of a church tower and one of the most important Belgian sites of memory.

Once-Lieve-Vrouwhoekje and Old Stuivekenskerke
Viconiastraat and the lane since the turn were both under water from the time of the inundations in 1914 and remained so thereafter. 'Old' Stuivekenskerke could only be reached from the Belgian front line by wooden plank walkways. Why is it called 'old'? Very unusually, a case had been made in 1867 to abandon the original and rather inaccessible village of Stuivekenskerke, which by then consisted only of the dilapidated sixteenth century Sint-Pieterskerk church and a few houses, and to build a new village some two and a half kilometres away. The old church was largely demolished in 1870, leaving only its 1572 west tower standing, and it is the base of this tower that remains today. The old village was briefly occupied by the Germans as they pushed the Belgians westwards in October 1914 but was abandoned by them as the inundations flooded the area. In poor weather this can be a most desolate place, isolated and windswept – a salutary reminder of what the garrison experienced – but on a fine day it is glorious and attracts many a cyclist and rambler, in addition to the battlefield tourist.

A small island, actually a twelfth century motte, was left when the water ceased to rise, leaving the church tower and other vestiges of the old village standing, which were re-occupied by the Belgian army from 3 November 1914 and which they set about fortifying. It was soon ringed by trenches, breastworks and barbed wire defences and acted as an excellent – if totally exposed – artillery observation post and a forward defensive position held by infantry and machine guns. The work became known as Grote Wacht Zuid (Great Watch South or, better, Main Observation Post South, or Grande Garde Sud). The nearby Reigersvliet Farm, which bears the same name as a drainage channel (Heron Brook), the small waterway that visitors will see near the church tower, was 900 metres distant and similarly fortified as the Grote Wacht

The stump of the old church tower and the Belgian Army Memorial Chapel at Oud-Stuivekenskerke.

Nord. Eastwards across the water, but still on the west side of the Yser, German forces held forward posts built around Den Toren Farm and Vandewoude Farm. The tower of the church and the other buildings nearby were gradually pounded to dust by German artillery. By 1916, the steeple had gone and the tower was only about half of its original height; by 1917 little more than a stump remained, surrounded by rubble.

Next to the remains of the base of the church tower is the beautiful, small Onze-Lieve-Vrouw der Zege (Our Lady of Victory) chapel, in memory of the Belgian army. It is surrounded by forty-one memorials to the units that held the Ijzer sector, with two larger memorials to the 5th Regiment Lansiers and the 1st and 2nd Karabiniers Wielrijders (cyclists). Visitors should not miss the especially fine stained glass windows depicting King Albert, Queen Elisabeth and Saints Maurice and Barbara (patron saints of the Belgian infantry and artillery respectively). Inaugurated in 1925, the brick-built chapel was instigated by Edouard Lekeux, known as Brother Martial, as he was a Franciscan friar. Born at Arlon in 1884, Lekeux had been in the army reserve until he entered the Franciscans in 1911. He became an artillery officer early in the war and was stationed at the observation post between December 1915 and May 1916. He was ordained to the priesthood after the war and in 1922 published a best-

The army chapel is surrounded by memorials to its regiments. This obelisk is to the 5th Lansiers, which was engaged on the Reigersvliet in 1918.

selling war memoir, *Mes cloîtres dans la tempête, Le Patelin de Notre-Dame* and *Passeurs d'hôtes*. Two of the windows in the chapel depict Lekeux. In one, he kneels by an unexploded shell, praying to the Virgin: it refers to an occasion on which a German shell entered his post but proved to be a dud.

The church tower was reinforced with concrete in 1916 and now has a good viewing platform on top. It is certainly worth the short but somewhat claustrophobic ascent if possible, for there are excellent views across the once flooded battlefield. An orientation table helps the visitor identify the key points, many of which are mentioned in this book. The Yser Tower provides the most obvious landmark, about three kilometres away; the Trench of Death is a thousand metres distant. A demarcation stone, the remains of a concrete bunker and some picnic tables complete the site.

Stained glass windows in memory of the royal couple.

New Stuivekenskerke and the Vicogne outpost
Return along the lane and turn right at the junction with Viconiastraat. A few metres after the junction, on the right, is an **Albertina Memorial** marking **Reigersvliet, Grote Wacht 1914–1918**. The position of the memorial is approximately between the two Grote Wacht outposts: the more northerly was 450 metres further on along the lane.

Continue for 1900 metres through an area that was, with the exception of the slightly raised lane itself, entirely flooded. Some areas on your right still are, but the pools that you see relate to the post-1945 extraction of clay from the land here. Some lanes turn off this twisting road to the left: make sure that you keep to the right, along Viconiastraat. You will now reach **'new' Stuivekenskerke** that began to develop in the 1870s around the new version of Sint-Pieterskerk.

The church and village was devastated during the war and everything you see today has been rebuilt or is a more recent construction. Pressed back during the Battle of the Yser, on the night of 22–23 October 1914 Belgian troops set fire to the church to prevent the Germans from using the tower later as an observation post. The tower of the new church was built to the same design as the original in the old village. There is a small shop and café near the church should you wish to visit.

The church site includes some interesting memorials and connections to the Great War. Bronze memorial plaques commemorate the 8th Line and the 1st, 2nd and 4th Karabiniers; the village memorial plaque is within the church; it also houses a statue of the Virgin that was removed from the church before its destruction in October 1914. A wall painting of the Virgin and Child has as its background a flooded and ruined landscape, flanked by a dead soldier and civilian. It is believed that the background is based on a watercolour by the German painter and Petty Officer Franz Eichhorst, which appeared in the regimental journal of the MarineKorps Flanders, *An Flanders Küste*, in 1916. Stained glass windows commemorate local soldiers Theophile De Keyne and Henri Omer Dewicke. The latter is also commemorated by a heldenhuldezerkje stone in the churchyard. Artilleryman Dewicke died of wounds at a hospital at Beveren-aan-de-Ijzer in 1918 and was originally buried at Isenberge but was later reinterred at Stuivekenskerke.

Passing the rebuilt church on your left, turn right onto Kasteelhoevestraat. In less than 200 metres you will reach the impressive gateway entrance to **Kasteelhoeve Viconia**, which has operated as an hotel for more than forty-five years. It occupies the site of the much rebuilt former chateau that originated as a monastery farm of a Norbertine abbey in France. Reconstruction commenced in 1924 and it now takes considerable imagination to reconstruct the wartime events

Tervate Bridge today.

here. The Germans captured the chateau and grounds on 21 October 1914 after their breakthrough at Tervate, but were ejected the next day by a counter attack mounted by the Belgian 1st Battalion of Karabiniers. On 24 October it fell again into German hands and was developed into one of their key outposts in the water. It remained a hotly contested spot, attracting much Belgian artillery fire and being the scene of several costly local offensive actions by both sides. Vicogne only returned permanently to Belgian hands during the final offensive in 1918.

Continue to follow Kasteelhoevestraat until the t-junction on the River Yser is reached, crossing the area that was inundated. Turn left onto Ijzerdijk. The German front line trench ran along this road, connected to the opposite bank by numerous plank bridges. Some 500 metres from the turn, you reach a house with an ornate 'Tervaete' title above its front door. Just beyond it is an **Albertina Memorial** marked **'Tervate Brug (bridge) October 21–23 1914'**. The modern lightweight bridge can be seen further downstream. This is not the easiest place to stop as the road is narrow; but drive on a few more metres and you should be able to park in front of houses that lead up to the bridge. Walk back to the memorial if you wish but then go to the new bridge. It is situated at the southernmost point of the wide looping turn that the river takes, across which there were three bridges in 1914: from north to south, Uniebrug, Schoorbakkebrug and Tervatebrug. As the Germans pushed to cross the river they became centres of desperate fighting. The

Schoorbakke Bridge over the Yser, taken before the war.

river bend effectively formed a salient in which the Belgian defenders came under fire from three sides, not unlike the larger salient that formed around Ypres. On 19 October 1914 Belgian engineers blew up Tervate Bridge: fragments of its foundations can be seen on both sides of the river. Three days later this position became untenable for the Belgians when they found themselves being outflanked from the north, when the Germans crossed the river near the Schoorbakkebrug. Withdrawal became inevitable. The hamlet of Tervate was completely destroyed, mainly by fire, during this period.

Continue along Ijzerdijk on foot, soon reaching on the left the obelisk **Memorial to the Belgian 2nd Battalion of the 1st Grenadiers**. This was one of two units (the other being the 1st Karabiniers) that attempted to counterattack from the

Memorial to the 1st Grenadiers, who defended the Tervate crossing.

Vicogne direction once the enemy had a footing on the west bank. It failed to reach the river by some 300 metres but slowed further German advance.

Return to your vehicle and continue along Ijzerdijk round the river bend: the eventual German front line followed it the whole way. In 4.1 kilometres from the Tervate Bridge reach **Schoorbakke Bridge**. Parking here is only practically possible by turning left onto the N302 Schorestraat, signposted for Veurne and Pervijze, and then pulling into the car park just before the t'Vissershuis restaurant on the right.

There are two **memorials** within a short walking distance, both situated on the bridge: they are to the **Belgian 3rd and 23rd Line Regiment and 2nd and 22nd Line Regiment** respectively. The original bridge was blown up by the Belgians on 23 October 1914, but by then the Germans were across the river and constructing a temporary bridge some 800 metres to the south. The bridge that exists today is a post-1945 construction, for the one rebuilt after the Great War was once again blown up but this time by French engineers in the withdrawal towards Dunkirk in 1940. Once Schoorbakke hamlet was in German hands in 1914, the Belgians withdrew to the railway line defence and the inundation rose to the west, from which point it became part of the German defensive system. Trenches and barbed wire ringed the hamlet on its western side and several plank walkways went out to a number of small outposts a few hundred metres away across the water.

Return to the N302 and go in the direction of Pervijze. This takes us back away from the German front, across the inundated area and to the Belgian defences. The spire of the church at Stuivekenskerke can be seen across the fields on the left. In 3.1 kilometres from Schoorbakke Bridge – the width of the eventual No Man's Land, with only the lonely and exposed outposts in the area being crossed - the Frontzate is once again reached. It is easily missed: look out for a pedestrian crossing and some large farm buildings on the left, just after the former railway line. On the right hand side of the road, on the village side of the former railway line, is the **reconstructed railway station**. It has long since been used as a private house and there is now nothing to hint that this was once an important observation post.

Now once again a pleasant and relatively large village, **Pervijze** had the misfortune of the inevitable destruction that came with being part of the Belgian defences. It was riddled with trenches, dugouts, barbed wire and concrete constructions. Everything you see is post-war reconstruction and there is now relatively little trace of these works. With a history dating back to the reclamation of this land in the twelfth century, before the war it had been home to some 1,500 people and was a busy centre of rural life that featured no fewer than six breweries. The cemetery surrounding St. Niklaas Church (easy to spot, on the right in the village centre) incorporates the **village war memorial**. In the centre of the village turn left onto the N35 signposted for Diksmuide. Immediately after a pedestrian crossing, Brouwerijstraat goes off to the right and adjacent to it is some car parking space. On the street corner is an **Albertina Memorial 'Observatiepost Pervijze'**.

Walk down Brouwerijstraat and the village's most striking remnant of the Great War soon comes into view. The fourteen metres high **observation tower** is a combination of work from both wars. The Belgian engineers constructed the main base of the tower during the Great War on the site of the former St. Katharinakerk, which was demolished in 1895: it gave an excellent field of view across the floods towards the German line on the Yser. Inevitably it attracted much attention from their artillery. A second Belgian trench system ran behind it, linked by communication trenches to a third system about 1500 metres further west, on the Oude Vaart Channel. The brick construction atop the original work was built by the Germans in the Second World War and incorporates a machine gun position at the top.

The extraordinary observation tower at Pervijze includes sections from both world wars.

This concludes the tour. If returning to Diksmuide or perhaps going on to Ypres, follow the N35 south.

Tour C

The Belgian Rear of the Yser Front

This tour can be undertaken on its own or in conjunction with the 'Towns of the Belgian rear'.

Start at the **Belgian Military Cemetery, Steenkerke**. The easiest way to reach this starting point is to leave Veurne by Iepersesteenweg. Turn left onto the N390, Albert I Laan, and follow it across the Lovaart Canal. Turn right onto Vaartstraat, signposted for Steenkerke. Go under the E40/A18 motorway and turn left onto Steengracht West and continue into Steenkerke village. At Sint-Laurentiuskerk Church, turn left and then right to park.

Although it is primarily a Belgian cemetery, it contains a plot of thirty British and Dominion troops, almost all heavy artillerymen who lost their lives in October and November 1917. It is instructive to find what happened to them, for their deaths took place a considerable distance from the cemetery, although they appear to have been brought directly here for burial. Amongst them is 24 years old Lieutenant Charles William Comyns and six men of the crew of Number 5 Gun

British graves in Steenkerke Belgian Military Cemetery.

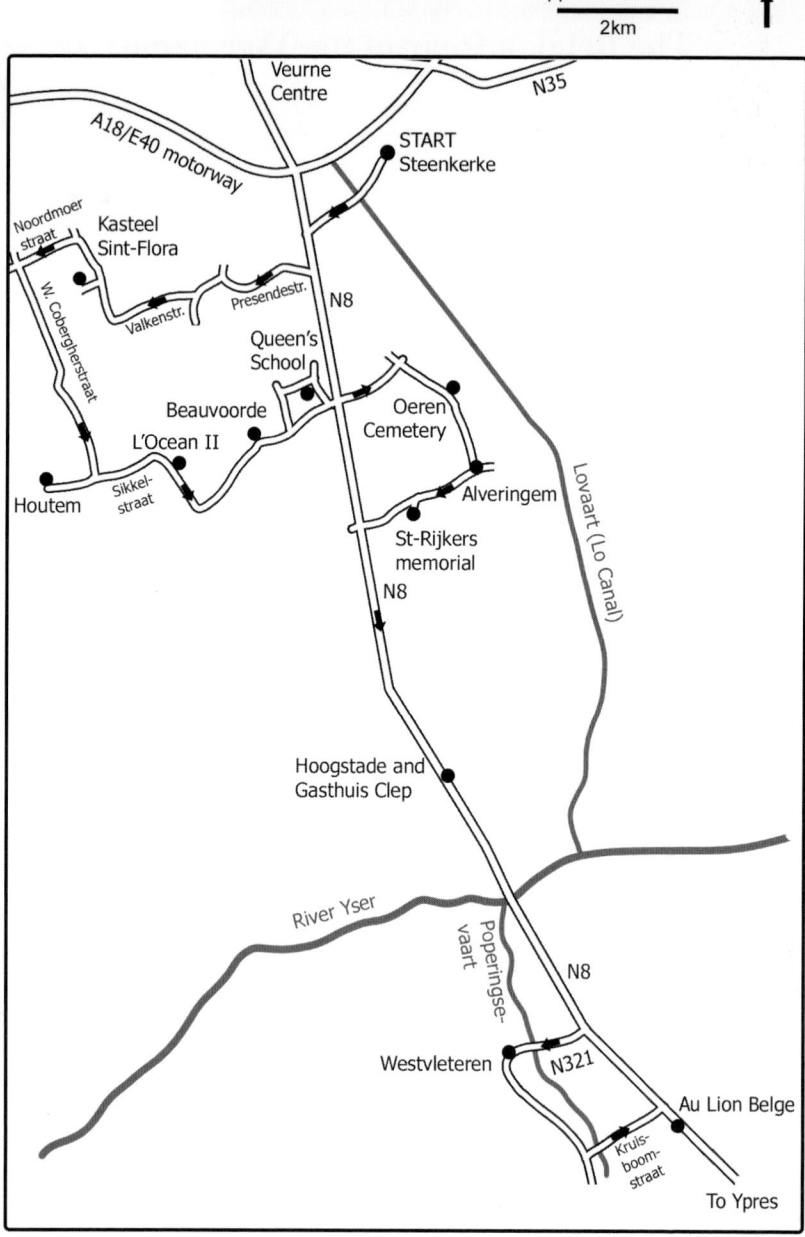

Tour C Route Map.

of the Royal Marine Howitzer Brigade, a huge 15-inch breech loading siege howitzer that had a maximum range of over ten kilometres, firing a 1,400 pound shell. He was decorated with the Belgian Chevalier of the Order of the Crown and the Croix de Guerre; but sadly these awards were only publicly announced on 20 December 1917, just over a month after he had died. Comyns' service record notes that *he has ability and is capable but is very impulsive*. Number 5 Gun had moved to Oostkerke on 15 October and had come into action there to support the Belgian raids on the Minoterie at Diksmuide.

Other graves in the cemetery include men of Number 2 and N Special Companies of the Royal Engineers who were killed by enemy artillery fire on 14–15 November 1917. These units were poison gas specialists that had been supporting the 2nd Belgian Division. 2 Special Company had recently fired a mortar gas bombardment on Diksmuide; N had been digging out its 960 Livens projectors after being in action firing oil and gas drums into the town on 5 November. Some twenty-seven of the projectors had been damaged by enemy fire and the men had been struggling to extract the equipment, which was embedded in ground below sea level, ever since. Their position was very close to the site of where the Yser Towers were later built, about thirteen kilometres from Steenkerke.

508 Belgian soldiers are buried in the main cemetery, of whom 492 are identified by name. The grave bearing the earliest date of death is that of married man 26 years old railway worker Englebert Moens, who was killed at Stuivekenskerke while serving with the 3rd Karabiniers on 22 October 1914. He was brought into the cemetery eleven years later. It is evident from the records that men who died in the first years of the war were brought into Steenkerke at later dates from original burial plots at Avekapelle, Eggewaartskapelle and Kaaskerke, all of which are nearby but closer to the front line of the time.

Many of the men buried at Steenkerke had succumbed to their wounds at the L'Océan II field hospital at Vinkem and appear to have been brought directly to this cemetery. An example is a Poperinge man, Joris (Georges) d'Hont, a 22 year old gunner who died of loss of blood due to wounds on the afternoon of 1 November 1917 and was buried at Steenkerke two days later. Joe English was at first also buried here, but his remains were later transferred to the crypt of the Yser Tower. Before this took place his grave here was the focus of the first *Ijzerbedevaart*.

There is a **village war memorial** to six local casualties inside the church and the graves of two British Second World War airmen in the churchyard.

Belgian royalty and army headquarters
Exit Steenkerke by going back along Steengracht West and follow it until reaching the busy N8, Iepersesteenweg. Turn left, signposted for Ieper. Immediately after passing a bus stop layby, turn right onto the narrow Presendestraat, signposted for Bulskamp.

Eventually reaching a junction, which is signposted left for Beauvoorde, the lane going right – which is actually still Presendestraat - goes into Bulskamp village. Take this direction. [There is an optional detour for this trip by carrying on into the village centre, which includes cafes, a few shops and a pharmacy. The village can trace its history back to the 1100s and is centred on the Sint-Bertinuskerk Church. There is a war memorial in the churchyard and illustrated local roll of honour inside.]

On the edge of Bulskamp – on the left if the detour is not taken, but on the right if coming from Bulskamp – is Beauvoordestraat, signposted for Houtem. Take this road and continue beyond the built-up area; the road bends left and then slightly right, and at time of writing there is a blue and white sign marking the Bergenvaart drainage channel, which the road follows. Turn right to cross a small bridge over the vaart onto a narrow lane: it is not signposted at all, but is called Valkenstraat. Continue along this lane for 1600 metres until what at first appears to be a t-junction is reached. It is in fact only a bend. Follow it to the right, at which point it changes name to become Debarkestraat. In a field on left, the now sail-less **Sint-Gustaafsmolen windmill** dates to around the time of the Battle of Waterloo and was still working at the outbreak of the Great War. This area is known as de Moeren and is below sea level. The mill was for pumping water to maintain the polder: the area was flooded by the Germans in the Second World War. Another mill, not far away and further up the road, is Sint-Karelsmolen.

Kasteel Flora, a temporary royal residence.

Some 550 metres after the bend and after passing Sint-Gustaafsmolen, Kasteelaan goes off to the left just after the white-painted house, numbered 2 (café "De Barke"). This lane is narrow and ends at private property. It not easy to park anywhere near the junction without some imagination but it is worth walking down for a photograph and appreciation of this location if possible: ask permission if necessary. On the right of the lane lies **Kasteel Sint-Flora**. This house is sometimes open to the public on open monumentendag. Dating to 1780, it was used by the Belgian royal family in 1917–1918 during the period when British forces took over the coastal sector. Consequently it was visited by many senior figures, including Joffre and Foch. Other buildings on the site includes a jenever distillery.

Continue along *Debarkestraat* and in 800 metres take the next left onto Noordmoerstraat. This really is the straight and narrow! Follow it for 1100 metres to the first crossroads and turn left onto W. Cobergherstraat. You will pass on the left hand side the unmarked far end of the straight drive from Kasteel Sint-Flora. Continue until the road bends to the right and becomes Moeresteenweg. Drive straight on for some 4.5 kilometres (which includes some sharp bends) to enter the village of **Houtem**, which in the past has been voted as one of the most beautiful villages in Flanders and enjoys an ancient history. In 2018 it had fewer than 700 residents but there were three times as many in the mid-1800s and still about 1400 when the Great War began. There is a café and a few shops. As the village centre is reached, the road bends sharp left: at which point, turn right into Sacramentstraat. In 200 metres turn left into Dorpstraat. Continue straight on for a hundred metres until it becomes Kerkhoek and park in front of Onze-Lieve-Vrouw-Hemelvaartkerk (The church of Our Lady of the Assumption), parts of which date back to as far as the 15th and 16th centuries.

The General Headquarters of the Belgian Army was moved from Veurne to Houtem on 23 January 1915 and remained there until 18 October 1918. King Albert was a frequent visitor, often coming to Houtem three or four times in a week, meeting his commanders and visiting dignitaries. On 5 January 1917 the Belgian Chief of the General Staff, Lieutenant-General Félix Maximilien Eugène Wielemans, 53, died here, said to be of pneumonia contracted while in the trenches. Before the war Wielemans had been Chief of the Military Cabinet to the Belgian War Office under Charles de Broqueville. The latter attended Wielemans' funeral (along with many dignitaries and senior military figures from the allied nations) and read a passage at his burial in the churchyard.

King Albert and Foch emerge from the Belgian headquarters at Houtem, 22 May 1918. (*Europeana*)

The grave of Wielemans overlooks his former headquarters at Houtem.

First enter the **churchyard** and follow the footpath, finding the tall obelisk memorial at Wielemans grave on the left. There are sixteen CWGC graves in the cemetery, all dating to WW2, as well as a *village memorial* to ten military victims of the Great War. A plaque inside the church portal records names twenty-seven military deaths amongst the villagers. The village war memorial is of interest in that only some of the names are given with dates of death, leaving others blank. The third named, Georges Meerschaert, was 19 years old when killed while serving with the 3rd Line Regiment at Sint-Katelijne-Waver on 1 October 1914. He is buried in the military plot in nearby Mechelen Communal Cemetery. The two preceding names are August Crombez and Georges Top. Both were named as missing in action and their bodies have never been found and identified. Top is said to have been killed on 19 August 1914. The fourth, Gustaaf Prinsier, is believed to have died of wounds at Lizerne (near Ypres) during the Second Battle in April 1915 but has no known grave. The final dateless name is of Jozef Verwarde, who died in hospital at Fécamp in France on 11 November 1915 and is buried there. Exiting at the far end of the churchyard, the path alongside takes the visitor to the entrance to the attractive **presbytery** buildings used by the headquarters. A **memorial plaque** gives details. It is easy to imagine this small and historic village crammed with the military staff, with despatch riders and transport in the busy streets, sentries guarding the headquarters and units billeted nearby. It is also easy to imagine it offering an ideal and obvious target for attention from the German artillery and bomber aircraft.

Retrace your steps to exit Houtem by Moeresteenweg and after leaving the village, where it takes a left-hand bend, turn right onto Sikkelstraat. Follow this for a kilometre until a crossroads is reached, at which take the right turn (it is signposted for Beauvoorde but you can only see this when coming from the opposite direction) into Joe Englishstraat. Continue to the first farm buildings that are near the road on the left, with a farm entrance turning to the left just past them, to find an **Albertina Memorial** marked '**Leger (Army) Hospital L'Océan 1917–1918'**. The location is often described as Vinkem but technically it is only within the boundary of that village, which lies some distance away. It is not easy to park near the memorial due to the narrowness of the lanes but a quick stop for a view and photograph should not be too much of a problem. The memorial recalls the site of the field hospital offshoot of the original L'Océan in De Panne. Amongst those treated here was the Flemish patriot and artist Joe English.

Continue along Joe Englishstraat to the crossroads and turn left onto Houtemstraat (it shortly becomes Gouden-Hoofdstraat), which soon brings you into Wulveringem.

Wulveringem

This pretty and historic village can be very busy with tourists and parking can be tricky, but all of the sights of Great War interest are within a short walking distance if you cannot park as suggested below.

Pass on the left hand side a former farmhouse-inn, In het Gouden Hoofd Afspanning, dating to 1594, soon after entering the built-up area. Take the second left turn onto Wulveringemstraat (a brown tourist road sign marks the turn): there are car parking spaces on the left. Ahead is the entrance to **Beauvoorde Castle**. A left turn in front of the entrance reveals some more spaces on the left hand side.

The castle has been called one of the best kept secrets in the Westhoek. Its origins are believed to date to the eleventh century; it was thoroughly renovated in the early 1600s. In 1875 the young but wealthy Arthur Merghelynck, froom Ypres, purchased it in a very delapidated condition and restored the buildings, created the garden and furnished the castle with a mixture of authentic and replica seventeenth century furniture and objects. In 1902 he donated the property – sometimes referred to as Merghelynck Castle - to the Belgian state and ultimately to the Royal Flemish Academy of Linguistics and Literature. The staff of the Belgian 6th Division used the property as its headquarters from December 1914 and arranged the transfer of the art to safe locations in France. Lieutenant General de Ceuninck, a former commander of the division and by then Minister of War, occupied the castle from March 1918. His timing was not good, for it came under heavy enemy fire in the April.

Facing the castle is the church of **Onze-Lieve-Vrouw-Hemelvaart** (Our Lady of the Ascension). It dates back in parts to the twelfth century, when it was constructed on raised ground: the area was often affected by the sea flooding unprotected, low-lying land. The church has been much developed and remodelled since, not least as it suffered a catastrophic roof and tower collapse in 1728. The interior contains much baroque furniture and a splendid art collection. The *village war memorial* is situated within the **churchyard**, near the entrance and there is also a plot of fifteen British Second World War graves.

Facing the church on Wulveringemstraat is a large house with a postbox on the wall of a small outbuilding. The house is **the former municipal school**, used in 1915 as a medical aid post. Its outbuilding, including a half-sunken basement, was used by the Belgian Army as a cell for prisoners held on bread and water rations for eight days and nights. Walk down the street to number 22 (on the right-hand side), where there is a small **memorial wall plaque** to the Belgian Army's **wireless school**.

Rejoining your vehicle, go to the end of Wulveringemstraat, turn left and then left again, rejoining Gouden-Hoofdstraat, signposted for Veurne and Ieper. After a kilometre or so, and approaching the left turn onto Boonakkerstraat (bean field road), you are close to the site of a wartime disaster. Just beyond the turn an ammunition dump at **Zwert Peerd Farm** (or zwart paard, the black horse, farm) blew up at 2.10pm on 8 November 1917. At least thirty men of 3rd Line Regiment lost their lives: some instantly, some succumbing at the L'Ocean II field hospital. Most of the victims lie in Steenkerke Cemetery. There is now no evidence of these events on the site, although Zwart Paard Farm still exists. The lane to it turns to the right off Wulveringemstraat but this tour heads left, onto Boonakkerstraat.

At the first right, after a house and farm buildings at the junction, turn into narrow Lobbestraat. In 400 metres you reach a crossroads; park where it is safe to do so. At the crossroads is an **Albertina Memorial** to the **Queen's School**. Its location, just twelve kilometres from the fighting front and thus exposed to the risk of long range gun fire and raid from the air, is a reminder of just how little national soil remained in Belgian hands. Its proximity, for example, to the ammunition dump at Zwert Peerd, underlines its vulnerability. The school was established here in September 1915 by Comtesse Maria van den Steen de Jehay (director of the relief organization 'Aide Civile Belge' and a lady-in-waiting to Queen Elisabeth) and Georgie Fyfe (a nurse of the Scottish Red Cross), with royal patronage and financial support.

The Comtesse had already played an important part in establishing a war time typhoid hospital in Poperinge and it was the bombardment of that town that drove the urgent need for the establishment of a school in a somewhat safer location (a smaller one was also established across the border at Caëstre). Practical help and teaching was provided by, amongst others, the Sisters Penitents of Poperinge. The school organised local and refugee children into two sections: 'Marie-José' for infants aged 3 to 8, and 'Charles-Théodore' for those aged 8 to 15. They were accommodated and taught in wooden huts until in 1917 the American Red Cross financed the construction of brick buildings. The Queen took a close interest in the school's affairs, ensured that the children received a religious education, that Flemish was spoken and that strict hygiene was observed. Many children received their first communion at the school. It was visited by many dignitaries, including French President Poincaré. The official announcement of the establishment of an international committee for the reconstruction of the Leuven (Louvain) University Library, destroyed by the Germans in 1914, was made at the school in August 1918. The school, which had educated many hundredsof children by the time of the armistice, continued to operate after the war during the years of reconstruction.

Continue to the end of Lobbestraat, turn right onto Molendreef and then left, once again joining Gouden-Hoofdstraat. Go straight on at traffic lights, crossing the N8 Veurne-Ieper road, and follow Oerenstraat, another narrow polder lane. After 1100 metres and immediately after crossing a small drainage canal, turn right: this is actually a continuation of Oerenstraat. Follow it into Oeren and the Belgian military cemetery is in front of the church of St. Apollonia.

Oeren

Laid out around the sixteenth century church, 642 soldiers lie in the smallest of the **Belgian National Military** cemeteries. In 1920 it held 629 Belgian, seventeen French and three German burials but the total changed as a consequence of repatriations and national cemetery concentrations. The first burials appear to have taken place in 1915; but there are now earlier dated graves of men whose remains were reinterred here after the war. They come from a wide area, notably the field hospitals at Vinkem, Fortem and Hoogstade, but also from Kaaskerke and Diksmuide. Many of the earliest victims were originally buried at the churchyard at Alveringem. The cemetery includes five AVV-VVK

Graves in the Belgian Military Cemetery at Oeren.

heldenhuldezerkjes, the last survivors from the 104 that began to be erected from August 1916. On the night of 9–10 February 1918 thirty-eight of them were vandalised: the letters AVV-VVK were covered with cement. They were restored next night with black paint, but this incident left a sour taste and its impact festered. The fourth Ijzerbedevaart pilgrimage was held at the cemetery in 1923 in honour of the restoration of the vandalised graves.

Amongst the graves with standard stones are brothers Jerome and Maurits De Caestecker, who came from Beerst. Their home and family were in German hands. Killed while serving with different units on 20 November 1917 and 28 September 1918 respectively, the brothers now lie in adjacent graves. Only two of their family of eleven siblings survived beyond the age of 25.

If the **church** is open (it often has art exhibitions in the summer) the interior is worth seeing, not least for a splendid example of twentieth century stained glass work. It is a 1965 memorial window, the work of the artist Ivo Baekelandts, dedicated to soldier Juliaan Heylen by his brother Alfons. Fatally wounded in the head while serving with the 5th Line Regiment, he died at the field hospital at Hoogstade in November 1917. Heylen was buried at Hoogstade and later repatriated to his home town of Mol, east of Antwerp. The window depicts a grieving soldier, kneeling by a comrade against the background of a church, while a fire burns on the horizon.

The fields east of Oeren were crammed with artillery positions, dumps, horse lines, tracks leading to the trenches and farms used for billeting. About two kilometres directly east and across the Lovaart Canal was Groot-Fockewaerve Farm, laid out in a typical Flemish moated, rectangular style. It billeted many a unit during the war but was also the site selected for a French 240mm long range gun. Not far from it is a modern, artistic interpretation of trench lines, laid in an area that was eventually entrenched as a third Belgian defensive system. Two brightly coloured and stone walls represent sinuous trenches. It is not on this suggested route but can be found on the eastern bank of the Lovaart, some 800 metres north of the Fortembrug Bridge, on the N319 east of Alveringem and at the corner of Groenedreef, opposite the cycle and footbridge over the canal. This lane leads on to Groot-Fockewaerve Farm.

A short distance along the road from the cemetery is **De Leute**, a building dating back to 1672. It was formerly the Oeren district's town hall and was used at times during the Great War as a bakery, shop, café, meeting place and concert hall. The mayor at the time, Carolus-Ludovicus Balloey, opposed the permanent construction of the cemetery. The café continues to operate today and is well worth a visit.

Alveringem

Continue on Oerenstraat through the village and continue to Alveringem: this was the first village behind this sector of the front line that continued to be occupied by civilians during the war and one which became an important place for the development of Flemish nationalism within the ranks of the army.

As the village is entered, do not follow the road as it bends to the right at a 30 kilometres speed limit sign, but take the left (physically it is straight on). You soon come to a t-junction with the N319, Nieuwstraat, and turn left (signposted Diksmuide) and park as soon as you can. On the front wall of number 52 (on the right) is a memorial plaque to the fact that it was in this house that an open letter to the King was published on 11 July 1917, imploring him to assist with improving the conditions for the Flemings. The letter was reproduced by troops of the Belgian 1st Division billeted here and was distributed widely: men found with a copy in their possession bore the risk of harsh treatment by the Sûreté Militaire. The plaque concludes: *Dit was het begin van de strijd voor zelfbestuur* (This was the start of the struggle for self-government).

Now turn around and head into the village centre. Park near the centrally positioned and large church of **St. Audomarus**. A lane runs all the way around its perimeter and there is usually relatively easy parking along it. Alveringem has a number of cafés and shops, all easily accessible from this spot.

Walk around to the far side of the church and enter by the main gateway on Putstraat. The **village war memorial** stands in front of the church. The statue figure of a soldier points to the north: it is believed that it was originally meant to be orientated to point to the front line, which of course lay to the east. Among those listed on it is Jeroom Bonte, one of many killed when the 13th Line Regiment attacked Violette Farm, just a few kilometres from his home, on 9 May 1915. His body was never found. How sad, therefore, to read in his record that as late

The village war memorial at Alveringem.

as 1921 his father was asking for his son to be brought back for burial in the churchyard.

Some of the dead who now lie at Oeren were originally buried in the churchyard. The last man named on the war memorial was buried here but was never removed. Julien Vansteene, who was born in Alveringem and lived on Putstraat, died of wounds at the field hospital at Hoogstade on 30 May 1918.

The highly controversial priest, poet and literary scholar and one of the driving forces behind the Front Movement, **Cyriel Verschaeve**, was chaplain at Alveringem from 1911 to 1939. He died in exile in Austria in 1949 and was reburied in Alveringem in 1973 after a clandestine transfer described elsewhere in this book. To locate his grave, walk from the war memorial to the right of the church and look for a high laurel hedge. Verschaeve has a larger than usual heldenhuldezerk and is now surrounded by eight others, including a stone to Julien Vansteene.

[You might be interested in **Appelstraat 7**. Belgian literary men in military service met at this location in 'Den Appel' in 1917–1918. A white glass plate with black etched letters reminds us of this: Here from 1917 to 1918 the Belgian literary men met in military service – 'Ici de 1917 à 1918 reunirent les écrivains Belges présents sous les drapeaux'.]

Cyriel Verschaeve's grave in the churchyard at Alveringem, flanked by other Flemish AVV-VVK stones.

Exit Alveringem by the N319, Sint-Rijkersstraat, signposted for Ieper. On the right, pass on a corner a community centre known as De Kwelle. This is on the site of a boys' school that was commandeered in October 1914 and turned into a military hospital. The name of the lane reminds the visitor that a windmill, de Kwellemolen, stood on it, just outside the village, and was there during the Great War. Next door to De Kwelle, at number 22, is the **Museum Cyriel Verschaeve** which is mainly based on a private collection of soldiers' letters and manuscripts, along with artworks.

Continue long Sint-Rijkersstraat until reaching, in some 900 metres, the **war memorial** to the dead of **Sint-Rijkers**. This is nowadays scarcely a hamlet, for it has no church, school or any other evident sign that it was ever a village. Even its last remaining estaminet, In den Dolfijn – which, like De Leute at Oeren, was also used for local administration - was removed to the open air museum of buildings at Bokrijk in 1965: the memorial stands on the site. The first death of a local soldier took place on 6 November 1914 when Gunner Camille de Schryver was killed near Ramskapelle. Buried in a nearby field, he was reinterred at Hoogstade in 1923.

The road continues until reaching the crossroads with the N8 Veurne-Ieper road, at which point turn left, in the direction of Ieper. Enter the village of Hoogstade.

Hoogstade

Just after entering the built-up area turn right onto the narrow Brouwerijstraat. It is signposted as a cul-de-sac but leads to **Hoogstade Belgian Military Cemetery**. Created during the war, it now contains the graves of 808 Belgian (and a row of twenty British) soldiers, those who remain of the 1100 men who had been buried here by the end of the war. All 150 French graves were removed as were a small number of Germans and many Belgians who were repatriated; on the other hand, others were brought in from scattered plots. The layout of the graves was remodelled in 1924–25 to the pattern as seen today.

The earliest of those originally buried in this cemetery appear to date to late May 1915 and are mainly men who had been evacuated to the Belgian field hospital at Gasthuis Clep, south of Hoogstade, where they succumbed to wounds.

The earliest British graves date to the same period. Privates Alfred Bristowe of the Middlesex Regiment and Frederick Foreman of the Buffs (East Kent Regiment) were wounded in fighting near St. Jean (Sint-Jan), east of Ypres, and had been taken out of the British sector altogether. It is not clear exactly why this was so, for the war diary of the medical

Hoogstade Belgian Military Cemetery.

units supporting their battalions show that they were located at Herzeele and Hoograaf at the time, but they appear to have been taken to the Belgian Field Hospital. Poor Foreman, a Special Reservist, had only joined his battalion thirteen days before his death. A third burial, Private George Trentham of the Royal Warwickshire Regiment, had also only been overseas for a matter of days.

Return to the main road and turn right. Almost immediately on the left is **St.-Lambertus Church**, but at time of writing it is rather obscured by trees. The village **war memorial** stands in front of it and a plot of sixteen British graves from 1940 can be found in the **churchyard**.

Continue for a kilometre, going through the rest of Hoogstade

Jérôme Renneboog, a lieutenant of the 9th Line Regiment, wounded in September 1915, later worked at the pharmacy of the Belgian field hospital at Gasthuis Clep. He was a prolific photographer: his collection of war time images is held by the archive of his home town of Aalst. (*Aalst Stadsarchief*)

and to the crossroads at Gapaard. Turn left onto Romanestraat and immediately on the right see the restored site of a **Belgian field kitchen**. It is possible to park near the entrance. The site was renovated in 2016–17 and is now a protected monument. It is a fragment of Camp des Américains, one of several built in this area in 1917. It housed one infantry battalion (around 650 to 750 men) and originally consisted of fourteen brick-built barrack blocks. Officers were billeted in nearby farms. The building that remains was used for some time after the war as a cattle shed. It had originally incorporated a kitchen, a dining room and a storage area. The renovation has included repair of the building, improved access and layout of the site and the installation of information boards and artefacts. A steel frame was added to illustrate the original extent of the building.

Return to the N8 crossroads and turn left. In 570 metres there is a large grey building with a modern extension on the left hand side of the road. There are bus stop lay-bys on both sides but no other parking, so turn if possible into the car park of the building. This is **Gasthuis Clep**, which at the time of writing appears to be rather run-down; a great pity for it is one of the key sites of historical interest in this area.

Established as an almshouse *for needy elders and ophans of Hoogstade* by the bequest of notary Joseph Clep (whose grave is in the churchyard at Hoogstade), it took in its first residents in 1876. A large

The buildings of the former Gasthuis Clep today.

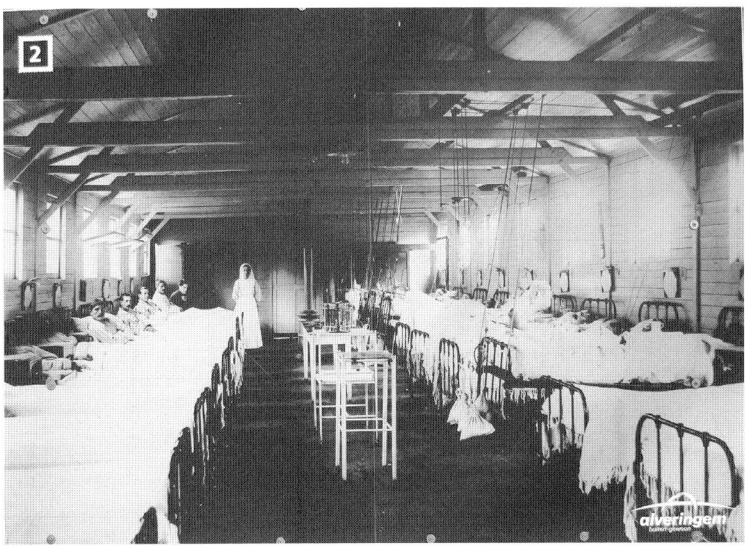

The interior of Gasthuis Clep Hospital, in a photograph that is on display there today.

two storey building, it was still occupied for its original purpose when in early 1915 the frequency of the bombardment of Veurne caused the staff of the Belgian field hospital there to be evacuated. While they were at De Panne and Dunkirk the authorities made a decision to evacuate the residents of Gasthuis Clep, and turn it over for use by the hospital.

All but a few very elderly inmates and a small staff of nuns left to care for them were removed by car to locations across the border in France. On the opposite side of the road, a field was commandeered for use by a Belgian motor ambulance convoy and the hospital came into operation from 15 May 1915 onwards. War volunteer and surgeon Charles Willems was appointed medical director, while its staff, then of twenty-six nurses, thirty orderlies and kitchen staff, were accommodated in its long attic room, with some half a dozen local laundry workers also employed. Several timber barrack huts were eventually erected behind and alongside the main building to expand its capacity and provide additional facilities; and an improved road and courtyard were laid to take place of the sea of churned mud that surrounded the hospital when it was first taken over.

The field hospital had facilities for the treatment of all manner of wounds but specialised in the more difficult surgical cases. A total of 1320 soldiers died while in the care of this hospital; many thousands more passed through its hands.

The plaque to Colonel Willems, commandant of the field hospital that operated at Gasthuis Clep.

On the front façade of the building is a bronze plaque memorial to the British section of the Belgian Field Hospital and another to Willems.

Continue south on the N8, crossing the Yser and passing through the scattered hamlet of Elzendamme to reach the larger Oostvleteren. The Belgians constructed a third defensive line that ran along and in parallel to this road. Turn right onto the N321, signposted for Poperinge, passing on your right the still operational Meestersmolen windmill, built around 1760 in Gijverinkhove and moved here in 1973.

Westvleteren
In 1500 metres you will reach the centre of Westvleteren, passing a **French military plot** of 200 graves in the **churchyard of St. Martinuskerk** on the left. Most of the graves are of men of the 38th Division d'Infanterie and the 87th Division d'Infanterie Territorial, dating from the first winter of the war. The village **war memorial** also stands in front of the church, opposite the village square on which there are cafés and a frituur (chip shop). It resembles the way it was during the Great War, where the Estaminet de la Forge continued to provide for the troops.

War came to Westvleteren on 16 and 17 October 1914 when French units arrived and were billeted in its church, schools, houses, barns and stables. It was used as a reserve area for the French forces holding the front line sector between Noordschote and Steenstraat, north of Ypres. As the Belgian army expanded and reorganised in 1915 it was able to take over this sector and it used Westvleteren for the same purpose. Some civilians remained in the area, which was a two hour march from the front and far enough away from it to avoid all but raids from the air and at times the most extreme-range shellfire, until they were finally evacuated on 28 June 1917. A field hospital was established in the girls' school, from which the more seriously wounded and sick men would be evacuated to the larger hospitals.

The **village memorial** records twenty-four military dead of the war. Loss soon came to the village when Jerome Sticker was killed at Bellaire, near Liège, whilst serving with the 9th Line Regiment on 5 August 1914. This was a matter of a couple of days after Germany had invaded Belgium and before any British soldier was on continental soil. He had enlisted in 1906; his unit was under the command of the 3rd Division, which was tasked with the field defence of the forts around Liège. Sticker was not brought home after the war and lies in Wandre Military Cemetery. A curious omission from the memorial is Camille Saesen, a Westvleteren-born soldier killed at Imde-Wolvertem, north of Brussels, on 24 August 1914. His burial place is unknown.

Follow the road as it bends left past the church and turn left into St. Martinusstraat to **Westvleteren Belgian Military Cemetery**. 1208 soldiers are buried here, including fourteen under heldenhuldezerkjes. Next to the cemetery was the Westvleteren girls' school, where a medical post was established in 1915. After the war several graves from the front to the west of the Ieper-Diksmuide road were concentrated into this cemetery, including 135 casualties who had been buried in the nearby churchyard. The French dead were repatriated after the war and several Belgian casualties were reburied in their home village. The Van Raemdonck brothers and Renaat de Rudder were also buried here before their removal to the Yser Tower. The men buried in the cemetery represent all phases of the Belgian's army actions from the Second Battle of Ypres onwards, with the majority from 1917 and 1918. Many died in the area of Boezinge, Lizerne and Steenstraat; but others come from the hospital at Hoogstade and from the battlefield area at Merkem. Thirty-three of the graves are of men who could not be identified.

Gunner 282150 Lewis Kennedy of 22 Siege Battery of the Royal Garrison Artillery is a lone British burial within the cemetery. His unit was positioned near Au Lion Belge (see below) when he was killed on 26 June 1916. Kennedy had enlisted in the Norfolk Artillery in 1901 but soon transferred to the regular army, in which he served until March 1913. He voluntarily re-enlisted just over a year before his death.

The buildings of 'Au Lion Belge' before the war.

On exiting the cemetery and rejoining the N321, here called Eikhoekstraat, turn left. This road leads eventually to the Trappist Abbey of Sint-Sixtus, an order supported by the commercial activities of its notable brewery, but on this occasion we must turn before we reach it.

Sint-Sixtus would be worth a visit in its own right, outside the tour described. It was the only such abbey in Belgium not to fall into enemy hands during the war, although at times it was occupied and used as a headquarters and lodging by the military forces of France, Britain (from May 1915) and Belgium (from March 1918). The site around the abbey developed into a large camp of huts. It has an uncommonly rich documented war time history through diaries and notes kept by three of the Cistercian monks whose home it was, other artefacts now in its archive, and is mentioned in many other diaries, memoirs and letters. They describe the arrival and passing through of hundreds of refugees after the first fifty-four arrived from Mechelen in early September 1914; the care and feeding of these unfortunates and the eventual clearance of the abbey for military use; the arrival of nuns and parish priests fleeing the enemy; of groups of evacuated orphans; the thousands of troops billeted in the area; of great visitors, including King George V and the Belgian royal family. Several of the monks were drafted into the Belgian army and trained as stretcher bearers or nurses. For a short time in 1915 a field ambulance of a Moroccan Division was located within the abbey. Seventeen French soldiers died within its care and were buried in a plot (no longer there) in a field behind what is now the vehicle access for beer sales. During the British military occupation, the abbey site was witness to a number of field punishments and on 12 June 1915 the execution on a charge of cowardice of Private 2779 Herbert Chase of the 2nd Lancashire Fusiliers. Buried on the site, he was reinterred at White House Cemetery, Sint-Jan, near Ypres, in 1919. Today the abbey site is mainly visited by those interested in its fine award-winning beers, which have been brewed on site since 1839.

After two kilometres turn left onto Kruisboomstraat: this is not easily spotted, indicated only by a yellow signboard pointing towards the 't Vleterhof Restaurant. If you miss the turn, seeing the 't Eikenhof bar just beyond the junction, on the left, will let you know that you have gone too far. Just 150 metres after the turn is made a small road bridge spans the little Poperingsevaart drainage channel, which originates as the Vleterbeek in the Flemish hills near Mont des Cats, flows through Poperinge and eventually meets the Ijzer. Its war time journey took it through many military camps and was used for watering horses, laundry work and to wash away effluent. It was also put to another use. A Royal Army Medical Corps report analysed the quality of the Vleterbeek water, which was drawn for rapid beer-making to supply the British: those with delicate stomachs should avoid this line of enquiry. Mind you, the St Sixtus beer drew necessary water from a stagnant looking pond that an overenthusiastic British sanitation officer had drained in 1917. Continue along Kruisboomstraat until reaching its crossroads with the N8, which is here called Woestenstraat. Turn right, in the direction of Ieper. Beware that this road can be both busy and fast.

The third Belgian system of defence ran south along the N8, and the fields now on the left were a complex warren of trenches, barbed wire and dugouts. Two of the strongpoints here were the Ouvrage Wellington and Ouvrage Cromwell.

Just 250m after the turn, pull off the road and park (there are lay-bys on both sides). In front of number 65 on the right is an **Albertina Memorial** marked **'Kantonnement Le Lion Belge 1914–1918'**. It recalls Au Lion Belge Cabaret, an important location behind the Belgian held front line of the Knokke-Steenstraat sector and was named after a substantial two-storey inn that stood here. A few metres away, a wall sign, Station Lion Belge, recalls that a tram line ran along this road. Other parts of the Au Lion Belge complex still stand, the next two houses after the station building. They are slightly modified from their pre-1914 appearance but can readily be matched to contemporary postcards.

Maurice Gabolde, a Sergent-Fourrier, a non-commissioned officer responsible within his unit for stewardship, accounting and sometimes logistical matters, with the French 69 Infantry Regiment, remembered the inn when he wrote a memoir from his hospital bed in late 1915.

> 'Located halfway between Ypres and Veurne, in the middle of a gamey and agricultural region, it was the meeting place for hunters, Sunday walkers, even neighbouring farmers who came there to talk about their business in front of a glass of beer. For the moment, empty of furniture, crowded with soldiers, it was a refuge from the rain for the wagon drivers and a meeting place for the troops who were billeted on the neighbouring farms. I often waited there for the battalion, once the quartering had been done, rolled up in a blanket or seated on some bench ... We had made the cantonment in the farms and my company was at the crossroads Reninge - Pypegale, just beside the big guns that fired forward of the Belgian front.'

In the fields behind these buildings, a standard gauge railway also came in from the west and inevitably the entire area around about became crammed with hutted camps, dumps and transport units. A tethered observation balloon floated above – often the target for German fighter aircraft - and two dressing stations were established close by. The French-speaking 'Center de Récréation au front Belge' set up a reading room in Au Lion Belge and in due course a theatre and cinema also came into operation.

This concludes the tour.

Follow the N8 south for Ieper or turn north for Veurne and locations on the coast.

Tour D

Drie-Grachten, Merkem and Steenstraat

This tour begins at **Woesten**, a village on the N8 Ieper-Veurne road, not far from Au Lion Belge, the concluding point of Tour C. It ventures from the rear and goes forward into the front line area that lay south of the main inundations and flanked the Ypres Salient. French and Belgian troops in the area covered by the tour often came into contact with men of the British Expeditionary Force, alongside which they fought during the Second Battle of Ypres and in the long months of positional warfare.

Park in front of the impressively large **Sint-Rictrudiskerk Church** in the centre of Woesten. The village remained behind the allied front line throughout the war and was garrisoned at different times during the war by French, Belgian and British troops. It became ringed by secondary defence trenches and barbed wire, beyond which there were many camps, dumps and stores. By 1917 a railway line ran across its southern side, passing down to Elverdinge and Boesinge at the northern limit of the Salient. The village sustained much damage from enemy shell fire; but vestiges of buildings and walls remained standing, providing dubious and inhospitable shelter for units moving into or from the front.

The **church**, whose fine tower dated to 1447, was a useful observation post but a roofless gutted ruin as early as 1915, by which date its grounds were being used for French military burials dotted around existing civilian graves. The church was reconstructed, largely to its original design with the exception of the highest parts of the tower, in 1921–26, but it was not until 1965 that the French graves were concentrated into a single plot.

The impressive village **war memorial** stands on the car park square, facing some shops. Topped by the statue of a soldier, it is formed from a beehive or cairn shaped pile of debris from destroyed bunkers.

Walk through the churchyard and take the path round its left hand side to the **French military cemetery** at its end. It is a reminder that, although the area travelled in this tour was Belgian-held for most of the war, French forces held Ypres and its northern flank throughout the first winter and remained here during the Second Battle of Ypres in April 1915. Of the 282 graves, about half are of men who died in the battle. A plot of eight British graves from May 1940 also lies within the churchyard. Six of the burials are of men of the 2nd Royal Ulster Rifles.

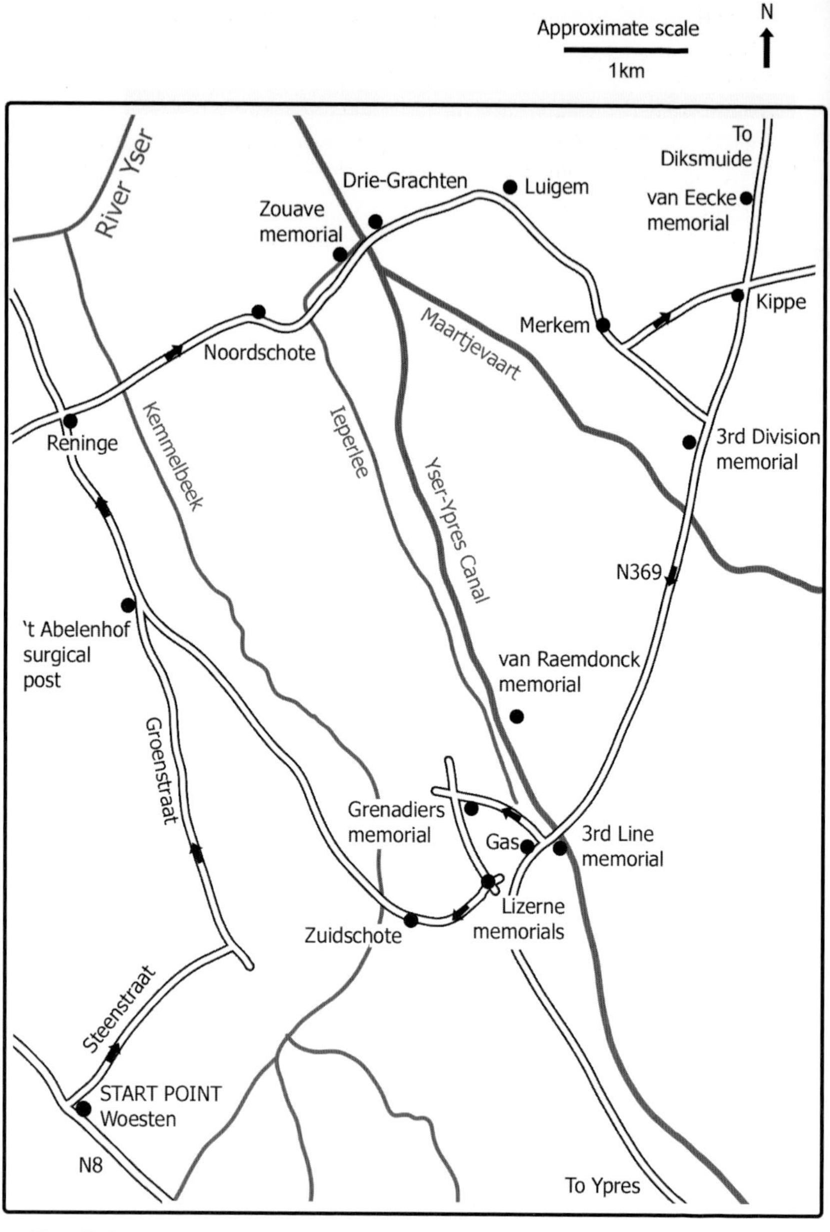

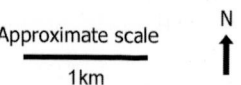

Tour D Route Map.

Leave the car park and take Steenstraat, which lies alongside the church. It narrows as it leaves the village and crosses the deep defences of the third Belgian line. Follow for about 1800 metres and turn a sharp left onto *Groenstraat*. A nicely decorated cottage lies on the right just before the turn and is a useful landmark. The second defensive line ran through the fields now on the right and parallel with the road, with the village of Zuidschote just beyond it. Follow Groenstraat for 2.8 kilometres, reaching the junction with the larger Zuidschotestraat. Park just before the junction at any convenient spot.

An **Albertina Memorial** at the junction marks the site of **the 't Abelenhof Surgical Post**. It was situated at a redoubt within the second line. The road junction was ringed by trenches and barbed wire and was named after the farm-inn In 't Abelenhof that once stood on the opposite side of the road to the modern house that now occupies the corner and which was destroyed by shellfire in 1917. The inn buildings had been incorporated into the second defensive line but its use as a specialist surgical post was a development of 1916. It was decided to establish a number of such posts at around two to five kilometres' distance from the front, with the intention of providing early treatment for men with abdominal and other wounds who were otherwise at serious risk of infection. Three were set up, each covering a defined zone of the front, at St-Jansmolen (Lampernisse), Grognie (Oudekapelle) and 't Abelenhof.

This latter received wounded from the central part of the Ieperlee sector of front between Steenstraat, Zuidschote and Noordschote. Stretcher bearers would bring the wounded from the forward aid post at De Ravelaer Farm via a footbridge over the Kemmelbeek Stream (which is across the fields opposite the Albertina memorial). Emergency surgery was carried out in the post, which was normally manned by three doctors and their necessary staff and a small fleet of motor ambulances, which further evacuated the wounded to the field hospital at Hoogstade. Two other aid posts operated nearby, at the convent of the Annuntiaten Sisters in Reninge and at Theophiel Segers Farm at Pijpegale.

Continue to follow Zuidschotestraat which leads on to Reninge; the second line ran in parallel on the right, coming rather closer to the road as the village is approached. Note that signs refer to Lo-Reninge: this dates to the creation in 1977 of a municipality incorporating both villages.

Reninge

On entering the built-up area of Reninge the road changes its name to Ieperstraat. Look out for house **number 13** on the right as the village centre is neared. It is the only remaining example of a post-

1918 **'temporary' home** in this area and one of very few in all of West Flanders. These houses were designed for quick construction in a similar way to the pre-fabricated homes built in Britain after 1945 and played a considerable part in the return to normality. The house is private property: please respect it as such.

Two more sites of importance can be seen along this road before the village centre is reached. On the right, just a few metres after number 13 and a side road also rather confusingly called Ieperstraat, is a large white building behind a wall, with a modern extension that faces onto the road. This is the reconstructed site of the **1816 convent of the Annuntiaten Sisters**. Beyond that, on the left of the main road, is an ornate turreted building on the left of the road: this is the reconstructed sixteenth century **Vilain Chateau**.

Drive past these locations into the village centre and park in front of **Sint-Rictrudiskerk Church**. There are cafés and shops nearby. The history of this village, which now has just over 1100 inhabitants, can be dated back to the ninth century when the land around was owned by the French abbey of Marchiennes, a seventh century foundation, east of Lens and north of Cambrai. It has always relied on agriculture and for some centuries had a thriving cloth trade (during which it was in conflict with Ypres). As with most villages and towns of this part of Flanders, its history also included terrible periods of plague, war and sacking by religious zealots. By 1914 it was a thriving small community, with a town hall just ten years old, brewery and dairy businesses, mills and links elsewhere by a tram line.

The convent had expanded its operations into the area north of the church, occupying a large site alongside the Steenweg, where shops and cafés now face the church, by 1914 and continuing further along the road. Much of it was occupied by a complex of buildings that had been used as a school but was by 1914 the Gesticht Vallaeys (Vallaeys' Foundation) elderly people's home. On 21 August 1914, even though fighting had not yet reached West Flanders, four of the sisters from the convent escorted fifty-four residents of the home to the safety of Sint-Sixtus Abbey at Westvleteren. It was a wise decision, for Reninge came under shell fire from October 1914.

The German advance was finally halted some two kilometres east of Reninge. From late October 1914 it came under frequent heavy shellfire that gradually razed the village centre, although the convent seemed to have a charmed life and remained standing longer than most buildings. It came under a particularly heavy bombardment on 27 February 1915, despite flying a red cross flag. Nuns, soldiers and wounded alike sheltered for hours in the cellars. It inevitably led to the nuns being evacuated to

France: they returned in 1919. The church went up in flames on 9 March 1915 and was gradually reduced to a jagged ruin. Understandably, most of the local people fled and Reninge became a military garrison with billets, stores, aid posts and stables. Those few civilians who remained lived under fire, often in the early days suffering the outrage of being accused of espionage. For a while the headquarters of the Belgian army was located in the convent.

On 7 April 1916 an evacuation order was issued to people still inhabiting the western side of the village; a second order in June 1917 cleared all of the brave (or foolhardy) souls still clinging on to their homes. Of the approximately 400 buildings that had existed in Reninge in 1914, around a quarter were declared completely uninhabitable at the end of the war. The Isidoor Grimmelprez Brewery and Sint-Antonius Dairy, both important in pre-war village life, could not be saved. The presbytery, Vilain Chateau and the convent were all partially destroyed but enough remained to provide a basis for reconstruction.

The layout of today's village is much as it had been in 1914 but inevitably much of it is rebuilt and bears little resemblance to the period, although the church was reconstructed to the same design, as were the convent and chateau. The area of the old Gesticht Vallaeys is one that residents of pre-war days would definitely not recognise for it has been considerably remodelled. Much of it is now occupied by the Hof te Yzer rest and nursing home complex.

A **war memorial** recording the names of seventeen soldiers of the Great War stands outside the **church**; inside is a copper plaque memorial recording the civilian dead. Among those listed are brothers Cyriel and Marcel Loonis, both of whom served with the 24th Line Regiment and succumbed to their wounds at the l'Ocean Hospital at Vinkem. Both were buried in the military cemetery at Steenkerke. They died within days of each other, on 30 October and 3 November 1917 respectively. Cyriel, the first of the brothers to enlist when he joined the army on 29 September 1914, was fatally wounded by the explosion of an aerial bomb. Born in 1894 and 1892, Cyriel and Marcel were a tailor and shoemaker. It is known that a further 171 men of the village served in and survived the Great War.

An aid post set up at the **De Smidse Inn** on Hoflandstraat, in the fields west of Reninge, was the cause of the establishment of a Belgian military burial plot. This cemetery remained in place until 1968, when 117 graves (mainly dating from 1915 and 1916) were transferred to Hoogstade. Another 123 men were reburied at Westvleteren. Twenty-one British and Canadian airmen and soldiers who had been buried in the cemetery during the Second World War were taken the long distance to Adegem Canadian War Cemetery and buried in a single plot.

[*Optional extra visit to a vestige* of **Reninge Cemetery** that requires a short detour. Leave Reninge by Zwartestraat, which is the left turn opposite Sint-Rictruduskerk. Its name soon changes to Oostvleterenstraat as it leaves the village. Take the first left turn after 930 metres, into Hoflandstraat and continue for 500 metres to house number 1. The front wall, with metal decoration, dating to the cemetery's construction in 1920, stands on the right hand side of the road and there is a central pathway with pollarded trees that can be walked. A **memorial** has been constructed near the front of the recently renovated site. Return to Reninge by the same route to recommence the tour.]

Leave the village by turning right on to Steenweg and pass the church on the right hand side. The road leads directly to the old front line. It soon leaves Reninge behind and crosses the Kemmelbeek Stream (today referred to as the Landdijkgracht Channel): most of the area between Reninge and the next village reached, Noordschote, was under water, swollen by the stream as its usual flow to the Yser estuary was disrupted. The road name changes to Noordschoteplein on reaching the village. Noordschote stood on slightly higher ground and was in the front line. The ground around it, notably on its southern side (the right as the road approaches it) became riddled with a network of trenches, breastworks and barbed wire. Enter the village and park near the church.

Noordschote
A smaller village than Reninge, Noordschote was little more than a cluster of houses tightly packed around its central 1498 Sint-Barnabaskerk Church. Today it is not dissimilar but is somewhat larger: even so, it is still little more than some houses, the church and a café. In the **churchyard** is a row of fourteen British graves from May 1940; men of the 1st Suffolk Regiment and 2nd East Yorkshires. Aside from the small village memorial, which stands alongside a small square at the church, the visitor may be forgiven for not realising that war had ever been this way. The village, whose name derives from 'schot' – higher land protruding amidst lower waterlands, is mentioned in records as early as 1146. For centuries it was relatively remote but by the early twentieth century the roads to Reninge and Zuidschote were paved and the tram link to Reninge was operational. In the front line from when the waters rose in 1914, the village was completely destroyed and everything that now stands is reconstruction or new.

The war memorial is sobering: it records three names of soldiers and five civilians. These were certainly not all of the Noordschote residents to perish, for at least three civilians not named on the memorial are known to have died in the period 1916–1918 and are buried at the Chartreuse of Neuville-sous-Montreuil in France.

Continue along the same road, Noordschoteplein. A small brick bridge just outside Noordschote takes the road over the little Ieperlee, which then bends and follows the road on its left hand side. The Ieperlee flooded as part of the inundations and water covered the fields on both sides.

Drie-Grachten and Luigem
The road now approaches Drie-Grachten, named because it is where three waterways, the Yser-Ypres Canal, the Ieperlee Stream and the Maartjevaart Drain meet. Some 1200 metres beyond it lies the hamlet of Luigem. The area saw intense fighting, concentrated along the road between the two, and it could be said to be the most northerly point of the Ypres Salient, although once the fighting stabilised in 1914 it was effectively in No Man's Land, occupied by advanced outposts by both sides.

Approaching from Noordschote, a small tram halt station building stood on the left of the road just before Grote Martjebrug Bridge over the canal and the tram line continued across it towards Luigem. To the left of the bridge, behind the tram station and on the far side of the Ieperlee, a sluice (l'Eclusette) controlled the flow of water from a network of field drainage channels into the canal. About 150 metres away on the right of the bridge, where the Maartjevaart joined the canal, Cayennemolen (built in 1796) corn and oil windmill stood along with outbuildings that would

The road to Luigem from Noordschote mainly remained above the water that flooded the land on either side of it.

The German outpost at Cayenne Mill, near Drie-Grachten, in April 1915.

later be known as **Chariot House**. It is mis-spelled as Cavennemolen on contemporary maps. The area is flat, with the exception of raised embankments at points along the canal and the foundations of the bridge and of the road running between Drie-Grachten and Luigem, which stood slightly higher than the surrounding fields. The inundation of the area from late October 1914 soon put the fields on the east side of the canal underwater, but the road itself remained passable – if only just.

On 15 October 1914 Belgian engineers destroyed the mill and bridge to deny them to the enemy. The tram station was very soon destroyed by shell fire; trenches and barbed wire turned the sluice into a small defence post; the area became one of considerable devastation; and gradually plank walkways snaked across the canal to forward posts on the east bank.

On 11 November 1914 the bridge, which lay just beyond the café, was held by the 1st Regiment of Zouaves, an exotic French colonial regiment originally raised in Algiers, with two of their machine guns deployed to cover the road ahead on the far side of the canal. A German column was moving on them from Luigem, which lies ahead down the straight road, but with a Zouave prisoner (or prisoners) pushed in front of them. The Germans called for the Zouaves to hold their fire, but a cry came from the prisoners *Shoot anyway, shoot, for God's sake!* The defenders opened fire; the prisoners and Germans died; and Drie-Grachten was held. The story may be apocryphal but the 1st Zouaves did have some men of its 11th Battalion captured the day before.

The Demarcation Stone on the road from Nordschote, nearing Drie-Grachten Bridge.

A brief study of the last resting places of some of the Zouaves who were killed or fatally wounded at Drie-Grachten is educational: some, like Henry Daviot, an Ardennes man who died of wounds on 31 October 1914, lie close by. He is buried in the French plot at Westvleteren Churchyard. Others are distant: Lucien-Claude Barel lies at Dunkirk, where he succumbed in hospital; Adolphe-Gaston Roux, who died of wounds on 21 November 1914, is on the other side of the country, at Rennes. Charles-Christophe Gabriel, killed on 30 October 1914, has never been found and identified.

Just before the few buildings of Drie-Grachten are approached from the Noordschote direction, a ***demarcation stone*** stands on the on left of the road and marks the deepest German advance here in early April 1915. This is not an easy place to stop but there is a bus lay-by a few metres further on, just before the Café de Drie-Grachten, with some space to park for a few minutes. Take care when walking back along the road. On returning from the stone, go beyond to see a **memorial plaque to the unknown Zouave soldier**, on the front wall of the former café.

Continue along the road, which is at this point called Noordeschoteplein, crossing the Ypres Canal by the reconstructed Grote Martjebrug Bridge.

French forces continued to hold Drie-Grachten until early 1915 when they were relieved by Belgian units, which extended down to Steenstraat. The Germans attacked on 29 March and forced a crossing on 8 April. They held it as a forward post until August 1917, when it was recaptured by French troops during the Third Battle of Ypres.

The memorial plaque to the 'Unknown Zouave' at Drie-Grachten.

An isolated but strong Belgian forward observation post stood in the inundated field on the right, immediately after the Grote Martjebrug bridge, and was known as **'Drie-Grachten Voorpost'**. Plank footbridges spanned the canal to reach it. The site is marked by an **Albertina Memorial** on the left of the road. It is possible to turn left off the main road and park nearby in order to examine it.

[**Optional detour**. Further down the canal to the right, at a distance of about 2.2 kilometres, was **Het Witte Huis** (White House) Inn, along with a ferry: the French named it the Maison du Passeur. There is an **Albertina Memorial** marking the site of the Belgian outpost there but it requires a short detour. Immediately after crossing Grote Martjebrug Bridge turn right onto Ieperleedijkstraat. This is a narrow dyke road that runs alongside the canal. It is mainly used by cyclists and has few passing places, so care is required. In 300 metres Cayennebrug Bridge crosses where the Maartjevaart meets the canal: continue straight on; the road is now named Westpoeselstraat.

The fields on the left were inundated and the German front line lay beyond the water at a distance of 250–350 metres. The Belgian front line was across on the right, 100–150 metres beyond the canal. After 700 metres the road begins to turn left and leaves the canal edge. There is space to park in front of the house and paddock that occupy the corner. To reach the memorial it is necessary to walk 1400 metres along the canal-side path (unless you are cycling, of course). Het Witte Huis, of which there is now no trace, was a large, fine building overlooking the canal from the Belgian side. It lay within the Belgian front line trenches and behind it was a second defensive line and three communication trenches leading up from the rear. A plank bridge was laid across to the German side and a small advanced and obviously very exposed

The Drie-Grachten to Luigem road saw both sides attempt costly advances in 1914.

Belgian post was established where the memorial now stands. It saw much fighting during the Second Battle of Ypres and was also the base for several Belgian raids against a German post some 400 metres to the north during 1916. Return to the vehicle and retrace the route back to Drie-Grachten Bridge, at which turn right.]

Return to the road, now called Drie Grachtensteenweg, and continue in the same direction through more of the inundated land. The road itself remained passable when the waters rose but was not in use until April 1915 as it lay in No Man's Land, between Drie-Grachten Voorpost and a German post ahead at Luigem. Once the Germans had crossed and captured Drie-Grachten, it became an exposed route to their front. After a right hand bend about a kilometre from Drie-Grachten Bridge, another **Albertina Memorial** stands at a small junction on the left of the road, with its text facing away from the direction of approach. It is usually easy to park here. This memorial recalls **Luigem Schiereiland**. Luigem is the name of the hamlet in which the memorial stands. It stands at the southern tip of a peninsula of slightly higher ground that remained above the rising water level.

Luigem was taken by the advancing Germans on 21–22 October 1914 during the Battle of the Yser. From the outpost of Drie-Grachten, the French aimed their machine guns along the road towards it in the hope of halting any incursion from the Luigem direction. On the night of 9–10 November a French force, including Zouaves, launched an attack along the road you have just driven. It became a fierce man-to-man fight, with heavy losses on both sides. The attack was repelled and the remnants of the attacking French troops withdrew. Two days later, on the night of 11–12 November, a German attack on Drie-Grachten similarly failed.

From the bridgehead at Drie-Grachten, Luigem was recaptured by another attack along this via dolorosa by the Belgian 2nd Battalion Karabiniers on 27 October 1917 as part of a large-scale attack, although it was held up elsewhere, especially towards Houthulst Forest, fought over the same terrible ground conditions so well-known between Ypres and Passchendaele.

Merkem and Kippe
Continue along the road, now called Westbroekstraat, into **Merkem**. In the village centre pass the church of St. Bavo on the right hand side and take the first right turn into Liniestraat. Park. The village centre has a few shops, banks and café-restaurants, many of which cluster around the small grassed square in front of the town hall, just 200 metres further along the main road. All of it is post-1918 reconstruction.

When the waters of the Maartjevaart rose, Merkem was inundated on its western side but the village itself was high enough to remain dry. The stabilised German front line ran parallel with Westbroekstraat at a distance of some 400 metres, with further outlying defences on the peninsula of slightly higher ground between the Maartjevaart and the Ypres Canal. One of the larger villages of the area – by 1900 it had over 3500 inhabitants – Merkem traces a history back to Roman times. It was dominated by the modern chateau of the de Coninck de Merkem family, which lay on the right hand side of the road behind St. Bavo's church and which was surrounded by its park and gardens. British war time maps show the castle as **Chateau Crocus**.

Refugees fleeing from the east began to arrive during August 1914, many coming from the area of Mechelen. On 13 September patrols of Uhlans passed through, probing forward as far as Proven (north west of Poperinge) without opposition. Others came through on 7 October on their way to Ypres and Poperinge. Just over a week later, with Antwerp falling and the Belgian army withdrawing westwards, German troops reached nearby Houthulst and Klerken. With much evidence and a lot of hearsay of atrocities, the people fled westwards. Merkem came under fire on 21 October and, along with Luigem, soon fell into enemy hands. When the front line stabilised it ran past the western boundary of the chateau grounds and provided the Germans with an excellent vantage point for observation across the area of Drie-Grachten and Maison du Passeur. The chateau continued to form part of the formidable defensive system that was constructed through the village. It included several concrete structures, of which only one is now left. The village was gradually destroyed by French, Belgian and British shell fire during the war, particularly during the earliest phase of the Third Battle of Ypres in July 1917, when French forces advanced across the Ypres Canal, recapturing Drie-Grachten and the peninsula.

Merkem itself was recaptured by French troops on 27 October 1917 in a phase of fighting coinciding with British attacks on Passchendaele. It fell to the 102e *bataillon de chasseurs à pied* (*la Gauloise*), a unit raised in 1915 and which was then under the command of 214 Infantry Brigade of the 133e Division. By 1917 this was an experienced formation, veterans of fighting in Champagne and the Battle of Verdun. It moved to the Dunkirk-Bergues area in May 1917 and took over the line between Bikschote and Drie-Grachten from 14 September. Beginning on 26 October, the division's attack took it across the inundations of the Saint-Jansbeek and Martjevaart, onto higher ground through Merkem and beyond, past Kippe and Aschoop. It was relieved on 6 November and moved to Nieuwpoort.

Belgian units moved into the sector and almost immediately faced local German counter-attacks. Advanced posts at the ruined farm buildings of Petit-Fils (which the British called Asbestos Farm) and Epernon, straddling the road from Merkem through Kippe to Nachtegaal and beyond, fell. On 28 Novembe, the Belgian 19th Line Regiment of the 3rd Division attempted to regain Epernon, only for the Germans to blow its concrete bunker up as they did so. Its 34 year-old adjutant, Jean Baptiste Marie Joseph Ghislain Taymans, was killed in the blast. A volunteer who had enlisted on 5 August 1914, he is commemorated by a **memorial at the remains of the bunker**, which was purchased by his family after the war. Two of his three brothers also perished in the war, dying within twenty-four hours of each other in October 1918. The brothers rest in Oostvleteren Communal Cemetery (their tomb marked in 2018 by a tricolour *Pro Patria* badge). Further German attacks on the Grand-Père Post were beaten off.

During the winter months the Belgians set about making the new line more defensible, linking it back to Merkem by plank tracks. It was on this line that the Belgians finest moment came during the German Tannenberg Attack during April 1918, described above in Chapter 4, in the section 'On the edge of the Ypres Salient'. The line was broken but restored by vigorous counter attacks and Merkem, while close behind the deepest German penetration, remained in Belgian hands. During late September 1918 it would see the start of the final offensive and the fighting soon moved eastwards.

There are several war memorials within the village. On the corner of Linestraat and the main road is the **memorial to the 19th Line Regiment**. The numerous battle honours featured on the memorial are testimony to its history; it also records the death of Taymans at Epernon. Turn left and walk a hundred metres to **Merkem's** *village memorial*, which is in front of the church of **Sint-Bavo**. On the left, as you approach, you pass the grounds of the rebuilt **Chateau Crocus**: unfortunately there is a high hedge but it is sometimes possible to obtain a glimpse through the growth. A German light railway ran across the road and through the grounds just before the church is reached. The church can date its original history to 886 AD. By 1918 it was in utter ruin, with only two arches from the original choir still standing amongst the rubble. The church was rebuilt in a similar style and on the original footprint.

The **churchyard** contains the graves of several veterans: they join the fifty-one men of Merkem identified by the Belgian War Graves Register. The memorial takes the form of a statue of the Sacred Heart of Christ, with panels listing military and civilian victims of both world wars. It also incorporates the coats of arms of Merkem, West Flanders and Flanders.

Turn back along Westbroekstraat, pass Liniestraat and continue until reaching, on the right, the grassed **square known as Baron de Coninck de Merkemplein**. On the façade of the town hall are **memorial plaques** to the **3rd, 11th and 13th Line Regiments**, which participated in the key battle at Merkem in April 1918; to **1 Battalion of 4 Jager te Voet**; and to the **Belgian Wireless Telegraphy Unit**.

At the crossroads adjacent to the square, exit by Stationstraat. Just after house number 13, on the left hand side, at the junction with Boterbloemstraat, is a 1986 bust of local **poet Sidronius Hosschius**. A village pump adorned with a bronze bust of Hosschius had been inaugurated in front of the church of Sint-Bavo in 1884. During 1918 Flemish soldiers painted in red on the stone base of the destroyed pump the text '*Hier ons bloed, wanneer ons recht*' (essentially 'Here is our blood, when do we get justice?'). The stone was transferred to the crypt of the original Yser Tower at Diksmuide in 1933 as one of the symbols of Flemish nationalism.

Merkem is now much expanded in this direction, an almost unbroken ribbon development built across the former Belgian defences of 1918 and the No Man's Land of 1914–1917. The extensions began very soon after the war in the development of the site known as **Elf Gemeten** (a gemet being an old measure of area). This was around the area on the right of the road that opens up to a broader space. This was the site of the former station halt on the tramway that led to Kippe. Elf Gemeten was in effect a housing estate of timber and corrugated iron huts, separated by pathways and garden plots, that also had temporary huts for a church and school.

The Belgian government in exile created the King Albert Fund with a view to the future need to address the issue of the vast war damage

Merckem Elf Gemeten.

The Elf Gemeten estate, built at Merkem during the post-war reconstruction.
(*Westhoek Verbeelt*)

to the country. From 1916 it became responsible for the provision of temporary shelter for the homeless but by the time of the Armistice it still had only some 150 timber shelters at its disposal. It purchased about 4500 corrugated iron and timber huts from the British army and during 1919–21 the restored Ministry of the Interior provided more resources, bringing the total to about 12500 homes of various sorts. Small estates such as Elf Gemeten were laid out in many towns and villages, usually situated along one of the roads and on the edge of the devastated centre.

Continue along Stationstraat and in 1100 metres reach the important **crossroads at de Kippe hamlet**. After the Allied advance in late 1917 the Belgian front line was established on the opposite side of the crossroads and work was carried out to to link it up with the British Second Army, not far away on their right (that is, south). Park on the right just before the road junction. An **Albertina Memorial** records the defeat of the German attack here on 17 April 1918.

East of de Kippe, directly across the crossroads but not visited on this tour, a moated thirteenth century motte was located between the Noord and Zuidwallandstraat. During the war the motte was used as the location of a German observation post and an underground field hospital.

Turn left onto the busy N369 Iepersteenweg. In 560 metres, just past house number 53 (on the left), park in one of the small laybys that are on each side of the road. Take care if crossing. Next door to the house is the **Memorial to Armand Victor van Eecke**, the 22 year-old adjutant of the 3rd Line Regiment who was killed in action here when leading an attack on 9 September 1918. Volunteering for war service in 1915, he served as adjutant from January 1916 and was highly regarded. Van Eecke came from Watou, near Poperinge, where he is both buried and named on the village war memorial. His family acquired the plot where his memorial stands and paid for its maintenance until 1982, when the responsibility was taken over by the municipality of Houthulst.

Turn around to head south back along N369 Iepersteenweg, pass the Kippe crossroads and the hamlet of Hoekske, which is identifiable from a fuel station on the left and a turn to Merkem on the right, next to which at the time of writing is the Steenen Molen café. Trenches of the German reserve line passed through Hoekske and crossed the N69 at this junction.

Less than 200 metres after passing through Hoekske, pull off the right hand side of the road into a small parking area adjacent to the unusual **Memorial to the Belgian 3rd Division**. Ringed by a chain fence mounted on shells, the memorial is a bronze plaque mounted on a large rock. This division began to acquire its battle honours with the defence of Liège in August 1914 and was involved in every significant Belgian action thereafter. The memorial is situated on the site of the deep German second line defensive system, with the trenches crossing the road here.

Continue along N369, all the while going deeper into the northern part of the Ypres Salient. In 500 metres the road crosses the Maartjevaart (which flows from here past Merkem to Drie-Grachten) at Langewaade. The spot can be identified by two small brick bridges. The land on both banks was inundated and the width of the flooded area was normally some 200–250m on either side of the vaart. During 1914 until the summer of 1917 the water separated the German reserve trench system from the front line beyond. The road is slightly embanked and was one of the few places at which men and material could pass to and from the front line.

Steenstraat and Lizerne

After another 2.6 kilometres, during which the Loobeek Stream is crossed and the road junction hamlet of 't Smiske passed, approach **Steenstraat**, an epicentre of the fighting in the Second Battle of Ypres. On the left is the ground of the Ypres Salient. Just as the village name sign is reached, a small lane turns off the road to the right. It is signposted **Monument Gebr. Van Raemdonck**. This is a narrow lane, mainly used by hikers and cyclists, and it is recommended that you park somewhere sensible (do not block the lane) and walk the 800 metres or so along the eastern bank of the Ypres Canal. The five metres-high hexagonal monument stands in the field on the right. It marks the place where the Van Raemdonck brothers and their comrade, Fievez, were killed during a trench raid at the Stampkot Position on 26 March 1917. Their story is told elsewhere in this book. The monument, which resembles a blockhouse, was erected in 1933 after a design by Karel De Bondt, who was also responsible for the portal of the crypt of the Yser Tower. It was inaugurated on 19 August 1933, the day before the 14th Ijzerbedevaart, which in that year was dedicated to the memory of the brothers and took place at the monument site. A walk further along the canal would bring the visitor back to the Maison du Passeur Albertina Memorial (see above).

Return to the main road and cross the canal bridge. The German front line ran along the eastern bank of the canal from April 1915 until late July 1917, when the allied line advanced at the start of the Third Battle: the canal was in No Man's Land. Immediately past the Steenstraete Café building on the left is a **Memorial to the Belgian 3rd Line Regiment** in the form of a tall white cross. It was erected in 1953 and has an unusual background: three original memorial plaques had been affixed to the railings of the bridge but were removed by a local resident for safe keeping shortly before it was destroyed by British troops on 28 May 1940. The plaques are now located at the new memorial.

In another 200 metres is the right turn onto Grenadiersstraat. At the junction is the large **Memorial to the victims of poison gas** released during the Second Battle of Ypres, with its fifteen metres' high cross of reconciliation. Should you choose to visit the memorial be aware that there is very limited car parking near to it (a paved area immediately in front of it on the main road) and once the turn into Grenadierstraat is made there is none without blocking the lane. The memorial was inaugurated in 1961 and replaced the 1929 French original, destroyed by the Germans in May 1941.

Go down the narrow Grenadiersstraat until, in 550 metres, the **obelisk memorial to the Belgian Regiment of Grenadiers** comes into view on the left hand side of the road. Although it is possible to stop with care immediately in front of it, a parked car will partially block the road so pull off if possible onto ground at the junction with the lane that goes off to the right, just before the memorial. Be careful not to block access.

Walk back along the lane for about thirty metres. The storage buildings adjacent to the lane belong to house number 4, Withof, and are on land that was open ground during the Great War but which belonged to the former Antwerp Farm. A reserve or support trench crossed the lane approximately where the buildings end. The trench passed a concrete machine gun post that still exists and is in remarkably good condition. Its two open gun embrasures are not easy to see from the lane, but they were for firing eastwards across the ground towards the canal and the Stampkot Position beyond it. The roof and walls of the post are apparently at least eighty centimetres thick.

Walk back to the memorial. It was unveiled on 22 April 1934, the twenty-ninth anniversary of the gas attack, by King Leopold III and was the first to be unveiled by him after he acceded to the throne following the death of King Albert. At the same time, the former Nieuwstraat was renamed as Grenadiersstraat and part of what had been the nearby Middelstraat was renamed Generaal Lotzstraat (maps now often omit the first word). The regiment played an important part in the defence of the area during the Second Battle of Ypres. Gustave Lotz was aged 52 at the time and was the commanding officer of the Grenadiers. He rose steadily in rank during the war and ended his career as a lieutenant general. Lotz is also commemorated by a memorial plaque in Boezinge.

A few metres after the memorial turn left onto Lotzstraat, signposted for Zuidschote. In 600 metres, on the right and on the front face of house number 15, is a wall plaque **memorial to the 2 and 4 Belgian Karabiniers,** units which also participated in the defence of the area in 1915. Just a hundred metres further on, at the **Lizerne Crossroads**, is a **demarcation stone.** No trace of the original Lizerne remains – which was never more than the café-estaminet *In de Zon Cabaret* (on the corner where the stone was erected), a few houses and farm buildings – for it was completely destroyed by mid-1915. For much of the war it was in an area of reserve trenches, dugouts and various shelters, not far behind the allied front line. The stone was unveiled in 1923 to mark the furthest progress of the Germans during the Second Battle. Lizerne was recaptured by a French counter-attack on 27 April 1915.

Turn right for **Zuidschote** and follow the road into the village. As the road bends right, notice on the left a small, ivy-covered **grotto containing a statue of the Virgin Mary**: it is constructed from lumps of former Great War concrete bunkers. In the **churchyard of Sint-Leonardus** on the left, the 1927 village **war memorial** stands just before a plot of seventy-six British graves from 1940 and five unidentified French graves from the Great War: a stark reminder of allied sacrifices in the First World War and that men were again dying here just twenty-two years later. The village lost five soldiers and four civilians in the war and was another that was completely devastated. Of the civilians, three died in shell fire in November 1914: after that the other residents fled or were eventually barred as the area became a militarised sector.

Tour E

The Towns of the Belgian Rear

This tour incorporates two of the larger towns of the Belgian coast, **Koksijde** and **De Panne**. They are seaside resorts and are always busy but especially so in the summer, at weekends and public holidays. The towns bear virtually no resemblance to the way they were at the time of the Great War but there are some important cemeteries, memorials and traces of the conflict to be found. Driving through them is rarely a problem in itself but parking can be difficult. There is extensive provision of paid car parking, both in car parks and at the roadside but (at time of writing) it is often possible to park free for up to thirty minutes. In some zones the driver will need to enter the registration number of the vehicle. Enforcement is taken seriously. The tours have been constructed to avoid the busy areas as much as possible but certain sites are deep within them: parking further away and walking to them would normally be a better option. To a lesser extent these comments also apply to the inland town of **Veurne**.

The tour begins at Oostduinkerke, the nearest village behind the Nieuwpoort sector of the front.

Oostduinkerke
Situated two kilometres inland from the sea, by 1914 the village had long since begun to grow from its traditional reliance on fishing and farming to develop as a seaside destination. The modest original village centre, linked to Koksijde and Nieuwpoort by tram and growing with the addition of estaminets and hotels, clustered around Sint-Niklaaskerk Church. A straight road took visitors through high dunes to the beach and the small resort of Oostduinkerke-Bad, centred on the fine, 1900 Grand Hôtel des Dunes and its renowned restaurant and cellar. The large chapel and convent of Très Saint-Sacrement was close by: it was used by Field Ambulances during the period of the British occupation of the area. Other hotels and large villas dotted the area.

Belgian troops first occupied the church on 16 October 1914 but a week later it was taken over by French troops. At about 1pm on 30 October a salvo of four German shells hit the village centre, damaging the church and nearby rectory, vicarage and the girls' school, as well as other

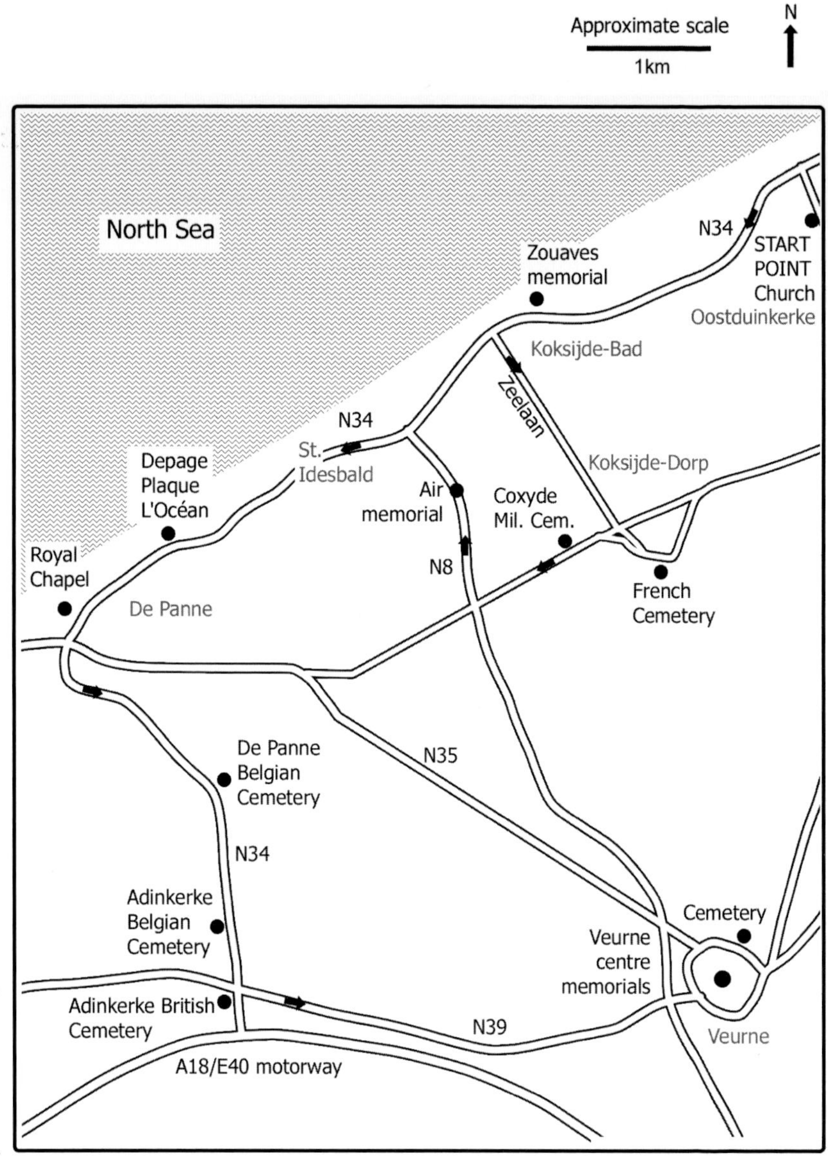

Tour E Route Map.

properties. Thirteen civilians, some of whom were refugees from the east, lost their lives, along with three French soldiers. The church was struck again on several occasions in 1915: it was rebuilt after the war and completed in 1920. The area became one of billets and camps during the war, and much of the French and British artillery covering Nieuwpoort was situated within close proximity. As such it was a legitimate target for German guns and raids from the air and, especially in 1917, also for poison gas. Among the victims was French Général de brigade Corneille Gustave Ernest Trumelet-Faber of the 81st Division Territoriale. A veteran of the Franco-Prussian War, Indo-China and North Africa, he was headquartered in the Grand Hotel and seriously wounded when a shell exploded on the sea promenade nearby on 7 December 1914.

Neither the village nor resort now resembles its Great War past, and in particular there is no trace of the original centre: the rebuilt church was burnt to destruction after bombing in 1940. It is a popular holiday area, with all of the shops, bars, restaurants, hotels and other facilities that go with such a trade.

Leopold-II-Laan is the road that links the original centre with the seaside resort. Situated on the left when driving from the old centre towards the sea is the impressive modern church of **Sint-Niklaaskerk**. It takes the name from the original church but is not on the same site. There is free parking in front of it. At the right of the entrance to the church site is the large 1924 **village war memorial**. It takes the form of a statue of a young woman supporting the body of a fallen soldier. The names of the dead of both world wars are incorporated. The cemetery includes a mass grave of those who died in the bombardment of 30 October 1914.

Continue along Leopold-II-Laan towards the sea and turn left at traffic lights onto the N34 Albert-I-Laan (also called Koninklijke Baan): beware and give way to the coastal tram that runs along the centre of the road. After the first block of buildings, pass on the left the former chapel and convent of Très Saint-Sacrement. It is one of the very few traces of the buildings that were here in 1914. The complex was rebuilt after much war damage and is now known as the Vrij Orthopedagogisch Centrum Rozenkrans.

Continue along the N34 until reaching Koksijde, passing en route on the left the intriguing 'Normandie' restaurant, constructed on the lines of the famous ocean liner.

Koksijde
The next village along the coast, Koksijde, was and remains a larger resort than Oostduinkerke and was some ten kilometres behind the

front line. In 1914 the seaside Koksijde-Bad was quite distinct from the inland old centre Koksijde-Dorp, but in recent times much development has merged the two. The resort began to develop largely as a result of investment by the Terlinck family, who had built a large seafront hotel in their name. A promenade was laid out and was gas-lit. Behind it, a number of small lanes were constructed in the dunes and large and ornate villas began to proliferate. The straight Zeelaan linked the resort to the village proper, which consisted of little more than a windmill and few buildings clustered around a church, and passing the highest dune on the coast, the Hoge Blekker. The buildings of the area were all taken over for military use and many camps were laid out in the dunes and hinterland.

About 500 metres after entering the built-up area, the road begins to bend slightly left and narrows from a dual to single carriageway. At this point, turn right onto Zouavenplein. There is car parking adjacent to the large **Zouaves Memorial**. Erected in 1934 by a veterans' group, the Union des Amicales Réglementaires de Zouaves, and designed by

This memorial to the French Zouave regiments is on the sea front at Koksijde.

a former member of a Zouave regiment, the memorial is in memory of more than 224 officers and 7427 men of the nine Zouave regiments who died on Belgian soil.

A plaque has been added to commemorate the fact that **Alexis Roger Hély d'Oissel**, who commanded the Groupement Nieuwpoort, stayed at the Villa Ravensteen in Koksijde between January 1915 and August 1916. He had begun the war as chief of staff to General Lanrezac of the French Fifth Army but was given command of a division in September 1914. Hély d'Oissel, by then aged 55, commanded the 38th Division on the Yser until promoted to command XXXVI Corps on this front in May 1915.

Across the main road, in a post-1918 development, an area of housing became known as the Village Sénégalais. It harked back to the occupation of this area by camps of French colonial troops.

It is possible to see Villa Ravensteen (it is situated at 7 Generaal Hély d'Oisselstraat, off Koninginnelaan, on the west side of Koksijde) but it is a little off the proposed tour route. The same is true of the large Villa la Vigie (Verdedigingslaan), which was constructed above the site where heavy British artillery fired on the German Tirpitz coastal battery. Concrete bunkers and tunnels are below ground but are not accessible to the public. Villa la Vegie continued to be used as a mess by Belgian Army officers until 1933.

From Zouaveplein return to the N34 and turn left. In 150 metres turn right, crossing the tram line, onto Lejeunelaan. Follow it until a large traffic roundabout, at which take the third exit onto Zeelaan, signposted for Koksijde-Dorp. Once in the village centre, go straight across at the traffic lights: the road soon changes name to Noordstraat. Then turn left onto Kerkstraat and reach the large **Sint-Pieterskerk** on the right. There is parking in front of and alongside the church site.

The **French Military Cemetery** is accessed by the footpath to the right of the church. It contains the remains of 135 men, mainly of the Fusiliers-Marins and the 42nd Division. Originally buried in and among civilian graves, they were later concentrated into a single plot. The whole cemetery contains much of interest, including graves of Belgian veterans. A large semi-circular plot of them, centred on statuary of a half-buried sword, is particularly striking. There are **several memorial plaques** inside the church.

Turn back along Kerkstraat, right onto Noordstraat and then take the first left onto Louise Hegerplein. At the end of it, on the left at its junction with Robert Vandammestraat, is the **Koksjide War Memorial**. It commemorates twenty-three military and seven local civilian victims of the war, with another five military and five resistance victims of the

The French cemetery at Koksijde.

Second World War. A total of 210 Koksijde men served in the Belgian forces. It is a striking and unusual memorial, depicting a galleon in full sail, said to represent Belgium in the stormy seas of war. Originally erected on Noordstraat in 1929, the memorial was moved in 1946 and again, finally, to this position, in 2004.

Turn left onto the N396 Robert Vandammestraat and continue for a kilometre beyond the village towards De Panne. On the right hand side lies **Coxyde Military Cemetery**. It is the largest Commonwealth War Graves Cemetery in the area covered by this book and is well worth a visit. Parking is very difficult in front of the cemetery and visitors may find it easier to pull into one of the two supermarket car parks situated on the left about a hundred metres before reaching the site.

The cemetery was begun by French units when they held the coastal sector; was then taken over when the British XV Corps was here in the summer of 1917; and then went back into French hands in the December. British naval casualties of 1918 were also buried here and the remains of forty-four British soldiers were brought into the cemetery after the war. Nineteen of them came from Furnes Road British Cemetery, made in July 1917 by the 2nd Manchesters and the 49th (West Riding) Division, and twenty-five (of whom twenty-two belonged to the 49th Division) came from Oosthoek Military Cemetery, near Adinkerke. The cemetery came into use again for the burial of 155 casualties sustained during the defence of the Dunkirk-Nieuwpoort perimeter in May 1940. The cemetery now contains 1,507 British and Dominion burials of the

First World War, the French graves from this period having since been removed. Belgian troops and airmen who died in the area were generally taken to Duinhoek Cemetery, near De Panne.

It is perhaps fitting in this seaside cemetery that the first and last British burials are of sailors: the first three, who were killed in a seaward bombardment of their shore siege gun, died on 26 April 1917 (I.A.37–39). Exactly three years later, the final man buried here was drowned when the salvage tug *Hughli* went down in poor weather in shallow waters off Westende at 8pm. It had been carrying food supplies but also explosives intended for clearing the channel into Ostend. The exact cause of the disaster has never been resolved but it was observed that a column of smoke poured from the stricken vessel. Engineer Lieutenant Thomas Gill RNVR (III.L.22) was one of the twenty-nine lives lost; some of the bodies washed ashore were wearing lifebelts.

For the most part the cemetery is an ordinary soldiers' graveyard: privates and gunners from generally unsung units, most of whom perished as a result of enemy shell fire and poison gas at Nieuwpoort, Oostduinkerke and Koksijde. They all have stories to be discovered. Amongst them lie men of the Royal Army Medical Corps and Army Service Corps of numbers 1 and 92 Field Ambulances, both hard hit by enemy shell fire during the Strandfest attack on 10 July 1917. The experience of the former is sobering: within minutes, the Ambulance lost nine men killed or wounded at Koksijde, had an Austin vehicle burned out on the road to the Main Dressing Station and also lost two of its mules. Among its dead here is 29 years old Staff Sergeant Norman Pirret (I.D.547). A former postman and army reservist, he had been awarded the Military Medal in October 1916 for his work in bringing in between fifty and sixty wounded officers and men during a recent attack on the Somme. His widow, Tina, left a personal inscription on his headstone, but did not mention their daughter Mary, just four years of age when her father died.

Another medical man of the same age was Captain Wilfred Sneath (I.H.9). Said to be the most promising student when he attended Manchester

The war memorial at Koksijde-Dorp.

University, he was awarded numerous prizes and scholarships before going on to become a house surgeon, first at the Manchester Royal Infirmary and then the Dreadnought Hospital in Greenwich. Sneath had earned the Military Cross and been mentioned in despatches while acting as Medical Officer to the 1/6th Welsh Regiment. He had only arrived back from home leave the day before he was fatally wounded. Sneath, who was by then the adjutant of 2 Field Ambulance, was with his commanding officer and a sergeant major, just returning to the convent in Oostduinkerke from the horse lines, when they were hit by fragments of a shell on 2 July. All were taken to the Belgian Red Cross Hospital L'Océan in De Panne. The others finally returned to duty ten days later; on that same date Sneath succumbed to his wounds.

Continue along the N369 and turn right at the first roundabout onto Leopold III-laan. This road did not exist at the time of the war: the area was entirely duneland. On reaching a second roundabout, note the lighthouse-like **memorial** which was erected here in 1951. It commemorates the Belgian and allied airmen who flew from the Great War airfield, situated south, on Ten Bogaerde farm, back on the far side of the N369. Continue towards the coast and on reaching the N34, Koninklijke Baan, turn left, signposted for De Panne and St. Idesbald.

De Panne

The largest of the 1914 seaside resorts, De Panne gained prominence when King Albert took over four of the large villas of the area for use as a family residence and as a headquarters location. This was an act of great symbolism as well as practicality. The town was connected to the formation of Belgium; on 17 July 1831 its first king, born Leopold von Sachsen-Coburg-Saalfeld, first set foot on the soil of the new country.

The Belgian government had left to operate at Sainte-Adresse, near Le Havre, in October 1914 and in effect De Panne became a forward post of the country's administration. The royal presence and the function of the town led to it becoming a centre of prime importance behind the Yser Front. Medical facilities, baths, laundries, headquarters, stores, barracks, offices, theatres, cinemas and shops proliferated; many occupied the pre-war hotels and villas. The royal family occupied the villas Bortier, the Terschueren, Saint-Joseph and Maskens, with the latter being used as the royal residence. At the suggestion of Queen Elisabeth, Saint-Joseph was used for an orphans' school operated by Portuguese nuns. The editors of the Flemish (but politically moderate) newspaper *De Belgische Standaard*, the only large scale Belgian publication that appeared in the unoccupied area, were housed in a villa on the sea front.

La Panne   L'Hôpital de l'Océan

Originally based in a seafront hotel, the L'Océan Hospital expanded across a large area of De Panne. (*Geneanet*)

De Panne has been much developed over the decades but behind the tower apartment blocks of the seafront promenade is a very pleasant town with a number of sites of Great War interest. The first few are clustered together within a short walk. As the dual carriageway N34 Koninklijke Baan enters the town and narrows to a single lane, take the second right onto Dr. A. Depagelaan and park. On the wall of number 13 is a bronze **memorial plaque** to Brussels professor **Dr. Antoine Depage and the Hospital L'Océan** that he founded here with the support of Queen Elisabeth in December 1914. L'Océan was originally a 1904 seaside holiday hotel, with four floors and thirty-seven beds, owned by the local Huysseune brewing family. They made the hotel available to the Belgian Red Cross and the first wounded soon arrived. More buildings nearby were gradually taken over and by its peak, in the summer of 1918, the hospital had a total of 1,800 beds ove a sprawling forty-six locations. More than 24,000 men received treatment there, making it the largest Belgian-run front hospital of the war. Little wonder that De Panne came to be called 'Depageville'.

Walk onto the sea promenade, Zeedijk, and turn left. Just past the first building on the left is a **Monument to Queen Elisabeth** and the hospital. Continue to pass Mijnstraat on the left, reaching building 45, which is **Villa Catherine (Kaatje)**, squeezed between apartment blocks. You will need to look up to appreciate it, for the ground-floor facade is modernised. The villa, together with the nearby Villa Ten Duine, was hit by the last German air raid on the town on 16 October 1918. The reader will appreciate how close it was to the hospital and also to the royal residence a few hundred metres further along the coast. The two villas were being used for administrative offices. Four civilians were killed in Ten Duine, while in Villa Catherine a young couple, Gustaf Devré and Hortensia Debruyne were killed. Their barely three-week-old daughter Paula survived, her crib being protected by being placed below a staircase. She was eventually adopted (her new mother Alma was employed as a seamstress at L'Océan). In 2012, Paula attended the opening of the exhibition 'The Queen's Hospital. Red Cross, L'Océan and De Panne 1914–1918' at the age of 94. She died on 28 April 2014 and lies with her adoptive parents in Nieuwpoort.

The notable Dr Antoine Depage, the key figure behind the development of the major military hospital l'Océan complex at De Panne. He was a royal surgeon, the founder and president of the Belgian Red Cross and a founder of the scouting movement in Belgium. His wife Marie died in the sinking of the *Lusitania* in 1915.

Return and turn down Mijnstraat and cross the main road to the Art Deco Hotel des Princes / Prinsenhof, one of many buildings of the style in De Panne. A notice tells the story of the military hospital. Take the left hand road, Leopold-II-Laan, to where it crosses Koninginnelaan. Turn left there and continue to building number 34 on the right: **Villa Belle-Vue**. This is the only building of the **L'Océan Hospital** to remain. It was some distance from the other buildings that were used, as it was assigned to patients with contagious diseases. Its use of heliotherapy was apparently effective and one of several medical innovations that originated at L'Océan. The Carrel-Dakin method of wound disinfection was used on a large scale for the first time, preventing what otherwise might have led to amputation. Continue along Koninginnelaan, take the first left onto Kunstenaarslaan, re-cross the main road, turn left along it and soon return to Dr. A. Depagelaan on the right.

[**A possible detour**: the destination is on a one-way road that is very complex to reach, goes in the wrong direction for the purposes of this tour and is always terrible for car parking! Intrepid readers may however wish to try it by going on foot. From Dr. A. Depagelaan, turn right and walk along the main road. Turn left at the traffic lights into Zeelaan. Take the second right into Albert Dumontlaan and continue until reaching building number 18, on the right hand.

Villa Zonneweelde dates to 1913 and at that time was known as Val d'Ante. For a while from January 1915 it was the billet of Captain Robert Thys and engineer Fernand Umé of the **Belgian Service d'Inondations**. They quickly dubbed it 'Au bon Génie'. Other men of the unit occupied the Villa La Roche nearby and the neighbourhood became the virtual headquarters of the hydraulic engineers. At a later date they relocated to a specially built barrack at Bulskamp.]

From Dr. A. Depagelaan, turn right onto the main road, which changes its name to Duinkerkelaan after passing the town centre. Pass, on the left, the tram stop at Koning Albertplein: behind it is the town's *war memorial*. As the area of central shops and restaurants is passed and the road begins to bend left, turn right just before a petrol station onto Pierre Bortierplein. Go straight across the next junction onto Kapellelaan and park. Now surrounded by blocks of holiday apartments but in 1914 isolated in the dunes, the **Royal Chapel** is easy to spot. The title was granted by King Albert in 1924 to what had been the Chapel of the Oblate Fathers, missionaries who had been in the town since 1906. The royal family regularly attended services held in the chapel during the Great War. There is a memorial plaque as a reminder.

Return to the N34 (Duinkerkelaan) and turn right, going straight on at the traffic roundabout in the direction of the E40 motorway and Adinkerke (follow the tram line). The road soon changes name to Kerkstraat. In abut two kilometres from the roundabout, reach a tram

The Royal Chapel at De Panne.

The Belgian Military Cemetery at De Panne.

stop, Moeder Lambic, on the left of the road. (If you pass a restaurant of that name, you have missed it; you may also get tangled in traffic for the 'Plopsaland' Play Park). There a small car parking area and the entrance to the **De Panne Town Communal Cemetery** and beyond it the **Belgian Military Cemetery**. Note that access is restricted to cemetery opening hours.

A lone identified British grave in section F of the civilian cemetery, just ten metres from the entrance to the Belgian Military Cemetery, is of another of the victims of the sinking of the *Hughli*, described earlier in this tour. John Cain, a 50 years old man from Liverpool, was the ship's assistant cook and a member of the Mercantile Marine Reserve. Sadly, a shipmate with him has never been identified. There is **a CWGC plot** of 259 Second World War dead towards the rear of the site.

De Panne was inaugurated as a Belgian war cemetery on 1 July 1918 but the first burials took place in March. It grew through the post-war concentration of smaller plots and isolated graves to become the largest such cemetery, containing 3,366 Belgian and thirty-six French soldiers from the Great War, to which were added 342 Belgian soldiers from 1939–45. Most regiments of the army are represented, with deaths ranging in date from the earliest days of the war in Flanders until well into 1919. Some of the men brought here died at hospitals and camps in France. Some were killed accidentally, some of illness, but most were those killed on the battlefield or who died of wounds on the line

British graves at De Panne of two victims of the sinking of the *Hughli*.

of evacuation. As such, the cemetery is a good representation of the Belgian army's experience. Burials continue to this day: in July 2018, four soldiers found at Diksmuide, three of whom were identified as being of the 12nd Line Regiment and killed on 24 October 1918, were reinterred here in row J (graves 198–200). Gérard Joseph Dethier, Félix Alphonse Jacquet and Pierre François Pintens were mentioned in the records of the battalion as having been buried together on the battlefield east of the Yser but were only conclusively identified after painstaking artefact, historical and genealogical research, including reference to DNA. The fourth man was believed to be French.

Elsewhere, the communal cemetery contains many marked graves of war veterans, some in entire plots of identical headstones, and there are many stories of interest to be found. There are some notable graves too, such as that of Maurice Calmeyn (1863–1934), a wealthy local landowner who observed at first hand the Belgian oppression of the Congo and turned increasingly to liberal politics and communism (grave C9). Another is of Dr. Abel Dewulf, who became the second mayor of De Panne after serving as the youngest medical officer on the Yser Front (C74). Gustaf Devré and Hortensia Debruyne, the parents of Paula, see Villa Catherine above, lie in grave F86.

Perhaps the saddest of all is the stone that lists the three young sisters and refugees Josephina, Bertha and Lina Gonsales, killed together when their temporary home was hit by a shell on 2 May 1917 (F15). The eldest was aged just twelve. It appears that she was killed outright but the others, the youngest being just six, sustained fatal injuries and succumbed on 4 May. Jane de Launoy, a nurse working at the L'Océan, recalled:

> 'It is perhaps the most horrible vision of war that we have before us. The mother [along with] one or two soldiers and all the children had dinner in a small fisherman's house on the old road. A shell pierced the table and burst on the ground, tearing off the legs of the unfortunate! The mother was brought to us (double amputation), soldiers (amputations) and three little girls who have five of their little legs torn off or crushed. I worked all day. ... until midnight we fight! We saved the men, we saved the mother ... but two little black and bloody corpses are side by side in the same bed. They were photographed to make propaganda in America against the unjust war and against Germany!'

The girls' father Henrik remained unaware of the fate of his family for some time, for he was a prisoner in Germany.

Now continue along the N34 Kerkstraat, pass the 'Plopsaland' play park and the tram line to enter the town of **Adinkerke**. Reach the railway line, with De Panne Station [sic: even though it is in Adinkerke] on the right. There is parking on both sides of the road should you wish to stop. Adinkerke is also well furnished with shops, cafés and restaurants.

The railway now seems fairly unremarkable but during the Great War it was of prime importance. This area became a key railhead on the line from Calais. The only other supply line into West Flanders came up from Hazebrouck towards Poperinge. Once Veurne began to come under fire from 25 October 1914, the casualty clearing hospital, which had until then been located there, moved into the old railway station of Adinkerke and to the outbuildings of the nearby new station. Not all units were informed at the time and for a while casualties continued to be transported to Veurne, causing a certain degree of chaos and no doubt loss of life. The hospital – often called "Duinhoek" – developed as a Franco-Belgian co-operative effort, with seven barrack blocks built and two tented areas established near the station.

During 1917 the British 24th and 39th, and the Canadian 1st, Casualty Clearing Stations [CCS] were established to the left of the road in an area referred to as 'Oosthoek'. 24 CCS, one of the first to arrive, had to cut barley crops and carry out work on neglected drainage ditches in order to clear the ground for its forty Nissen huts. Despite the site being flooded and the hut roofs leaking after heavy rain in early August, the Matron-in-Chief, Maud McCarthy, noted on her visit on 2 September that she found 24 CCS *particularly good, being composed entirely of huts, which are most wonderfully arranged, hot and cold water laid on, electric light and all the conveniences of a small base hospital.*

Continue further into Adinkerke and take the first right turn, into Heldenweg alongside the Sint-Audomaruskerk church. Go to the end and park at the entrance to **Adinkerke Belgian Military Cemetery.**

Adinkerke
The position of Adinkerke as a railhead and major medical centre led to a proliferation of associated activities, including a military joinery works for production of coffins. Before the war it was a small place, centred on the railway and the crossing of the Dunkirk-Veurne Canal, which lay to the south of the centre, with two windmills in the vicinity and with commerce flowing from its position near the international border.

The cemetery was begun early in the war and used mainly for those casualties who died of wounds at one of the nearby hospitals. By 1920 it held over 2000 Belgian and almost 500 French graves but the number was reduced by repatriation and it now contains 1,651 Belgians, one Frenchman under a Belgian stone and sixty-seven troops in a British extension. The latter include eight privates of the 3rd British West Indies Regiment, killed together when a long-range German shell exploded and blew up an ammunition train they were unloading at St Idesbald Station, on the coast. The Belgian casualties who died at Adinkerke formed the basis of the original cemetery, but many others were later brought in from

The Belgian Military cemetery at Adinkerke. The destruction of AVV-VVK stones here encouraged activists to build the Yser Tower.

The barracks of the large Belgian cantonment camp on the Cabour Estate near Adinkerke.

a wide area of the Yser battlefields. Early photographs show a profusion of different designs of private memorials, all eventually removed in 1924–25 and replaced by the standard headstones. Heldenweg (Heroes Road) is itself a place of memory and controversy, for it was reported that about 140 heldenhuldezerkjes were removed from the cemetery and broken up to pave the road. The desecration of the stones gave impetus to the campaign for a Flemish national memorial and the eventual construction of the Yser Tower. **Sint-Audomaruskerk Church** contains memorials to the military and civilian war dead of the town, as well as a plaque in memory of five men of the 2nd Fusiliers-Marins who were originally buried in the churchyard in 1914–15.

[Detour: Go to the end of Heldenweg and turn right on Stationstraat. The first left is Noordhoekstraat, which leads to the site where the British casualty clearing stations were established. The site now shows no sign of its occupation by these units but can be located by continuing until the railway crosses the road.]

South west of Akinkerke, across the canal and stretching down to the border with France, was a large estate, centred on an impressive chateau built by Dunkirk businessman Charles Cabour. In April 1915 the establishment of a large military hospital on the site was sanctioned and within a month the first buildings had been erected and were in use. In part it was paid for by the Antwerp British Hospital Fund, the original purpose of which had long since ceased to exist. Under the leadership of Dr. Paul Derache, the hospital grew greatly during the war, eventually becoming a 500-bed unit housed in twenty-two barrack huts with modern facilities. The surgical unit remained and was active at Cabour until March 1917 and carried out around 2,500 operations. An extensive water supply system was also developed on the estate, supplying many of the camps and hospitals of the Westhoek, whilst much dune sand was excavated for use in production of concrete. Sadly there is little left of this once-impressive facility, although there is a small museum dedicated to its role in the Second World War, situated along Moeresteenweg.

Return to your car and proceed along Heldenweg, turning right onto the N34, which in this area is called Stationsstraat. Continue across the canal bridge and turn right at the traffic roundabout onto the N39 signposted for Bray-Dunes. The first turning on the left, Kromfortstraat, is signposted for **Adinkerke British Cemetery**. The gateway to the cemetery is reached in 260 metres, on the left of the lane. The cemetery is reached by a walk of some one hundred metres along a pathway.

The cemetery contains 168 British burials of the Great War and fifty-five from the Second World War, along with 142 Czech and German war graves. The busy main road to Veurne that is now just behind it did not exist then: the cemetery was in open fields. Most of the British burials relate to 1917, when XV Corps occupied the area; the German graves are of late 1918, after the final Belgian offensive. The earliest death recorded is of a flying ace: Flight Commander Arnold Jacques Chadwick, a Canadian from Toronto who had scored eleven victories while a pilot of the 4th Squadron of the Royal Naval Air Service, based at Dunkirk. On 28 July 1917 he attacked a formation of nine German aircraft but sustained damage and was forced to ditch into the sea off De Panne. His drowned body washed ashore on 17 August, six days after the *London Gazette* notified the public that he had been awarded the Distinguished Service Cross for *exceptional gallantry and remarkable skill and courage ... in repeatedly attacking and destroying hostile aircraft* in May and June 1917. He had been shot down before, in 1916, but made his way back via the neutral Netherlands. Chadwick, who was still just 21 years of age, lies in row G, grave 1.

Lying next to Chadwick is another RNAS Flight Commander, a holder of the DSC, 27 year-old Irishman Francis Dominic Casey. He had shot down nine enemy aircraft between March and May 1917 but tragically died while on a test flight on 10 August 1917. The rate of loss due to flying accidents is brought home by the adjacent burials in G8 and 9 of 18 year-olds Lieutenants Frank Leonard Cattle and Frederick Philip Pemble of 213 Squadron Royal Air Force. They died on 29 June 1918 when their Sopwith Camel aircraft collided. Both men had previously survived accidents in the previous weeks. Pemble's grieving father renamed his home 'Adinkerke' in his honour.

A reminder of the breadth and global nature of the war is the burial near A.37 of Nafar (Private) 8267 Sabit Harun Mohamed of the 80th Company of the Egyptian Labour Corps, which was working near Bray-Dunes when he died on 6 September 1917; and four Russian members of the 33rd Siberian Regiment, who died in April 1919. Their story remains obscure.

Turn back along Kromfortstraat and turn right onto the N39 for the roundabout passed earlier. Continue straight across, on the same road, signposted for Veurne. It follows the canal on the left hand side and after passing below a road bridge crosses the canal as the town is entered. Carry straight on at a small roundabout into Duinkerkestraat and follow that until it is necessary to comply with a left turn into one-way Zuidstraat. At its end it bends right to enter the central square or Grote Markt. Park.

Veurne

This town can trace its history to the ninth century and to defences made for protection against the Vikings and it still contains many (mostly repaired) buildings from the Spanish and French occupations of this region. In the early 1700s it was once again fortified in the style

Veurne's glorious architecture.

King Albert, standing, during a review of his troops held in Veurne's Grote Markt in November 1914 (The Sketch).

The bust memorial to Karel de Cogge in Veurne.

of Vauban. Although it was the first city to welcome King Leopold after he landed at De Panne in 1831, Veurne remained rather undeveloped as a provincial market town in the decades up to 1914. Today it benefits from a substantial economy based on tourism and commerce and the battlefield tourist will usually have no problem in finding suitable refreshment, toilets and shops as well as the many traces of history.

The town hall was used as the Belgian military headquarters until it moved to Houtem in early 1915, and a major hospital operated in the nearby college in the early days of the war. It is said that Marie Curie visited the hospital for a demonstration of X-ray technology. One of the most commonly seen postcard images of the Belgian front is of the King on ceremonial duties in the Grote Markt in November 1914. Steps were taken to protect and preserve the town from damage as far as was possible, but even so it sustained much damage from long range shellfire and aerial bombing. In 1920 the French government awarded Veurne the Croix de Guerre, even as the restoration of the historical centre was only just beginning to get underway.

Walk diagonally across Grote Markt to exit onto Noordstraat. After the first block of buildings on the left, the pavement widens at the rear of St Walburga Church, where there is a 1927 **bust memorial to Karel Cogge**, one of the heroes of the inundations. Return to the square and turn right, passing a row of café-restaurants towards the splendid **town hall** of 1596–1612. Exhibitions and shows are often held within, many on Great War themes, but the interior is

The exotic Spahis, French North African cavalry, drawn up at the Veurne Review in November 1914.

worth visiting in its own right. Just before reaching the façade is a right turn which takes the visitor below the belfry tower to face the **church of St Walburga**. Within is a plaque memorial to twenty-four of the town's civilian casualties from bombing and shell fire, including seven children, who died in 1915, 1917 and 1918. Of particularly tragic note is the entry for Marie-Louise Dequidt, killed along with her five children on 10 July 1917. The youngest child was just eight months old.

A walk around the side of the church brings you into Heldenplein, where a number of plaques and memorials to both world wars have been gathered. There is also a memorial to artist Paul Delvaux.

Head diagonally back across the Grote Markt (ie heading south east) to exit onto another square, Appelmarkt. Set in a niche on a wall on the left, just on entering the square, is a **bronze memorial plaque to Lieutenant General Baron Augustin Édouard Michel du Faing d'Aigremont** (1855–1931). He commanded the Belgian 4th Division throughout the war (under his surname Michel). His commemoration at Veurne recognises, amongst his other accomplishments, the steps he took to minimise damage suffered by the town by directing troops and material around, rather than through, it. **Sint Niklaaskerk Church**, further along the square from the memorial, can trace its history back to at least the twelfth century. It houses **several memorials**: to forty-six civilians who lost their lives in the Great War; to the town's twenty-three military dead; and to three men of the 2nd Battalion of Fusiliers-Marins who were buried in the cemetery here in 1914.

Return to your car and exit the Grote Markt onto Nordstraat. At the first junction, keep right by following the signs for Diksmuide and Nieuwpoort, but almost straight afterwards take the first right onto Smissestraat. Follow it until its end and park.

The large building on the right that takes up most of Smissestraat is the **Atheneum School**. Near the end of the street is a bronze **memorial to pupils and teachers** of the school who perished in the Great War.

The street exits onto Oude Vestingstraat. Walk across it and enter the **town communal cemetery**. Amongst the many graves with Great War connections is that of **Karel Cogge**, in section 3H, on the left of the central pathway. His stone reads: 'Pray for the soul of Karel Lodewijk Cogge - supervisor of the Noordwatering of Veurne - knighted in the Leopold Order by His Majesty King Albert for his indispensable and effective cooperation in the flooding of the Ijzer. Born in Veurne on 31 January 1855 and here died on 15 June 1922. Along the left hand side of the cemetery is a **French military plot** containing the remains of 225 men: 145 in individual graves, eight in two collective graves and seventy-two together in an ossuary. It appears that fourteen of the original graves were emptied and the men's remains repatriated for home burial after the war.

In grave 179, near the French plot, lies **Petty Officer 220196 Samuel George Mann RN**, with an unknown serviceman buried next to him. Mann, who came from Harrowden, near Bedford, had served since 1904 and died of wounds on 20 January 1915. He was working as a gun layer aboard ship when struck in the stomach by shrapnel, piercing his intestine. His wounds were beyond the medical facilities available at sea and he was landed: newspaper reports say he died at a hospital in Dunkirk but this may be incorrect. The grave next to him is intriguing, for CWGC records show that it was originally thought to be Cavalier 2e Classe Charles Cardon, a 24 year old from Reims, who died of wounds on the same date as Mann, having been hit while his cavalry regiment, dismounted, was holding the front line at St. Joris, near Nieuwpoort. Next to the French plot is a **CWGC Extension** to the cemetery, containing seventy-seven graves of the Second World War, almost all from May 1940.

The cemetery concludes this tour.

Other Notable Sites in the Area

The following sites are too far from the suggested tours to be included within them but are all well worth seeing and all relate to the fighting on the Yser.

The Lange Max Site, Clevenstraat 2, 8680 **Koekelare**. The site surrounds the immense concrete platform of the 38cm armoured German gun 'Lange Max' of Leugenboom, which was also known as the Batterie Pommern. The largest gun in the world at the time, it first came into action in June 1917 and fired on targets as distant as Dunkirk.

Enamelled photographs of every casualty are a feature of this Flemish village memorial.

The site includes a small museum with useful explanations of the history of the battery, a brasserie for refreshment and various memorials and vestiges of the war time site. It is one of few sites or museums in this area to have a focus on German operations. Opening days and times are limited: check with the museum website www.langemaxmuseum.be before travelling. It is located off the N33 Torhout-Ostend road, about three kilometres north of Koekelare.

Houthulst Belgian Military Cemetery, Poelkapellestraat 44, 8650 Houthulst. On the N301 road to Poelkapelle, south of Houthulst. The graves of 1,731 Belgian and eighty-one Italian soldiers, mainly of the late 1918 offensive, lie in this cemetery, which was created in 1923. The Italians died as prisoners in German hands, brought to the area to act as labourers. As with all of the Belgian cemeteries, the dead were relocated from a wide variety of locations. There are a few graves of men who died in the Battle of the Yser in 1914, around Diksmuide and Stuivekenskerke, and sprinklings of others throughout the period before the final offensive. There is a substantial crypt below the lawn as you enter the cemetery, which is (as of 2021) still open for burials.

Vredesmolen, Klerkenstraat, 8650 Houthulst. A former oil and grain windmill on the highest point in the area, used and reinforced by the Germans as an observation post. It was an obvious target for allied shell fire and was gradually brought to ruin. When I first visited it in 1983, what remained of the mill was in a terrible state of dilapidation and I fully expected to be crushed by falling masonry. A large section had already fallen. I did not tarry! It is now renovated, completed in 2013, and can be ascended by a spiral staircase, which allows today's visitor the view that was so valuable to the German gunners.

Vladslo Kriegsgräberstätte (German Military Cemetery), Houtlandstraat 3, 8600 Diksmuide. This is a concentration of burials of more than 25,600 men (and a small number of women) of the German military forces of the Great War. Vladslo is one of only four German cemeteries in West Flanders that remain after a succession of concentrations of many (several hundred of them) smaller cemeteries. The others are at Hooglede, Langemark and Menen. Situated within Praetbos Wood, the cemetery includes the notable sculptural group **Mourning Parents** by Käthe Kollwitz. Her 18-year-old son Peter is among those buried here, transferred from a smaller nearby cemetery; his gravestone is amongst those near the front of the memorial.

The general appearance of Vladslo Cemetery will be familiar to those who have seen Langemark or Menen. At various places along the boundary hedges a number of original headstones can be found.

The Belgian 4th Division Memorial, Veurnekeiweg, 8670 Koksijde (but beware this address is misleading. The memorial is situated on the N39 road, north east of and just outside Wulpen). This impressive memorial is unfortunately not the easiest place to stop if travelling by car: slow down well in advance. It is possible to park, with care and good vehicle and life insurance, in the space between the road and cycle lane

Vladslo, near Diksmuide, is the only German cemetery in the area covered by this book.

on the memorial side of the road. The 4th Division, a predominantly French-speaking formation, had defended Namur in August 1914 before it made its escape. It subsequently saw service at Antwerp and on the Yser. The significance of the location of its memorial is due to the division having been in this area, headquartered in nearby Wulpen, for much of the rest of the war. The origins of the memorial can be traced to a concept by its commanding officer, Lieutenant General Michel, with 1916 designs by engineer corporal and architect Georges Hendrickx of the 4th Line Regiment and soldier and sculptor Louis Jacquemotte of the 8th (later 18th) Line.

The first building blocks were assembled during the war, including stones from the debris of Nieuwpoort and marble from the destroyed halls of Ypres. The memorial as seen now was erected in 1919 and unveiled on 11 July 1920 in the presence of King Albert, who significantly delivered a speech in both French and Flemish. It is, aside from the 3rd Division, which is represented at Merkem, the only Belgian division with a memorial. There was a certain amount of early controversy at the sole use of French on the memorial.

Appendix

The Belgian Army

Commander in Chef: King Albert of the Belgians
Chief of the General Staff: Generals Antonin de Selliers de Moranville (to 6 September 1914); Félix Maximilien Eugène Wielemans (to 5 January 1917); Louis Rucquoy (to 11 April 1918); Cyriaque Cyprien Victor Gillain.

The Belgian Order of Battle in August 1914: The Field Army after Mobilisation
The basic composition of a division was a number of mixed brigades; one cavalry regiment; one artillery regiment; a battalion of engineers and a transport unit. The latter three each took the number in their names from the division.

    Each mixed brigade had two line regiments of infantry (Line Regiments, Foot Jagers, Grenadiers or Karabiniers), a machine gun company and an artillery group, the latter two numbered after the brigade, and a platoon of gendarmerie. For simplicity and to avoid repetition, the machine gun companies, artillery groups and gendarmerie of each brigade have been omitted below.

The 1st Division (Lieutenant General Baix)
- 2nd Mixed Brigade (2nd and 22nd Line Regiments)
- 3rd Mixed Brigade (3rd and 23rd Line Regiments)
- 4th Mixed Brigade (4th and 24th Line Regiments)
- 3rd Regiment of Lansiers (cavalry)
- 1st Field Artillery, Engineer Battalion, Transport Battalion

The 2nd Division (Lieutenant General Dossin)
- 5th Mixed Brigade (5th and 25th Line Regiments)
- 6th Mixed Brigade (6th and 26th Line Regiments)
- 7th Mixed Brigade (7th and 27th Line Regiments)
- 4th Regiment of Horse Jager (cavalry)
- 2nd Field Artillery, Engineer Battalion, Transport Battalion

The 3rd Division (Lieutenant General Leman)
- 9th Mixed Brigade (9th and 19th Line Regiments)
- 11th Mixed Brigade (11th and 31st Line Regiments)
- 12th Mixed Brigade (13th and 32nd Line Regiments)
- 14th Mixed Brigade (14th and 34th Line Regiments)
- 2nd Regiment of Lansiers
- 3rd Field Artillery, Engineer Battalion, Transport Battalion

The 4th Division (Lieutenant General Michel)
- 8th Mixed Brigade (8th and 28th Line Regiments)
- 10th Mixed Brigade (10th and 30 Line Regiments)
- 13th Mixed Brigade (13th and 33rd Line Regiments)
- 15th Mixed Brigade (1st and 4th Regiments of Foot Jager)
- 1st Regiment of Lansiers
- 4th Field Artillery, Engineer Battalion, Transport Battalion

The 5th Division (Lieutenant General Ruwet)
- 1st Mixed Brigade (1st and 21st Line Regiments)
- 16th Mixed Brigade (2nd and 5th Regiments of Foot Jager)
- 17th Mixed Brigade (3 and 6 Regiments of Foot Jager)
- 2nd Regiment of Horse Jager
- 5th Field Artillery, Engineer Battalion, Transport Battalion

The 6th Division (Lieutenant General Lantonnois van Rode)
- 18th Mixed Brigade (1st and nd2 Grenadiers)
- 19th Mixed Brigade (1st and 3rd Karabiniers)
- 20th Mixed Brigade (2nd and 4th Karabiniers)
- 1st Regiment of Horse Jager
- 6th Field Artillery, Engineer Battalion, Transport Battalion

Army Troops (that is, those not under command of a division but under General Headquarters) included the few resources of heavy artillery; engineer reserves; railway, telegraph, balloon and air units. It also included eight regiments of volunteers (VrijwilligersKorps), organised into four brigades; and a small corps of Congolese volunteers. Corps is perhaps too strong a word for the latter, for there were but thirty-two of them. Many of these volunteers, including the Congolese, found themselves drafted into the regular infantry.

Armament
In 1914 the standard armaments in use by the Belgian field army were the 1889 and 1895 pattern Mauser rifle, firing .301 and .275 inch rounds

respectively; the 1895 Mauser carbine, also .275 inch, and the Browning .301 pistol for officers. Smokeless powder for the rounds fired by these weapons was manufactured by the Cooppal factory at Wetteren, near Ghent. It was captured by the Germans on 7 October 1914. The Cooppal employees who had not fled refused to work for the Germans, who brought in about 150 men from Germany to man the factory. It proved to be an unsuccessful venture, partly due to sabotage, and efforts to run it were abandoned in 1915. The employees were provided with clandestine company funds brought across the border from the Netherlands. Marcel van Vijve, one of the sons of the company's director, went to England, where he played a part in supervising the establishment of munitions supply for the Belgian army. His father, Georges, and brother, Raymond, went to Italy, where they too helped establish munitions production. Marcel eventually joined them there.

During the war, the army received about 7000 Chauchat machine rifles of French manufacture, converting about half to employ the .301 inch (7.65mm) rounds rather than the 8mm variant normally used for the Chauchat.

The field artillery was equipped with the 8.7cm Krupp breech-loading field gun, and the horse artillery with the 7.5cm version. It possessed northing larger. It was eventually re-equipped, mainly with French 75mm, 105mm, 120mm, 150mm and 155mm guns and a variety of trench mortars. The latter included the 75mm Schneider, 142mm Delattre and 58mm and 90mm Van Deuren types.

Selective Bibliography

Official or semi-official histories:
Tasnier, M and Overstraeten, R.: *La Belgique et la Guerre. III. Les Opérations Militaires* (Brussels: Henri Bertels, 1926).
De Legerbode (war time journal of the Belgian Army).
Moniteur Belge (official journal of the state).
Les Armées Françaises dans la Grande Guerre (French Official History).
Journal Officiel de la République Française (official journal of the state).
Der Weltkrieg 1914 bis 1918: Die Militarischen Operationen zu Lande (German Official History).
War Office: *Handbook of the Belgian Army 1914*.

Other works:
Breton, Willy: *Les pages de gloire de l'armée Belge* (Paris: Berger-Levrault, 1915).
Cammaerts, Emile: *Albert of Belgium: defender of right* (London: Ivor Nicholson and Watson, 1935).
Debaecke, Siegfried: *Het drama van de Dodengang* (Koksijde: de Klaproos, 1998).
De Launoy, Jane: *Infirmières de guerre en service commandé* (Paris: Desclée De Brouwer, 1936).
Deryck, Luc: *Terug naar niemansland* (Koksijde: de Klaproos, 1996).
Draper, Mario: *The Belgian Army and society from independence to the Great War* (London: Palgrave Macmillan, 2018).
Gabolde, Maurice: *Les carnets de Sergent Fourrier: souvenirs de la Grande Guerre* (Paris: Editions l'Harmattan, 2013).
Hallett, Christine E: *Nurse writers of the Great War* (Manchester: Manchester University Press, 2016).
Hoorebecke, Ladislas van: *La bataille de l'Yser* (Ghent: Philips & de Schaepmeester, 1927).
Jacobs, Kristof: *The Nieuwpoort Sector 1917* (London: Uniform, 2018).

Lampaert, Roger: *De inval: België tijdens de Eerste Wereldoorlog* (Erpe-Mere: De Krijger, 1995).

Lampaert, Roger: *Stabilisatie in Vlaanderen* (Erpe-Mere: De Krijger, 1995).

Le Goffic, Charles: *Dixmude: The Epic of the French Marines* (London: William Heinemann, 1916).

'L.F.R: *Naval guns in Flanders 1914–1915* (London: Constable, 1920).

Lucas, Andrew and Schmieschek, Juergen: *Fighting the Kaiser's War* (Barnsley: Pen & Sword, 2015).

Mabire, Jean: *La bataille de l'Yser: les Fusiliers-Marins a Dixmude* (Paris: Fayard, 1979).

Macnaughtan, S: *My war experiences on two continents* (London: John Murray, 1919).

Rash, F. and Declercq, C. (ed): *The Great War in Belgium and the Netherlands. Beyond Flanders fields* (London: Palgrave Macmillan, 2018).

Sheldon, Jack: *The German Army at Ypres 1914* (Barnsley: Pen & Sword, 2010).

Souttar, H. S: *A surgeon in Belgium* (London: Edward Arnold, 1915).

Ureel, Lut: *De kleine mens in de Grote Oorlog* (Brugge: de Klaproos, 2008).

Western Front Association-België: *Shrapnel. WFA-België tijdschrift* (Quarterly journal).

Anon: *La campagne de l'armée Belge d'après les documents officiels* (Paris: Bloud et Gay, 1915).

Anon: *A war nurse's diary* (New York: Macmillan, 1918).

Index

The River Yser and the towns of Diksmuide, Nieuwpoort and Veurne are mentioned at frequent intervals throughout the book.

Military units and formations
Belgian
General Headquarters, 8–9, 19, 50, 54, 183, 237
Burgerwacht, 10
Cavalry, 9–10, 14, 26, 31, 34–5, 123–4
Sapeurs-Pontonniers, 53, 57–8, 76, 117, 149–51, 229
1st Division, 8–9, 16–17, 19, 26, 28, 33, 38, 95, 106, 190
2nd Division, 8–9, 14, 16–17, 19–21, 25, 32, 39, 43, 54, 112, 116, 119, 181
3rd Division, 8–10, 12, 14, 19, 26, 31, 37, 39, 73, 79, 102–103, 107, 164, 197, 216, 243
4th Division, 8–10, 12, 26, 29, 39, 99, 106, 238, 242–3
5th Division, 8–9, 26, 31, 34–5, 39, 121
6th Division, 8–9, 14, 26, 31, 33, 35, 39, 41, 91, 93–4
9th Division, 102
10th Division, 102–103
1st Mixed Brigade, 35
5th Mixed Brigade, 119
6th Mixed Brigade, 32
7th Mixed Brigade, 32
17th Mixed Brigade, 35
18th Mixed Brigade, 35
34th Brigade, 8
5th Lansiers, 123–4, 172–3
2nd Engineers, 107
1st Grenadiers, 51, 65, 94, 176
2nd Grenadiers, 35
6th Grenadiers, 41
2nd Guides, 31
1st Foot Jager, 42, 44, 103, 107
2nd Foot Jager, 39, 46
3rd Foot Jager, 35, 121
1st Karabiniers, 123, 172, 174–6
2nd Karabiniers, 98, 123, 172, 174, 212, 218
3rd Karabiniers, 154, 181
4th Karabiniers, 174, 218
1st Line, 35, 45–6
2nd Line, 44, 177
3rd Line, 40, 44, 61, 177, 183, 187, 216–17
4th Line, 42, 51, 61, 243
5th Line, 61, 63, 119, 183
6th Line, 37, 40, 61, 64, 158
7th Line, 18, 32–3, 37, 43, 61, 77, 136, 155
8th Line, 40–2, 44, 106, 174, 243
9th Line, 37–8, 42, 44, 103, 109, 193, 197
10th Line, 33, 44
11th Line, 38–9, 47, 102–103
12th Line, 38–9, 47, 84, 103, 164, 231
13th Line, 44, 58, 103, 106, 190
14th Line, 45, 64, 155, 158
15th Line, 119
16th Line, 117
18th Line, 243
19th Line, 103, 213
21st Line, 18
22nd Line, 78, 177
23rd Line, 177
24th Line, 95, 205
27th Line, 32, 34
6th Volunteers, 58

British
  6th Destroyer Flotilla RN, 27
  Expeditionary Force, 6, 12, 24, 26, 36, 87, 201
  Second Army, 102, 214
  I Corps, 34
  IV Corps, 19, 21–4
  XV Corps, 88, 91, 146, 153, 224
  XIX Corps, 115
  1st Division, 89
  7th Division, 19, 22
  32nd Division, 89–91
  49th Division, 91, 224
  66th Division, 91
  97th Brigade, 90
  1st Royal Naval Brigade, 20
  Oxfordshire Hussars, 17
  1st Northamptonshire Regiment, 89–90, 146
  2nd King's Royal Rifle Corps, 89–90, 146
  2nd Lancashire Fusiliers, 199
  2nd Manchester Regiment, 224
  3rd British West Indies Rgt, 233
  11th Border Regiment, 90, 146
  15th Highland Light Infantry, 146
  17th Highland Light Infantry, 90
  Portsmouth Battalion, 20
  Army Service Corps, 146
  Egyptian Labour Corps, 236
  Royal Air Force, 235
  Royal Army Medical Corps, 225
  Royal Engineers, 17, 116, 118, 121, 181
  Royal Marine Artillery, 17, 115–16, 181
  Royal Marine Light Infantry, 17
  Royal Naval Air Service, 235
  Royal Naval Division, 19–20, 23, 65, 145
French
  Cavalry, 34–5, 85
  Fifth Army, 9, 12
  XXXVI Corps, 91, 97, 99, 223
  38th Division, 64, 196, 223
  42nd Division, 39, 42, 223
  45th Division, 93
  51st Division, 97
  133rd Division, 213
  81st Territorial Division, 65–6, 148, 221
  87th Territorial Division, 18, 20–1, 24, 33, 93, 186
  89th Territorial Division, 24, 33
  76th Brigade, 64
  83rd Brigade, 43–4, 46
  84th Brigade, 42
  214th Brigade, 213
  8th Chasseurs, 46
  16th Chasseurs, 64, 158
  19th Chasseurs, 46
  102nd Chasseurs, 213
  69th Infantry Regiment, 200
  94th Infantry Regiment, 46
  151st Infantry Regiment, 42, 45, 64
  162nd Infantry Regiment, 45, 50
  273rd Infantry Regiment, 98
  Fusiliers-Marins, 18, 21, 24, 26, 29, 34–5, 38, 43, 45–6, 48, 65–6, 93, 98, 223, 234, 238
  Goumiers Marocains, 34
  7th Tirailleurs de Marche, 86
  8th Tirailleurs de Marche, 64
  Tirailleurs Sénégalais, 46
  1st Zouaves, 208, 222
  4th Zouaves, 64, 94, 222
German
  First Army, 9
  Second Army, 9–10
  Fourth Army, 24, 26, 37, 39
  Liebeshuzaren, 10
  11th Uhlanen, 58
  III Reserve Corps, 10, 16, 24, 26–7, 29–30, 37, 39, 61
  IX Reserve Corps, 13
  XXII Reserve Corps, 24, 26, 36, 38, 39, 44
  XXIII Reserve Corps, 24, 26, 35–6, 93, 95
  XXVI Reserve Corps, 24, 26, 39
  XXVII Reserve Corps, 24, 26, 39
  MarineKorps Flandern, 65, 84, 89–90, 102–103, 106, 174
  4th Ersatz Division, 16, 24, 32, 37, 39, 45, 61, 65
  5th Reserve Division, 16, 29, 37, 50, 61

6th Reserve Division, 16, 33, 37, 50, 61
6th Bavarian Division, 102–103
30th Division, 14
58th Division, 102–103
214th Division, 124
43rd Reserve Division, 38, 46–7, 59, 66, 111
44th Reserve Division, 38, 50
46th Reserve Division, 94
54th Reserve Division, 120
1st Landwehr Division, 102–103
19th Landwehr Division, 97
20th Landwehr Division, 112, 120
1st Ersatz Brigade, 19
12th Landwehr Brigade, 13
27th Landwehr Brigade, 16
37th Landwehr Brigade, 20, 24
38th Landwehr Brigade, 16, 65
6th Jaeger, 13
103rd Infantry, 103
106th Infantry, 103
8th Reserve Infantry, 63
26th Reserve Infantry, 41
48th Reserve Infantry, 63
52nd Reserve Infantry, 63
203rd Reserve Infantry, 59
204th Reserve Infantry, 59
248th Reserve Infantry, 121
2nd Bavarian Reserve, 121
31st Landwehr Regiment, 103
33rd Landwehr Regiment, 103
84th Landwehr Regiment, 103
388th Landwehr Regiment, 99

People
Acland-Hood, Lady, 69
d'Aigremont, General, 238
Albert, King of the Belgians, 1, 11–12, 17, 19, 23, 30, 32–3, 54, 73, 82–4, 91, 96, 100, 113, 127, 142, 172, 183, 226, 229, 237, 243
Albrecht, Duke, 24
Alexander of Teck, Prince, 72
Van Averbeke, R, 131

Bacon, Admiral, 87–8
Baekelandts, I, 189
Barel, L-C, 209

Baudouin, Lieutenant, 117, 120
Baudoux, Médicin-Adjoint, 31
Bauwens, Corporal, 120
Bernard, Colonel, 108
Berryer, Paul, 6
von Beseler, General, 10, 13, 16, 19, 21
Bidon, General, 65–6
Binnie, W, 146
Blairon, Major, 41
von Boehn, General, 13
Bollaert, C, 124
Bonte, J, 190
Bontinck, Sergeant, 120
Borriemans, Captain, 94
Borthwick, J, 69
Bradford, A, 146
Brialmont, Henri A., 2, 14
Bristow, A, 192
de Broqueville, C, 126, 183
de Broqueville, Lieutenant, 71
Bryan, M T, 68
von Bülow, General, 9

de Caestecker, J and M, 189
Cain, J, 230
Calberg, Lieutenant, 149
Calmeyn, M, 231
Carr-Gomm, Mr, 69
Carter, C, 146
Casey, Commander, 235
Cattle, Lieutenant, 235
de Ceuninck, General, 93
Claudon, Colonel, 45, 50
Chadwick, Commander, 235
Chase, H, 199 Chisholm, M, 70, 73, 75
Churchill, Winston, 17–19, 87
Churchyard, A, 145
Clifton, J and V, 70
Cogge, K, 55, 237, 239
Comyns, Lieutenant, 116, 179
Congreve, C, 68–9
Cooper, C, 70
Costenoble, A, 60
Couffez, A, 60
Crombez, A, 183

Daignon, Henri, 9
Dallas, Colonel, 17

Daviot, H, 209
Davis, Richard H., 11
Debongnie, Médicin, 31
Debruyne, G H and P, 228, 231
Decker, Miss, 75
Delage, Captain, 29
Delcourt, Major, 34
Deguise, General, 15, 19–21
Deleu, A, 129
Delobbe, Colonel, 33
Depage, Doctor, 227–8
Deprez, F, 130
Dequidt, M-L, 238
Derache, Doctor, 234
Devijver, Captain, 117
Dewicker, H, 174
Dewulf, A, 231
Dingens, G, 53
Donies, Captain, 94
Dossin, General, 26, 64, 154–5
Dresse, Lieutenant, 58
Drubbel, General, 112–13, 115, 119
Dubroecq, Major, 35
Dufour, General, 8
Duguet, Doctor, 48
Dungelhoef, Captain, 34
Dupont, Lieutenant, 117–18
Durand-Gasselin, Lieutenant, 47

Van Eecke, Adjutant, 216
Eichhorst, F, 174
Elisabeth, Queen, 19, 73, 82–3, 172, 226–7
English, J, 130, 132, 135, 181, 185
Evrard, Colonel, 117

von Falkenhayn, General, 24
Feilding, Lady, 70–5
Fiévez, A, 95–6, 130, 217
Foch, General, 28, 30, 66, 85, 183
Foreman, F, 192
François, Lieutenant, 50, 54
French, Field Marshal, 87
Funck, Colonel, 33
Fyfe, G, 72, 76

Gabolde, M, 199
Gabriel, C-C, 209
Gartside-Tipping, Commander, 145
Gavin, Miss, 68
Geeraert, H, 54, 57, 151

Gill, Lieutenant, 225
Gillespie, J, 146
Gleeson, A and H, 70
Goethals, Lieutenant, 117
Gonsales, B J and L, 231
Grossetti, General, 42–3, 45, 64
Gurney, E, 70

Haig, General, 34, 96
Halahan, Commander, 72
Hancock, M, 75
Hellebaut, A, 129
Hély d'Oissel, General, 223
Hendrickx, G, 243
Heylen, J, 189
d'Hont, J, 181
Hood, Rear-Admiral, 27–8, 31–2
Hunter-Weston, General, 87

Jacuemotte, L, 243
Jacques, Colonel, 38, 107, 164
Jacquet, G, 231
Jagger, C, 146
Jeanniot, Captain, 48
de Jehay, Comtesse, 187
Joffre, General, 9, 12, 22–3, 183
de Jonghe, Priest, 50

Keith-Johnstone, Lieutenant, 153
Kennedy, L, 197
de Keyne, T, 174
Kitchener, Lord, 17–18
Kollwitz, K and P, 241
Knocker, E, 70, 73–5
von Kluck, General, 9
Kusters, F, 130

de Landtsheer, C, 132
de Launoy, H, 232
Lederosay, Colonel, 107
Lekeux, E, 172
Léman, General, 8–9, 83
Léopold II, King of the Belgians, 2
Léopold, Prince, 84
Lock, Second Lieutenant, 118
Loonis, C and M, 205
Lotz, Colonel, 94, 218

MacDonald, R, 72
Macnaughtan, S, 74
Maes, Councillor, 33

Mann, S, 239
von Marwitz, General, 10
Maude, Dr, 70
Max, Adolphe, 11
McCarthy, Matron-in-Chief, 232
Meerschaart, G, 185
Meisser, Colonel, 38
Michel, General, 8, 29–30, 243
Moens, E, 181
Mohamed, S, 236
de Moranville, General, 5
Morgan, O, 68
Munro, Dr, 70–1, 73–5

Nuyten, P, 55

O'Gorman, Colonel, 69
d'Oultremont, Major, 42

Paris, General, 19
Pau, General, 22
Pauwels, Chaplain, 41
Pauwelyn, Sister, 36
Pearson, A, 146
Pemble, Commander, 235
Pintelon, C, 78
Pintens, P, 231
Pirenne, P., 65
Piret, Staff Sergeant, 225
Pollet, C and M, 161
Prinsier, G, 183
Pynaert, F, 106

Raemdonck, E and F, 95–6, 130, 132, 134, 197, 216–17
Rawlinson, General, 21, 88
Reece, L, 70
Renneboog, Lieutenant, 193
Renton, D, 70
Ronarc'h, Contre-Amiral, 21–3, 29–30, 34–5, 38, 40, 47, 73
de Rossart, Lieutenant, 35
Roux, A-G, 209
de Rudder, R, 130, 132, 197
Rupprecht, Crown Prince, 66
de Ryckel, General, 5

Saesen, C, 197
Salpetier, Major, 41
Schmidt, W, 121

von Schröder, Admiral, 65, 89
de Schryver, C, 192
Schwink, Captain, 46
Secker, J, 70
Shaw, E, 70
Simons, F, 138
Sinclair (or St Clair), M, 70
Sneath, Captain, 225–6
Somers, Mr, 68
Spegelaere, Farmer, 33
Stack, M, 70
Sticker, J, 197
Streatfield, Reverend, 70
Stuckens, A, 77
Sutherland, Duchess of, 67

Taymans, Adjutant, 213
Top, G, 183
Thuret, Lieutenant, 86
Thys, Captain, 54, 76, 151, 229
Trentham G, 193
Trumelet-Faber, General, 221

Umé, Captain, 57, 151, 229

Vallet, Colonel, 64
Van der Linden, F, 130
Vansteene, J, 191
Varney, Captain, 29
Verhaege, Lieutenant, 117–18
Verschaeve, C, 130–1, 134, 166, 191–2
Verwarde, J, 183
de Vlaeminck, Labourer, 33
de Vos, Jan, 20
van der Vreecken, F, 58

Wakefield, C, 70
Warmoes, J, 60
Wauthier, Captain, 158
de Wiart, Count Carton, 43
Wielemans, General, 55, 66, 183
Willems, B, 130
Willems, C, 195–6
de Winde, B, 130
Winterbottom, G, 68
Wise, Lieutenant, 37–8, 153
de Witte, General, 9–10, 14
Wynne, H, 72

Cities, towns and villages
Aalst, 74, 193
Aarschot, 10–12, 58
Adinkerke, 49, 58, 131, 138, 166, 232–6
Alveringem, 36, 51, 89, 130, 190–1
Andenne, 12
Antwerp, 4–6, 8, 12–14, 17–22, 24, 26, 58, 69, 75, 134, 212, 243
Avekapelle, 31, 36, 72, 181

Becelare, 39
Beerst, 26, 30, 32, 34–5, 38–9, 41, 59, 189
Berchem, 20
Bergues, 54
Bikschote, 96–7, 213
Blaasveld, 17
Boesinge, 26, 93, 124, 197
Booitshoeke, 43, 45, 51, 61
Bovekerke, 34–5
Brielen, 93
Bristol, 41
Bruges, 18–19, 27, 29, 31, 87, 135
Brussels, 6, 12, 23, 67, 126

Calais, 33
Cassel, 17–18
Chatham, 88
Le Clipon, 88–9
Coxyde *see* Kokside

Deinze, 23
Dendermonde, 13, 71
De Panne, 31, 39, 83–4, 138, 194, 219, 226–31
Diest, 12
Dinant, 12, 58
Doel, 15
Drie-Grachten, 26, 81, 93, 96–8, 100, 139, 207–13
Dunkirk, 17–18, 21, 27, 31, 39, 48, 54, 61, 71, 75, 87–8, 194, 209

Eekloo, 19
Eernegem, 24
Eggewaartskapelle, 181
Esen, 22–3, 34, 38–9, 47, 58–60, 161

Fortem, 89, 116–17

Gemmenich, 8
Ghent, 8, 19, 21–2, 71, 74
Gistel, 29
Graville Ste. Honorine, 78

Halen, 10, 30
Le Havre, 10, 18, 226
Heist-op-den-Berg, 16
Hofstade, 36
Hoogstade, 66, 70, 107, 118, 138, 189, 192–3
Houtem, 183, 237
Houthulst/Forest, 24, 26, 31, 39, 97–9, 102, 120, 138, 212, 241

Jabbeke, 29

Kaaskerke, 29, 38, 40, 47–8, 107, 116, 118, 129, 181
Kapelle-op-den-Bos, 13
Kasteelhoek, 33, 41
Keiem, 26, 30, 32–4, 39, 138
Kemzeke, 20
de Kippe, 97, 99, 102–103, 213–14
Klerken, 22, 34, 89, 212
Kloosterhoek, 43–4
Koksijde, 89, 146, 219, 221–5
Kortemark, 23
Kortrijk, 23

Lampernisse, 26, 31, 64
Langemark, 31, 91, 97, 100, 102
Langewaade, 96–9
Ledegem, 59
Leke, 30, 34
Leugenboom, 88, 240–1
Leuven, 8–10, 12–14, 58, 61, 135
Liège, 2, 4, 8–10, 12, 16, 36, 126, 216
Lier, 15–16, 18, 36
Lille, 17, 24
Lizerne, 91, 94–5, 197, 216–17
Lo, 107
Lokeren, 13
Loksbergen, 9
Lombardsijde, 26, 32, 36–8, 40, 42, 45, 48, 65–6, 84–5, 88–9, 146–7, 150
Luigem, 26, 31, 96, 99, 207, 211–12

Mannekensvere, 26, 32–4, 40, 43
Mechelen, 12–13, 16–17, 21, 36, 183, 213

Malo-les-Bains, 88
Melle, 22, 30, 71
Menen, 23, 36
Merkem, 26, 66, 81, 96–7, 99, 103, 124, 197, 212–13
Merlimont, 88
Middelkerke, 31–2, 35, 88, 153
Moerbeke, 20
Mons, 8, 12, 126

Namur, 2, 4, 8–12, 16, 68, 243
Noordschote, 96, 118, 197, 206

Oeren, 131–2, 138, 166, 188–9
Ondank, 31
Oostduinkerke, 153, 219, 225
Oosthoek, 224
Oostkamp, 30
Oostkerke, 38, 79, 107, 116
Ostend, 10, 17–19, 21–2, 27, 30–1, 35, 69, 74, 87–8, 153, 225
Oudegem, 13
Oude God, 18
Oudekapelle, 70
Oude-Stuivekenskerke, 26, 41–6, 50, 66, 105–106, 123–4, 171–2

Passchendaele, 102
Pervijze, 35–6, 39, 42, 44, 46, 51, 61, 73, 79, 81, 107–108, 177–8
Perwez, 8
Pilkem, 97
Poesele, 66
Poperinge, 20, 24, 213
Praatbos Wood, 38
Putte, 16

Ramskapelle, 43, 61, 64, 81, 106, 138, 150, 152, 157–9, 192
Rattevalle, 26, 32, 37
Reninge, 81, 129, 203
Roeselare, 22–3, 35, 59, 126

Saint-Omer, 24
St.-Gillies-bij-Dendermonde, 13
St.-Gillies-Waes, 20
St.-Jans-Kapelle, 26
St.-Jacobs-Kapelle, 38, 46
St.-Margriete-Houtem, 10
St.-Pieters-Kapelle, 28, 33

Sint-Joris, 26, 32, 37, 39, 43, 45, 152
Sint-Rijkers, 192
Sint-Sixtus Abbey, 198, 204
Schaffen, 12
Schoonaarde, 19
Schoorbakke, 26, 32, 34, 37–41, 44–5, 81, 156, 175–7
Schore, 26, 32–3, 36, 41
Selschotter, E, 51
Sennelager, 14
Slijpe, 33, 37
Soltau, 14
Staden, 31, 35, 59
Steenkerke, 132, 138, 179, 187, 205
Steenstraat, 66, 91, 93–6, 132, 197, 216–17
Stuivekenskerke, new, 94, 105, 123, 174, 177, 181

Tamines, 12
Termonde *see* Dendermonde
Tervate, 26, 34, 39–44, 175–7
Thielt, 22–3, 30
Tienen, 8–10
Tongeren, 10
Tremelo, 12

Vieu-Dieu *see* Oude God
Vijfwegen, 31
Vilvoorde, 12
Vinkem, 136, 181, 205
Vladslo, 22, 34–5, 38–9, 59, 141, 241–2
Vladslovaart, 33

Waregem, 30
Watou, 128, 216
Wavre, 8–9
Westende, 31–2, 37, 42, 65, 85
Westroozebeek, 39
Westvleteren, 96, 132, 138, 196–7, 209
Woesten, 201
Woumen, 22, 38
Wulpen, 63, 149, 242–3
Wynendale Forest, 24

Ypres, 20, 22–4, 26, 34, 36, 39, 41, 54, 61, 66, 95, 102, 115, 213

Zarren, 31, 38, 58, 60
Zeebrugge, 19, 22, 27, 87
Zelzate, 20
Zuidschoote, 81, 94–5, 218
Zwijnaarde, 71

Waterways
Arkevaart, 53
Blankaart, 58
Broenbeek, 103
Brugsevaart, 52
Corverbeek, 102
Ghent-Terneuzen Canal, 23
Grote Beverdijkvaart, 50, 55, 157
Handzame Canal, 35, 38, 112, 116, 121, 165
Klein Beverdijkvaart, 44, 50, 105
Koolhofvaart, 63–4, 160
Loobeek, 103
Loo Canal (Lovaart), 79, 102, 189
Maartjevaart, 97–9, 207, 213, 216
Nieuwbedelf, 52
Nieuwendamme (Old Yser), 53–4, 58, 152
Noordvaart, 45, 53–4, 57–8, 106
Plassendale Canal, 26, 32, 37
Reigersvliet, 44, 105, 108, 123, 171, 173–4
River Dender, 13, 16
River Demer, 11, 14
River Dijle, 12, 14, 16
River Grote Gete, 9
River Ijzer *see* River Yser
River Leie, 13
River Meuse, 9
River Nete, 13, 15–16, 19
River Rupel, 13, 15
River Scheldt, 13–15, 17, 19, 21
River Senne, 12
St. Jansbeek, 96–7, 213
Steenbeek, 103
Venepevaart, 46
Veurnevaart, 53, 85
Veurnevaart, old, 53
Willebroek Canal, 16
Ypres Canal (Ieperlee), 34, 66, 91, 96, 103, 207

Farms and battlefield locations
't Abelenhof, 203
Affenberg, 85, 89
Aschoop, 102, 213
Au Lion Belge, 80, 197–201
Berkelhof Farm, 105
Blockhuis Farm, 32
Boyau des Templiers, 151
Britannia Post, 103
Busbrug, 33
Calvarieberg, 168
Cayenne Mill, 208
Champaubert, 103
Denain Post, 103
Den Toren Farm, 26, 45–6, 65, 105
De Smidse Inn, 205
Deux Pommiers Post, 123
Dodengang (Trench of Death), 38, 105, 108, 112–13, 123, 168–9, 173
Epernon Farm, 213
Etang Trench, 117
Equerre Trench, 117–18
Forts 1 to 4 (Antwerp ring), 20
Fort Breendonk, 13
Fort Knokke, 33, 58
Fort Koningshoekt, 16
Fort Kruibeke, 14
Fort Loncin, 9
Fort Merksem, 14
Fort St.-Katherine-Wavre, 16–17
Fort St. Marie, 14, 20–1
Fort Walem, 16–17
Fort Zwijndrecht, 14
Ganzepoot (Goose Foot), 38, 52–4, 81, 85, 148, 151–2, 160
Gasthuis Clep, 70, 75–76, 107, 118, 192–5
't Geuzengat, 33
Gourbi Post, 103
Grote Bamburgh Farm, 37, 53
Grote Hemme Farm, 156–7
Grote Wacht, 105, 123-124, 171
de l'Hermine, 103
Hexenkessel, 85, 87
Hibou Farm, 103
Höhe 17, 85
Honoré Post, 102–103
In de Predikboom Cabaret, 89
Jesuitengoed Post, 102–103
Kasteel Flora, 182–3
Kloosterhoek, 105
Maison de Passeur, 99, 118–19, 201, 212

Mazeppa Farm, 103
Minoterie Diksmuide, 29, 48, 109, 111–12, 115, 117–21, 123, 130, 165
Molenbrug, 33
Mondovi Post, 103
Montmirail, 103
Novel Trench, 151
Obusiers, 103
L'Océan Hospital, 185, 225, 227–8
L'Océan II Hospital, 136, 181, 185, 187, 205
Palingbrug, 38, 45, 50, 85, 89, 147
Pelican Bridge, 85
Petroleum Tanks, 43, 107, 123, 170
Poitiers Post, 102–103
Railway line, 44, 57, 157
Sardine Works Trench, 150
Stampkot, 95, 217–18
Steenbakkerij, 160
Ten Bogaerde Farm, 226
Ter Stille Farm, 106
Uniebrug (Union Bridge), 32, 34, 37, 106, 155, 175
Vandenwoude Farm, 105
Verbrande Smis, 103
Vicogne (Viconia), 41, 43, 66, 105, 174–5
Violette Farm, 106–107, 190
Violon Farm, 61
Vredesmolen, 241
Zwert Peerd Farm, 187

Miscellaneous
Antwerp City Council, 20
Armoured cars, 34
AVV-VVK, 128–9, 131, 136, 140, 147, 188–9, 233
Battle of the Marne, 14
Battle of the Silver Helmets, 10
Belgian army chapel, 171–2
Belgian Field Hospital, 69–70, 193, 196
Belgian military law, 3
Belgian mobilisation, 5–6
Belgian War Graves Service, 138
Cabour Estate, 234–5
Congo, 1, 2
Costenoble Brewery, 59, 162
Dover Patrol, 27
de Duinengalm, 33
Elf Gemeten Estate, 214
Elisabethville, 78
Groote Nord Nieuwland, 45
Heldenhuldezerkjes, 128, 130–1, 136, 140, 147, 165–6, 189, 234
HMS *Adventure*, 27
HMS *Amazon*, 32
HMS *Attentive*, 27, 31–2
HMS *Foresight*, 27, 31–2
HMS *Humber*, 27–8, 31
HMS *Marshal Ney*, 146
HMS *Marshal Soult*, 146
HMS *Mersey*, 28, 31
HMS *Sapphire*, 27
HMS *Severn*, 28, 31, 37
Ijzerbedevaart, 131–2, 134, 136, 165, 181, 189, 217
Ireland, 32
Munro's Ambulance, 71, 76
Parti Ouvrier Belge, 3
Queen's School, 187
Red Cross and Order of St John, 68, 71
Touring Club de France, 141
Treaty of London, 1
Vaderlandjes, 79
Vierboete lighthouse, 32
War Heritage Institute, 138
Women's Emergency Corps, 70, 72
Women's Motorcyclist Club, 72
Ypres League, 141
Yser Tower, 96, 130, 132, 136, 165, 167, 173, 181, 197, 217
Zeppelin, 9, 13, 153
Zusters van Liefde, 36